Timber!

Terrace Books, a trade imprint of the University of Wisconsin Press, takes
its name from the Memorial Union Terrace, located at the University
of Wisconsin–Madison. Since its inception in 1907, the Wisconsin
Union has provided a venue for students, faculty, staff, and alumni to
debate art, music, politics, and the issues of the day. It is a place where
theater, music, drama, literature, dance, outdoor activities, and major
speakers are made available to the campus and the community. To learn
more about the Union, visit www.union.wisc.edu.

Timber!

The Story of the Lumberjack

World Championships

Lew Freedman

Terrace Books
A trade imprint of the University of Wisconsin Press

Terrace Books
A trade imprint of the University of Wisconsin Press
1930 Monroe Street, 3rd Floor
Madison, Wisconsin 53711-2059

uwpress.wisc.edu

3 Henrietta Street
London WC2E 8LU, England
eurospanbookstore.com

Library of Congress Cataloging-in-Publication Data
Freedman, Lew.
Timber! : the story of the lumberjack world championships / Lew Freedman.
    p.   cm.
    Includes bibliographical references.
    ISBN 978-0-299-28454-1 (pbk.: alk. paper)
    ISBN 978-0-299-28453-4 (e-book)
    1. Logging—Competitions—Wisconsin—Hayward—History.   2. Sports—
Wisconsin—Hayward—History.   I. Title.
SD538.2.W6F74 2011
634.9'8079—dc23
2011017749

Special thanks to
Diane McNamer and **Bonnie Salzman**
for all of their help in the writing of this book.

Contents

Preface

Feats of strength have fascinated mankind since caveman days. It is not difficult to imagine hairy guys with neither cell phone nor Internet capability sitting around the fire they invented wondering what to do with their free time after they've finished hunting and gathering for their families.

In the 2000s, such idle time usually results in either the commission of crimes or the creation of some new, magnificent product that we can't do without. In the 2000s BC, men might well have come around to the topic of who was the strongest. Their next move might have been to see who could pick up the heaviest boulder and heave it the farthest.

Chopping wood must be one of the oldest pastimes or work responsibilities known to man. For centuries it was either cut wood for winter or die. So there was considerable incentive to develop a talent for woodchopping. And as any sober woman or drunken man can tell you these days, once you get guys involved in such elementary activities it's never enough to know that they are simply doing the good deed of providing for their families. They have to know who is the strongest, toughest, or fastest so they can brag.

These traits have defined mankind under the umbrella of survival of the fittest since before Charles Darwin figured it out and informed society. From a sporting perspective, most talents, regardless of the sport itself, grew out of those three traits. Reduced to an even more elemental form, the strongest throw things, the toughest knock opponents out with their fists, and the fastest win the gold medal in the 100-meter dash.

This is how we end up with football player Lawrence Taylor, heavy-weight champion Joe Louis, and gold-medal sprinter Jesse Owens. But it's also how we end up with human powerhouses such as Mel Lentz, Jayson Wynyard, Dave Bolstad, Dave Geer, and Ron Hartill as kings of the lumber-jacks. They have impressed audiences of thousands at the Lumberjack Bowl in Hayward, Wisconsin, over the years with their own brand of feats of strength, their own coordination and speed.

While most of the events contested at the Lumberjack World Champion-ships since 1960 would have seemed alien to those bored cavemen, wood-chopping would not. They would be fascinated by the equipment in use, whether it was the sharpened ax blade with the smooth wooden handle or the two-man saw. Someone transported from the past might check out the double buck sawing and say, "Now why didn't I think of that?"

Of course, none of those prehistoric characters could have pictured large-scale logging, in which entire forests of pine trees would be cut down. They were happy just to be able to find enough wood to start a little home fire, never mind stockpiling enough wood to keep it burning for months. Timber sports, the lumberjack games, grew out of the logging industry's evolution during the nineteenth century. Just like among good old boys everywhere, while taking their relaxation in the logging camps at the end of a long day, talk pretty much got out of hand and it naturally turned to who was the strongest, toughest, and fastest.

Seeking the answers within the context of their own lives and professions, the lumberjacks sometimes challenged one another to contests of skill, chopping wood with an ax, cutting it with a saw, or balancing on logs floating in the nearby river. Whether the winners gained much more than bragging rights, payoffs such as tobacco or small amounts of money, the details are not known.

Gradually, as the natural resource—trees—was reduced in areas such as Maine, the Upper Midwest, and the Pacific Northwest, all places where logging helped carry the economy, logging also declined as a profession that always had job openings and would embrace a young man with no experience moving from the city.

Lumberjack games, always in a small way, persevered. The communities in Oregon and Washington, southeast Alaska, upstate New York, and Wisconsin, Michigan, and northern New England, where logging was important, either staged regional competitions or incorporated them into local fairs or festivals. The athletes who entered held other jobs. No one could make a living solely by going on the timber sports circuit, such as it was.

Beyond genuine competition, some entrepreneurs created lumberjack shows that approximated some of the competitions under the guise of show business. The characters who demonstrated their logging skills were lumberjacks, but with acting ability. Probably every live show aimed at the public in the last century that commits to history or romance in frontier America in any way owes a debt to Buffalo Bill Cody and his Congress of Rough Riders.

Buffalo Bill was indeed a buffalo hunter, Indian fighter, and western icon, yet his fame increased a hundredfold when he scripted his live Wild West show and took it on the road in front of adoring audiences across the country and even across the ocean. Cody's troupe of onetime cowboys, ranch men, and Plains Indians, coupled with dazzling horseback riding and the magical shooting prowess of Annie Oakley, transfixed little boys in Boston and royalty in England. Cody's shows, as much as reality, contributed heavily to the long-term perception of the West. Cody's shows elevated the West from hardscrabble reality to mythological romanticizing. And even though the real West was lodged in not so old minds, the revamped West in Cody's telling took hold and altered the way Americans would think about frontier days forevermore.

Except for driving behind a heavily laden logging truck on a winding road in one of the continuing staple areas of logging, or being called to by a particularly attractive flannel plaid shirt, the average person living hundreds or thousands of miles away in the desert of Arizona or the steamy south of Little Rock, might not think about the logging world at all. Yet just about everyone in America flipping the channels of a television set is likely to pause for a moment when they stumble on wood chips being sent skyward by a hot saw or young women being dunked in the water when they flail and fall while logrolling.

At the least that channel surfer will know what he or she is seeing: "Oh, that lumberjack stuff, I watch it all the time. I love it." And they do. The casual fan has only a slim idea what he or she is watching and the technique that goes into it, but there is no mystery about the winner once an event ends. Either the visual evidence provides clarity to the naked eye or precision timing, to the hundredths of a second, sorts the competitors' placement out swiftly. In this sense, timber sports are primitive, fundamental, simple. Either a man can chop wood more quickly than his foe or he cannot.

Like Buffalo Bill's cast of thousands in spectacular Wild West shows a century ago, and in rodeo now, the Lumberjack World Championships serve as a connector to the past. People can't jump into time machines to return to an old-fashioned lumber camp. This is the best they've got, and the skillful way the Lumberjack World Championships mesh history, show business, and sporting events into one pitch creates a lollapalooza of a setting.

To the man on the street the events contested are foreign. To those who have educated themselves by studying up via television, they are less so. But there is a presumption that the four thousand fans who daily attend the annual late July championships have a rudimentary knowledge of the sport. They are not talked down to but are included in public address announcements as if they are in the know.

The Lumberjack World Championships have become a natural tourist draw for Hayward, along with the other popular attractions strongly rooted in the community.

Key Names and Terms

American Birkebeiner—Dreamed up by promoter Tony Wise, the American Birkebeiner in Hayward, Wisconsin, is a cross-country ski marathon of 55 kilometers contested each February. Racers are of all calibers, from world class to citizen participants. Begun in 1973, the annual race has attracted nearly ten thousand entrants in a single year and is a cornerstone event on the world marathon racing circuit.

Hayward, Wisconsin—The community of Hayward has a population of approximately 2,100 people and is located in the north woods of Wisconsin, roughly 150 miles northeast of Minneapolis, Minnesota. The area around Hayward was a prime logging center decades ago, and the community counts logging as one of the most influential industries that created and perpetuated the town. Hayward is surrounded by forests, lakes, and rivers and is a popular outdoor recreation destination in winter and summer.

Historyland—Although Historyland is no longer in business, it was one of Tony Wise's earliest enterprises. He said he founded it to tell the story of Wisconsin's history and that the exhibits were authentic re-creations of a Native American village.

Lumberjack Bowl—The Lumberjack Bowl is the stadium in Hayward where the annual Lumberjack World Championships are contested. In a former life it served as a holding pond for cut logs being shipped from the north woods to be sold. The bowl is surrounded by metal bleacher seats.

Lumberjack World Championships—Held annually since 1960 in Hayward, Wisconsin, the championships represent a gathering of the finest timber sports athletes in the world. Men and women compete for fifty thousand dollars in prize money, trophies, and bragging rights.

Muskies—Hayward, Wisconsin, bills itself as "The Muskie Capital of the World" because the huge fish are prominent in local waters. People travel great distances to fish for the muskellunge in nearby lakes and rivers. Guided fishing trips and local resorts are big business in Hayward. The main reason Hayward can claim to be the capital of muskie fishing is its history. Between 1939 and 1949, four world-record muskies were caught near Hayward, three by a salty gent named Louie Spray. Despite many challenges to the veracity of the claim, Spray's catch of a 69-pound, 11-ounce muskie on October 20, 1949, is recognized by the National Freshwater Fishing Hall of Fame in Hayward as the record.

National Freshwater Fishing Hall of Fame—Symbolized by a 140-foot-long building in the shape of a muskie on the premises, the Hayward-based hall of fame honors accomplished anglers and contributors to the sport of fishing with some fifty thousand artifacts. The hall is also a world- and American-record governing authority that reviews submissions for recognition annually.

Telemark Ski Resort—Telemark was Tony Wise's first major undertaking when he returned to Hayward after World War II. Technically located in nearby Cable, the resort was transformed into a first-class ski resort and event center. It housed restaurants and bars that attracted dinner parties and the like for events beyond skiing.

Tony Wise—The late Tony Wise, who died in 1995, was a visionary promoter who in the decades following World War II worked tirelessly to make Hayward a tourist destination. Wise, who grew up in Hayward, returned home in 1947 with a pocketful of schemes after serving as an officer in the war. He opened a ski resort, constructed a series of buildings for a history exhibit, started one of the most popular cross-country ski races in the world, and in 1960 founded the Lumberjack World Championships as we know them. For nearly fifty years, Wise hustled and poured his heart into popularizing his enterprises and hometown.

Lumberjack World Championships Events

All-Around Title—This is the most prestigious title to win. The man who takes home this award is regarded as the best all-around lumberjack of the year. Points are accumulated event by event throughout the competition, and the individual with the most points is the winner. The award is named the Tony Wise All-Around Champion. The All-Around Lady Jack title has been awarded since 1997.

Ax Throwing—In this event competitors stand back from a target, as if they are taking aim at a dartboard or an archery target, and flip their axes end over end. They must stick to earn a score. Often the ax throwing is held away from the premises of the Lumberjack Bowl at another location in Hayward. The neutral site attracts the attention from tourists who might not know the Lumberjack World Championships are going on.

Boom Run—An event that stresses balance and agility, the boom run is usually dominated by competitors who are lightweight rather than heavyset. Logs are lashed together end to end in the Lumberjack Bowl pond and competitors must race from dock to dock over them. They start on one side, dash to the other side, run around a marker, and then sprint back across the floating logs again. If a competitor falls into the water, he can get up and continue but only by lifting himself back onto the log in the spot where he fell into the pond. The women's boom run was introduced in 1995.

Double Buck Sawing—This is two-man tandem sawing relying on an old-fashioned long saw with handles on both ends. Duos cut in synchronization, pulling back and forth in rhythm in order to sever a single slice of wood from a pine log 20 inches in diameter. Teamwork is essential to success in this event.

Hot Saw—This event requires the lumberjack to slice through a pine log that is 20 inches in diameter, making three cuts with a power saw—down, up, down—as fast as he can. This hunk of equipment is a single-cylinder, single-motor power saw that makes about as much noise as a car without a muffler. The sawdust flies when a lumberjack cuts with one of these babies. In the hot saw, more power is supplied by the machine than by the man. The battle is ostensibly against the clock, and the fastest sawyer wins the title. The loggers of the late nineteenth and early twentieth centuries relied on hand-pulled saws, which later morphed into chainsaws. The hot saws at the championships are generations improved in power and efficiency.

Jack & Jill Double Buck—Husband-and-wife teams, father-and-daughter teams, and teams of friends make up the competitor lists in the Jack & Jill sawing in the only co-ed event at the Lumberjack World Championships. It has been contested since 1985.

Logrolling—This crowd-pleasing event appeals to people with lightweight, cross-country-runner-type builds rather than the bull-like physiques of the strong men of timber sports. Harkening back to the days when loggers had to break river jams free by carefully stepping out on floating logs, logrolling is all about maintaining balance. Also called birling, logrolling requires competitors to go head-to-head on a single log, trying to toss the other guy into the water by forcing him to lose his balance.

In the early going the competition is best two out of three. Once the event reaches the semifinals and finals, the winner must take three out of five falls to advance or capture the trophy. When the competitors are equal and can't throw the other fellow within a specified time period, officials blow a whistle and start them again. Sometimes to make the challenge more difficult in a close match, and as a way of settling things, officials might switch the log to one with a smaller circumference.

This is the one event in which women were truly embraced in the lumberjack championships from the beginning. Women were part of the program in 1960 and always have been in logrolling.

90-Foot Speed Climb—Sometimes in the forest a lumberjack must climb a tree and trim its high branches or crown of leaves. This climb requires a competitor wearing spiked shoes to scamper up a 90-foot-tall cedar. The entrant must touch the top of the tree before heading down—a descent that can only be described as free fall. They do use ropes for safety and land on thick cushions.

Relay—While the word *relay* implies the passing of a baton, as is done at a track meet, this relay is actually a compilation of co-ed individual scores for a team. As an example, in 2009 the winning team consisted of Karmyn Wynyard in single buck sawing, Guy German in the 60-foot pole climb, Tyler Fischer in the boom run, Alyse Schroeder in the boom run, Matt Cogar in the underhand chop, Rick Halvorson and Alastair Taylor in the masters double buck, and Brad Delosa in the standing chop.

Single Buck Sawing—In this event an individual wields a one-man bucking saw (a buck saw with very large teeth) to cut slices of 20-inch-diameter pine logs down to size. The power is supplied by human muscle, and the competition ends when one cut is made. This event is consistent with the image of one man sawing down a tree in the forest. The women's single buck sawing competition began in 1995.

60-Foot Speed Climb—This event is similar to the 90-foot speed climb, only shorter. On the descent, the climbers must touch the cedar every 15 feet.

Springboard Chop—This is an axman's event. Simulating the type of work that might be required in the forest, the chopper must advance up a tree trunk. The next step is cutting a deep enough gash into the trunk to insert a board (the springboard) that will hold his weight. As the competitor works his way up, a second gash is slashed and another board inserted. As the lumberjack stands on each slat he is working to get close enough to chop up a 12-inch-diameter aspen log on top of a nine-foot-tall pole. The fastest competitor to finish all of these steps is the winner.

Standing Block Chop—In this axman special, competitors stand on level ground when wielding their axes. An aspen log that is 12 inches in diameter and 28 inches long is placed on a flat surface. When the 3-2-1 countdown hits go, the lumberjacks start belting the wood with their axes in an attempt to cut right through the block.

Tree Topping—Tree topping takes the 60- and 90-foot climbs one step further in degree of difficulty. Not only does the competitor have to ascend the tree, but while on top he must carve up a block of wood, 12 inches long with a 3-inch starter cut, using a crosscut saw he has carried with him. This event was contested for stretches between 1960 and 2000 but is no longer part of the championships program.

Underhand Block Chop—In this event, an aspen log the same size as that used in the standing block chop—12 inches in diameter and 28 inches long—is assaulted with an ax. The difference is that instead of swinging levelly, as if stroking a baseball with a bat, the lumberjack stands above the log, feet straddling it, and swings the ax from over his head. This event is an accident waiting to happen. Although no lumberjack has severed a foot or toes with an errant swing yet, such a mishap looks ripe to occur at every single competition.

Women's Events—When the Lumberjack World Championships were founded in 1960, there was only minimal female involvement in organized sports. Little League was for boys. High school and college sports teams were for guys. Just about the only opportunities women had for high-level competition were in the Olympic Games. But as time passed and women took a more active and routine role in sports, the Lumberjack World Championships responded by adding more and more events for female competition, primarily in 1995. Traditionally, a lumberjack was a man, but eventually, whether they had actually worked with wood or never set foot in a forest, an equivalent term was coined: *lumberjills.*

Timber!

Introduction

 "Yo ho!" The words echoed at the Lumberjack Bowl, repeated and chanted by a crowd of thousands on cue following dramatic developments at the Lumberjack World Championships.

The simple exclamation bridged the space between the world of lumberjacks and lumberjills and that of the fans who roared at their accomplishments. "Yo ho!" It was almost like a children's game, with a nattily attired lumberjack poser orchestrating spectators' responses as if they were kindergartners.

Some may deem it silly, but the cry of "Yo ho!" captures the spirit of a rollicking sporting event that is deeply rooted in American history and legend. For several days at the end of July each year, Hayward, Wisconsin, becomes the timber sports capital of the universe, a place where the men and women who are the best, the strongest, and the fastest sawyers, tree climbers, and logrollers gather for a festival celebrating a nearly bygone way of life that helped build the United States.

During this gathering of the clan, the uniform is plaid, the tools of the trade are gleaming axes and saw blades, and the muscular competitors are the twenty-first-century links to Paul Bunyan and Babe the Blue Ox.

The lumberjack of yore is a cornerstone of the American story. He is a gruff, tough, well-muscled man who plied a hard trade and risked his life to make a living. He paid a steep price, enduring frigid winters in the remote north country woods of Maine, the Upper Midwest, and the Pacific Northwest, transforming towering trees into logs that became the boards that built homes as the nation grew.

Just as one generation of youths dreamed of going west to become cowboys, their successors imagined themselves unconstrained by delicate society, living in the woods with other unshaven men, by brute strength felling trees that would be used for the common good. You didn't need much book learning to train as a lumberjack. For the most part it was about want. If you wanted to do it badly enough, you did it. You set out from home on your own to make your own way. There was no rule against having smarts, but it took more brawn than brains, power in the shoulders and stamina in the chest, to make a go of it in the forest.

The pioneer spirit in the hardiest of Americans who settled the West, who moved the nation ever westward from the Eastern Seaboard, was envied by the respectable men who stayed behind and wore neckties when going to work. Becoming a lumberjack wasn't for everyone, but everyone seemed to admire them to a degree. It was good, honest labor and the notion took hold that cutting and chopping in the great outdoors under God's blue sky equaled a freedom of sorts.

And once that happened, the lumberjack joined the mountain man, the minuteman, and the cowboy in the pantheon of romantic American heroic figures. America was a land where anybody could grow up to become president, but it was also a land that embraced the rugged individual. Logging was a hard profession, but that was part of the mystique.

Lumberjacks came in all shapes and sizes and from every corner of the globe. The lumberjack world included Native Americans like Ojibwes, Potawatomis, Menominees, and other Indians wherever the pine trees grew tall. It was a profession that also attracted immigrants to U.S. soil, many of them French Canadians in the Northeast, where Maine touched Canada, as well as Germans, Finns, and Swedes in the Midwest. It was more important to swing an ax proficiently than to speak English precisely.

The lumberjack, like the cowboy and mountain man, grew in stature in the telling and retelling of stories, true, partially true, or out-and-out fabrications, and long after the lumberjack's role has diminished in the everyday working world, the image of the lumberjack as one of the great, swaggering characters of nation building still touches a chord in Americans who are no more likely to pick up a fine-toothed saw than steer a plow.

"It is the romantic in people," said Lumberjack World Championships executive director Diane McNamer. "This is the larger-than-life man. It's John Waynesque. This is the man that will conquer the wilderness. You marvel at their ability."

John Wayne was a football player named Marian Morrison at the University of Southern California before he became John Wayne, the ultimate good guy with laconic but firm speech, who seemingly tamed the West by his lonesome with six-guns in each fist and the reins guiding his horse in his teeth.

Paul Bunyan is the John Wayne of the lumberjack world, the superhero, patron saint of ax wielders and sawyers everywhere. There are children's books galore exploring the exploits of a man who grew into a giant and always did the right thing. Of course, there is a Paul Bunyan for almost every occasion. Apparently, in the old logging camps where the men told bawdy stories, there existed a Paul Bunyan who was quite a randy guy. Those stories were not written down.

Tracing the roots of the Paul Bunyan figure takes one down a slippery slope. Some origin stories credit a series of French tales dating to 1837 for the creation of Bunyan. In these stories, passed on by generations, Bunyan was a National Football League–sized lumberjack in Quebec who distinguished himself in a battle against the British.

Probably only one in a million Americans can cite that story in connection with Bunyan, and some researchers have discredited it.

Paul Bunyan as we know him, a giant capable of phenomenal feats with goodwill toward all, dates in print to 1906. That year a Michigan journalist named James MacGillivray wrote some newspaper stories featuring a character called Paul Bunyan. A hundred years later, August 10, 2006, was celebrated in Michigan as Paul Bunyan Day.

However, in the days before the Internet, when every sentence uttered in any forum spreads like wildfire, MacGillivray's authorship of stories in a small, out-of-the-way newspaper called *The Press* in Oscoda, Michigan, would not have sufficiently spread the Bunyan story.

Others took up their pens and contributed details to the emerging Bunyan persona. One writer described the bearded giant as eight feet tall and weighing three hundred pounds. Others gave Bunyan a faithful companion in Babe the Blue Ox.

In 1916 an advertising copywriter named William Laughead molded the commonly known Bunyan legend, borrowing details from here and there and unleashing his own imagination. Laughead the writer had once been Laughead the lumber camp worker. Bingo. Laughead had a hit on his hands. Appropriately enough, he sold his handiwork to the Red River Lumber Company. The company adopted Bunyan, and its first advertising brochure featuring the big man was called "Introducing Mr. Paul Bunyan of Westwood, California."

Interestingly, in an age well before frequent-flier miles would have made Paul's travels easier, he was spotted working the forestry circuit in the Northeast, Midwest, Pacific Northwest, and West. He was everywhere. Bunyan's universality was swiftly established, and a century later there are statues in tribute to him all over the land.

Eau Claire, Wisconsin, is home to a Paul Bunyan statue. So is Westwood, California. But so are Maine, Michigan, Minnesota, and New York. Consistent with the legend of Bunyan being a very big dude, many of the statues are also extra-large roadside attractions; the statue in Klamath, California, is just shy of fifty feet tall with a faithful thirty-five-foot-tall Babe erected next to it.

Communities in all of those states declare a specific kinship with Bunyan and, using one line of reasoning or another, claim that they are his hometown. Their claims revolve around the attraction of the tourist dollar. Indeed, whether Bunyan is on one knee leaning on an oversized ax in Akeley, Minnesota, or standing (very) tall in Portland, Oregon, he is both a formidable sight and a wonderful photo op.

One reason why Bunyan endures in American legend, likely as popular as ever, is because he has no skeletons in his closet. He is a perfect hero with no blemishes on his record. There are two common denominators in post-1920 Paul Bunyan stories. One is his prodigious strength. The other is that when confronting the forces of evil he is always on the right side of the law and the moral imperative, standing up for the little guy, protecting the weak.

This made Bunyan a superb spokesman for lumberjacks everywhere. He may have been too good to be true, but truth is often the first casualty in advertising. The subliminal message imparted was good publicity for loggers.

Sometimes in Paul Bunyan stories you find him involved in lumberjack games. It wasn't as if anyone could give him any competition, but just because he could cut down more wood than anyone else didn't mean the games weren't worth playing.

Loggers holed up in winter camps in the forest, minus the finery of civilization and the company of ladies, often became bored. In their idleness after long days of work and hot, hearty meals, if they didn't play card games or read books they didn't have much to do.

Timber sports, or the linear descendents of those events contested at the Lumberjack World Championships, got their start in the logging camps. As a rule, alcohol was not allowed in the camps, but people will always drink if they can obtain the juice. In the camps, that was true during free time, but the lumberjack presence was also strong in any nearby saloon. It is no stretch to picture a handful of lumberjacks lolling around camp shooting the breeze when a challenge was issued.

"I bet I could cut down that tree faster than you could," one logger might have said.

"Hah, not if I gave you a three-ring head start," another might snort in return.

"A dollar [pretty big stakes in those days] says you can't."

"You're on."

No doubt within minutes the axmen would line up, now surrounded by cheering friends making their own bets, and start swinging. Soon enough the men (and they were all men) would expand the games, adding one-on-one logrolling or sawing a downed log into many even-sized slices. Lumberjack games were for private amusement in a camp. But they moved from camp to camp with the loggers themselves.

At the end of winter logging seasons, the cut logs were transported to market on rivers, guided by "river pigs" whose talents at the dangerous occupation often drew crowds along the shore. These were men at work, not play, and the spectators admired their skills.

Author Robert W. Wells makes the case in his book *Daylight in the Swamp* that the favorite pastime of loggers was starting fights and engaging in vicious brawls. There was some logrolling, he wrote, but "Such milder sports as birling never replaced the barroom brawl in popularity."

Wells does describe one epic logrolling competition around 1900 that pitted the champion of Michigan against the champion of Wisconsin. For seven hours the men clung to their logs without dislodging the other. For over six and a half hours the next day, including an hour lunch break, they went at it again. Finally, the Wisconsin chap prevailed and won a hundred dollars.

Reviewing reportage of historians such as Wells, as well as individual lumberjack diaries dating from the mid–nineteenth century, it would seem that lumberjack sports ranked in this way: (1) drinking, (2) fighting, (3) lynching, (4) whoring, and (5) birling.

Perhaps the oldest birling, or logrolling, event to draw a crowd in the thousands dates to July 6, 1879, in Toledo, Ohio. University of Wisconsin authority James P. Leary has said, in a paper delivered in 1998, that Upper Midwest loggers started competing in birling in public in the 1880s.

Some aspects of timber sports spilled over into the world at large. Starting in 1910, a fair in Goshen, Connecticut, chose a Woodsman of the Day based on a lumberjack sports competition. The Mountain State Forest Festival was inaugurated in West Virginia in 1930. A Paul Bunyan Day was declared in Concord, New Hampshire, in 1939. In the Pacific Northwest lumberjack competitions date to the early twentieth century.

None of those loggers in the early twentieth century who were having a few laughs, fooling around, and collecting bragging rights would have believed that a century later the main connection between loggers and the average American citizen would be the games, not the lifestyle in the woods. The first response those axmen of the past would have uttered if told that thousands of people would someday travel hundreds or thousands of miles and pay good money to watch lumberjacks create sawdust is "G'wan, you're pulling my leg."

They may have found it easier to believe that the forests they knew so intimately, the woods they worked so hard, the places where they lived in strenuous conditions, would one day be logged out. Some may have seen it coming, the full-speed-ahead cutting that provided them with jobs but denuded lands. They would be more amazed to see how much forestland Americans have sealed off from logging in national parks and other protected areas. Instead of becoming building materials, millions of acres of trees have been placed under government protection so that those loggers' grandchildren can admire the scenery and their grandchildren's grandchildren can camp in the wilderness.

As a profession, logging has declined, with limited job opportunities of any type recommended by high school guidance counselors. Logging is hardly extinct, but there have been continuous developments in technology over the last century, so that today a small number of machines do the work that once employed hundreds in a single place.

In the American mind, as part of the past that made us what we are today, lumberjack stalwarts are kept alive through competitive timber sports, seen on television and watched in person in selected logging-experienced states, above all in Hayward, Wisconsin. There the lumberjack is hero and superstar athlete rolled into one.

The Lumberjack World Championships is where Paul Bunyan legends, the nostalgia of the old logging world, and the modern lumberjack overlap. It is where the wood chips still fly.

JR's Miracle

He had been weaned on the Lumberjack World Championships, and when he was a teenager, when he felt invincible, JR Salzman was the king of the world, champion again and again in the men's logrolling competition.

Salzman was a tightrope walker on wood, a Flying Wallenda on a round log floating in water rather than on a high-wire over open space. He had the balance of a figure skater and the savvy of a street fighter, able to employ strategies that tumbled his foes into the water time after time while he stayed dry.

Logrolling, being part of the lumberjack games in Hayward, Wisconsin, where he grew up, was part of his identity. Hayward is a small town, but everyone knew him not just as one of the local kids but as the best in the world at what he did. Not that it was any surprise that Salzman took up logrolling, or that he excelled at it. Three older sisters preceded him in what is essentially a game of chicken in which the loser gets dunked while trying to stay upright on a balance beam as it bobs in the water.

Older sister Tina Salzman Bosworth won ten world titles, and JR wanted to emulate her. When he was six he asked his mother, Bonnie, if he could try logrolling. All of her kids participated in a wide variety of sports, and Bonnie figured that JR would pass through his logrolling phase and go on to something else. He surprised her.

"That was twenty-three years ago," she said during the summer of 2009.

The Lumberjack World Championships are not a huge conglomerate with a gleaming office structure headquarters. It is an outfit that operates on the sweat and time of many volunteers. As long as her kids were going to be involved, Bonnie Salzman, who loved the games anyway, thought she should be, too. She was executive director for nine years and on the organization's board of directors for twenty. Today, even without an official title, she helps with various tasks.

When ESPN, the omnipresent sports television network, took an interest in timber sports and created its own Great Outdoor Games, logrolling was on the agenda, and JR Salzman was one of the invited athletes. Good choice. Over the years, as he matured from lanky teenager to young man, Salzman won so many medals that he could have filled his own treasure chest.

Salzman was a talent in his sport, a star in the timber sports subculture. He was a *somebody* whom people admired, if only because of his quick-footed genius in mastering an obscure skill.

Salzman accumulated six world titles, but unlike in basketball, baseball, or football, there is no chance of making a comfortable living as a logroller, and he enrolled at the University of Minnesota, seeking a college degree. After the terrorist attacks of September 11, 2001, Salzman felt he wanted to do something for his country. So he joined the National Guard. Since he was living in Minnesota at the time, it was the Minnesota National Guard.

As the wars in Iraq and Afghanistan escalated, more troops were called up, and Salzman's guard unit was deployed to Baghdad. During his first months in the Middle East in 2006, the personable Salzman maintained a website on which he recorded stories from the front. He called it "Lumberjack in a Desert." It was a blend of his personas.

A few months later JR was back in Wisconsin, visiting his wife Josie and family over Thanksgiving. It was a happy occasion, and anxiety over Salzman's fate ran no higher than it had when he was first sent overseas, though everyone realized that is not an emotion to take for granted.

When Salzman left home to return to Iraq on December 3, his father Darrell had a premonition that something was different, and he feared for his son's well-being. "Something's going to happen," he told Bonnie. She told him to shut up and never say such a thing again. But the worry did intensify. Soon after Salzman returned to action he informed his parents he was distraught over the death of a fellow soldier. It was the first time, Bonnie Salzman said, that she felt her son's confidence had been shaken. A couple of weeks later she heard not from her son but about him.

JR and Josie maintain a home in Menomonie, about a hundred miles from Hayward. It is a drive of about two hours. The younger Salzmans are close enough to Hayward for easy visits but are not next-door neighbors. This means they don't just drop by unannounced. When Salzman was wounded, the military contacted Josie. Rather than pick up the telephone, she drove to Hayward to tell Salzman's parents that JR's life was in jeopardy.

When Bonnie saw Josie at her door, she knew something was wrong. Her first sentence was, "Just tell me he's alive."

He was. It was Christmas Day.

Bonnie felt that if he could muster his will and other talents, JR would survive. It's a given that successful athletes are competitive and fight hard when confronted with adversity. But she thought JR had another advantage. When he was young he had taken violin lessons.

"I thought that might give him an extra edge in knowing how to concentrate," she said.

The suddenness and randomness of casualties in war have always played havoc with men's minds. One minute they are fine, sometimes in the middle of a conversation with a buddy, and the next they are bleeding or dead. It is a horror of war and unforgettable for those who live through it.

Salzman was commander of a scout vehicle, just completing a short mission in Baghdad and headed back to the U.S. Army base as part of a convoy, when an Iraqi explosive device was hurled through the open window of his Humvee. The explosion was powerful, concussive, damaging, and potentially fatal. The well-placed bomb injured only a few men, but one was Salzman.

The explosion knocked Salzman out, giving him a serious concussion. When he regained consciousness, he willed himself to reach for the Humvee door, but the message never connected because his right arm had been blown off.

"My arm was gone," Salzman recalled.

Maybe it was his athlete's background, but Salzman neither panicked nor lost his awareness of the situation. He stayed calm and asked the closest soldier for a tourniquet to wrap around the stump of his arm and halt the blood flow. It may sound odd, but Salzman believes that his logrolling experience helped him in that devastating moment.

"In logrolling, you look around and evaluate the situation," he said.

He looked around, recognized the urgency of his situation, and simply requested the tourniquet. That's what he thought he needed. It turned out that Salzman needed a lot more medical help than that, and he has memory gaps of some of the hours that followed.

Salzman knows something of what made his survival possible as events played out. Today's standard of battlefield medical care is considered by far the best of all time, and on-site rescues of casualties and the ability to move them to sophisticated hospitals in other countries far removed from the front are unparalleled. Salzman was a beneficiary of this network.

In the immediate aftermath of being wounded, Salzman was carried out of the danger zone and spent his first night being treated at a U.S. Iraqi medical center. By the second night he had been evacuated and flown to Germany, where there has long been a major American military presence with some of the most advanced war hospital care in the world.

While Salzman was in and out of consciousness, fighting for his life with the strength of a body built muscularly through sport and military training, doctors examined injuries that included a severely bruised brain, the loss of his right arm, and wounds to his left hand. Two surgeries sought to repair the initial damage.

On Christmas Eve of 2006, Salzman was transported to Walter Reed Hospital in Washington, DC, his home for the next nine months and the place where he endured five more operations.

The Salzman family began a DC vigil, keeping JR company, boosting his spirits, encouraging his initially weak efforts at rehabilitation, and just being there for him as the days, weeks, and months dragged on.

Salzman was right-handed. That meant he had to learn to write with his left hand. He was missing the ring finger on his left hand. That meant it was extra hard to tie his shoes. "When it's cold, I can't tie my shoes," he said. The brain injury complicated matters. Salzman had to learn to walk properly again—his balance, always one of his biggest strengths in logrolling, was affected. He had memory loss, no recollection of certain time periods, and lapses in concentration.

Rehab was draining. It was a long, frustrating, boring, demanding haul. Salzman wanted everything to be fixed, but everything was not going to be all right ever again. When he departed from Walter Reed in 2007, he had a prosthetic right arm. His motor skills and other injuries were still healing, and he was far from the fit athlete he had been.

Yet for all the weaknesses, all his losses, JR was rebuilding, and one way he could measure his recovery against his full-strength past was to return to his roots and the sport he loved most. In the summer of 2008, Salzman decided to enter the Lumberjack World Championships again. At the time he was a six-time men's logrolling titleholder. He was far from his peak, but mentally he needed to try to regain something precious that he had once owned.

The eyes of the public were on Salzman big time when his turn came in the logrolling prelims at the Lumberjack Bowl. For all of the timber sports fans who make pilgrimages to tiny Hayward—population 2,129 it says on the community signs—the championships are still very much a homegrown product. Most of the fans are from Wisconsin. Most of the competitors have been in the sport a long time. So easily 75 percent of the spectators knew Salzman's backstory and understood what he was trying to overcome.

When Salzman got out on the log in front of the typical four thousand fans who attend each session of the championships, it all felt familiar. But at the same time it did not. The setting matched his memory, but his muscle memory was out of sorts and his skills were rusty. In logrolling, two competitors balance on a log in the water and through trickery and fast feet attempt to make his or her foe lose traction and tumble into the water. The event is best three out of five rolls.

At his best, when he was younger and sharper, with his body intact, Salzman had the maneuverability to splash opponents by kicking up water in their faces and distracting them while keeping hold of the log himself with his short-spiked shoes. He used body language to distract. He head faked. His comprehensive strategy, combined with his dexterity, made him a winner.

But when Salzman resumed competition after suffering his wounds, he no longer could control his opponents. He could not make the same moves as quickly or successfully. Seemingly, his gift had deserted him. Friends and family were uplifted because Salzman had fought back well enough to put himself back into the arena. That wasn't good enough for him. His standards had been top flight. Go for the gold. But he did not contend for first place.

"I did pretty terrible," Salzman said with twenty-twenty hindsight, evaluating that comeback. "I was a train wreck."

For someone used to winning his specialty all of the time, being an also-ran entrant didn't cut it. Salzman was still trying to regain his equilibrium. As he and Josie managed their household, Salzman resumed his college studies and kept tuning up his body, adapting to his limitations and maximizing what he still had going for him.

In 2009 Salzman signed up for the lumberjack championships again with the goal of doing much better in logrolling than he had the season before. It's not as if he had no residual effects from his wounds. He did and always would. If it was cold, his "good" hand, the only one left, might go numb and he wouldn't be able to feel a thing. He was healthier, stronger, but how good could he be in the logrolling event? That he didn't know.

There were several other top contenders entered, including more recently crowned, younger champions who had taken over the event in Salzman's absence.

"It's a young man's event," Salzman said with a laugh. He was thirty years old that year. "I feel thirty," he said.

The logrolling battle stretched over three days. Athletes were eliminated one by one as the field narrowed to the gold, silver, and bronze contenders. Each time JR Salzman climbed up on a log, there was drama. By his standards, his comeback had failed in 2008. His struggle this time captivated the Lumberjack Bowl audience, thousands of watchers wanting to turn back the clock to a time when Salzman was whole.

No one could replace his arm and only he could restore his soul. The spectators were on the outside looking in. Salzman would keep working on his logrolling comeback mission.

A Land of Big Trees

If a tree falls in the forest and no one hears it, did it really fall? Yes, if it can be turned into lumber and converted into planks of wood to build homes.

At least from the days of Thomas Jefferson's presidency, Americans were fascinated with expansion westward, with exploration of the great continent they felt they owned and had won through hard work and the fight for freedom with the British. Many claimed that the birthright of Americans was to settle the vast lands east of the Mississippi, on the Great Plains, in the Rocky Mountains, and along the coast of the Pacific Ocean.

From Maine to Wisconsin to Washington and Oregon, there were millions of acres of trees for the chopping, a natural resource of great plenty that could be harvested to build a country. Through the muscles in their shoulders and the effort in their hands, men could build homes for their families. The United States was blessed with millions of pine trees, and their harvest became a fundamental industry of the country.

For those who didn't own the land, or have the wherewithal to obtain it, there was logging, and most professional lumberjacks worked for large corporations, which cut the trees to fulfill America's gargantuan appetite for lumber. Many were young men with a glint in their eye and romance in their souls, anxious to leave home and impatient to establish their own lives separate from their families. They might be transients in the profession, working the forest until they could set aside a substantial poke to stake the next phase of their lives. Others came to the woods temporarily and stayed, making lumberjacking their livelihood.

There were costs, however. Men learned by trial and error that logging was an extraordinarily dangerous job. Men died in various and dramatic ways when chopping and sawing went wrong. Trees cut to fall one way fell in another, crushing the life out of loggers in seconds. Fingers and limbs could be lost to wayward slashes with sharp blades.

Risks and the hard work drove some men off. They had seen enough, experienced enough, lost friends, and didn't want to push their luck. Ultimately, the U.S. Department of Labor proclaimed logging the most dangerous job in America, with 118 deaths for every 100,000 workers. It was a dubious title, and the number illustrated what the men on the ground already knew.

Logging worked its way west as settlement spread and American cities sprang up with a desperate clamor for building materials. Logging began in earnest in the 1840s and for most of the next hundred years was either an expanding or a stable industry, providing a product to match demand.

Yet even as Yellowstone was established in Wyoming and Montana as the first national park in the world in 1876, there was little or no environmental consciousness in society. There were no checks on business expansion and no recognition that once a forest was clear-cut it was gone. Beauty was not a consideration when money was involved. Until Teddy Roosevelt's presidency between 1901 and 1908, virtually no one made the argument that future generations might deplore what some have described as the pillaging of the land. The word *rape* has also been applied frequently to what the early logging companies did to the nation's old-growth forests.

It was not a time to question logging barons, though Louie Blanchard, a nineteenth-century logger, did express a tinge of regret on looking back at an abandoned camp. "They left behind a sorry looking land," he wrote in a diary he left behind. "Miles of stumps and brush, piles of branches where the swampers and skinners trimmed the trees, roads that never growed up again."

Up until about 1870 a forest worker was called a shanty boy. After that the term *lumberjack* came into vogue. John Emmett Nelligan, a man whose woods career spanned that time period, was like most men of the day who spent time in the forest. They just wanted jobs. But in his memoir *A White Pine Empire*, Nelligan briefly wrote about the guilt he felt over denuding the land. "It was almost a crime against Nature to cut it," he wrote of a pine forest. "But we lumbermen were never concerned with crimes against Nature. We heard only the demand for lumber, more lumber, and better lumber."

These were statuesque, 400-year-old, 200-foot-tall pine trees being leveled. They were five to ten feet in diameter, bigger around than people could hug. The size of the trees and the scope of the fields of trees spread before loggers also provided them with the feeling that they were accomplishing something when they cut one down. Their mission was a large one, the sheer size of the trees told them, and thus an important one.

The gradual but seismic shift in public perception that a tree was more than just a commodity and something to admire, something that might have a different, aesthetic value just by standing there, ultimately helped transform the logging business.

For the better part of a century, trees were treated like rocks, like inanimate objects, not living, breathing plant life. Men with the means and power to do so denuded millions of acres of the American landscape at will, slashing their way through forests as if they were raging fires. Tremendous tracts of land in the Northeast, Upper Midwest, and Pacific Northwest that had once been canopied woods looked liked battlefield remnants with ugly stumps remaining where thousands of lush trees once stood. It was a decades-long process, but careless cutting with no planning for the future devastated many areas. Some areas were so foolishly overharvested that they could not be regenerated. Others would take a half century or more to replenish.

As for the lumberjack himself, if his conscience bothered him he had to get out of the business. If a logger said, "Hey, what are we doing here?" to a foreman, he would be laughed at. If he took a complaint or observation about what logging meant for the future of the land, he would either be dismissed as some kind of radical or fired. Maybe both. Logging was about finding work, not about scientific study.

According to *There's Daylight in the Swamps* by Mert Cowley, for about a fifty-year period spanning the last part of the nineteenth and the first part of the twentieth centuries, annual employment topped 112,000 in Wisconsin, Michigan, and Minnesota. This was the area popularized and still known as the "north woods." A great portion of the laborers were immigrants whose second language was English and whose educations were limited.

"If it was work you were looking for, chances were that you would find a job in the lumber industry that would suit you," Cowley wrote.

Men who could handle saws and axes were admired, but men were also needed to cook the meals to keep the workers productive, teamsters to handle horses, blacksmiths to shoe them, and assistants for all of them. It is interesting to note that in a chart of monthly wages for the 1899–90 season the cook and blacksmith were likely to be paid forty to forty-five dollars, highest on the scale, while a head bucking sawyer commanded just twenty-two to twenty-four.

The theory behind the payments is sound. It is said that an army marches on its stomach, and a logging camp was like a military encampment. Men couldn't work long hours if they didn't ingest enough calories. Likewise, the horses that moved sledges laden with logs had to be kept fit. Men who fit the bill for those tasks must have been at a higher premium than wielders of axes and saws. The idea was probably that a man of the right build and temperament could be trained to cut wood, but a master of the culinary arts was a prize catch.

The Julia Child of the logging camp was someone who knew how to cook in bulk, how to fill empty stomachs with hearty food that piled on calories and left a man feeling full and satisfied. A hungry work force wouldn't do. Yet there were limitations. In the early days of logging there was no refrigeration, and the cook had to make do with a certain budget and foods that didn't spoil quickly.

In another book, *Beyond the Shadows of the Pine*, Cowley listed numerous foodstuffs that showed up on logging camp dinner tables. Biscuits, flapjacks, and pancakes slathered with molasses and syrup were staples of the breakfast menu. Other meals included hot soups, beans, rice, and barley dishes. Bacon or sowbellies were served so often they were as likely to be on the long dinner table as were a knife and fork. And beans were available nearly on demand. In an era when meat was an important part of the daily diet, especially if hunted by the head of the household, fresh meat was scarce in the camps. Loggers wanted to stay on the good side of a cook. The man who provided the meals was too powerful to irritate.

In the interests of efficiency, and eating in shifts of thirty to forty, there was no talking at the table. This was not a time for relaxation, chatter, or reflection but a time set aside on the cook's schedule to down grub and replenish strength. There was time enough for jokes, storytelling, and idle talk later.

Logging was not commuter work. Once a man went into the woods, he did not return to the city overnight to hang out with friends in saloons. He did not return home to visit his family. Except for the occasional night out at a nearby town, he stayed. A man might not see his family for months, until the following spring. Logging camp workers lived in wooden bunkhouses in cramped quarters. Their bunks were hard and constructed close together. One bunkhouse might house a hundred men.

These were basically no-frills accommodations, designed to allow a worker a good night's sleep, a hearty meal, and a beam to throw his wet outer gear on to permit it to dry out before he went back out for another shift. Wool pants and long underwear hung from walls and ceilings and could create an obstacle course weaving through the bunkhouse. Most men slept in their clothes, never took baths, and accumulated lice. A stove attempted to heat the low-slung building, but it was still cold indoors in winter. There were no windows or light entering the building, which was little more than a shanty. This was the wrong setting, too, for a man concerned with privacy. Loggers were hardy men, not frightened off by the Upper Midwest's long, cold winters. They wanted to work.

Given the inside of the bunkhouse, where a stove could provide only so much heat, and outside, where the men worked all day, they might go for weeks at a time without being truly warm. The logging season was winter, when the big sleds pulled by draft animals could haul the cut trees long distances over snowy paths. Each morning, usually by 5 a.m., the cook shouted the wake-up call of "There's daylight in the swamps!"

Idle time in the camps gave birth to the first lumberjack games, mini-competitions designed to alleviate the boredom. Timber sports got their start in much the same way as rodeo. Cowboys who were camped on the range during a cattle drive were also prisoners of their environment and had time on their hands. They, and the ranch hands back at headquarters, were looking to kill time and make their activities interesting with a little bet here and there. A century later what the cowboys did for hire is the sport of rodeo.

Lumberjacks sought amusement, but they also wanted to live to tell the tale at the end of the season. Whatever safety procedures were recommended or followed, lumberjacks knew they had to follow their own common sense first and foremost, lest they become accident victims. For the most part they worked alone on a tree, hopefully within shouting distance of another lumberjack if an emergency arose and hopefully not too close if another tree fell in an unexpected manner.

If not as Paul Bunyan or with axes over their shoulders, the most vivid way lumberjacks are pictured and remembered is wearing brightly colored flannel shirts. This attire was attractive, but above all it was utilitarian. A lumberjack could be better seen in the woods if he wore a bright shirt that stood out against the background of forest colors. In a worst-case scenario, if he was injured, knocked unconscious, or partially trapped by a falling tree, the splash of color would make it easier for his rescuers to spot him on the ground.

In the early days of American logging, the weapon of choice was the individual ax. It was man against tree, one-on-one, like an encounter in a boxing ring. Near the end of the nineteenth century, tools evolved. The two-man saw, with its sharp teeth, came into vogue. Men worked as teams and increased their output.

Although it was not a game as such, loggers did compete informally among themselves and with other logging camps to see how high they could pile freshly cut logs on the sleighs their workhorses, or in some places oxen—if any were named Babe it was not publicized—pulled. The trees would be sliced and diced and readied for shipment to the outside world. Then, just before the horses started the trek out of the woods, lumberjacks posed with the haul. Some stood next to the horses, some climbed atop the load. In a famous picture that Cowley identifies as "the largest load of pine logs ever hauled on logging sleds in Wisconsin or Minnesota," two men are seen atop a pile of logs that is at least twelve logs high formed into a near square shape. One immediately wonders how the logs will make it to market without tipping over.

That photograph is dated March 17, 1909. The log pile was measured as 19 feet wide and 24 feet high, and it was estimated that the logs contained 71,770 board feet of wood.

That feat may have topped even Paul Bunyan's greatest effort.

Once they were loaded, in the Midwest the logs might be transported to steamships on the Great Lakes or sent to a river. They were sometimes rolled down an embankment directly into the water, using their own weight to propel them, and then floated downriver in a log drive, which was the lumberjacks' version of a cattle drive.

This was a solid system when it worked, but logjams were frequent. If too many logs piled up at a bend in the river, lumberjacks had to force them free. This was no easy task and definitely a very dangerous one. The loggers had to scramble out on the logs in either their tilted, jumbled-up, jammed-solid positions or as they floated. It was from this assignment that the sporting event of logrolling grew. The lumberjacks, who used poles known as peaveys to push the logs apart, had to maintain their balance on the round surface.

While lumberjacks might go head-to-head on logs in a protected watery inlet for sport, there was no amusement or laughter attached to the job of clearing a logjam. Men could fall into the water and drown. They might be crushed by logs. In what was possibly the worst logjam accident in American logging history, according to Cowley, eleven men perished by drowning on July 7, 1905, in the Chippewa River in Wisconsin.

In a wild, reckless form of sporting behavior, the finest river men disregarded their own safety in a bow to reputation building and rode logs over rapids. Some died taking the chance. Others, reports Cowley, were rewarded with a stamp of approval legitimizing their bravery. If they made it through the rapids, they were forevermore called "whitewater men."

Louie Blanchard, a lumberjack born in 1872, left behind a diary, which was published as a book called *The Lumberjack Frontier*. He said that he and his brothers had learned "to ride logs before we was knee high to a grasshopper."

Official record keeping of Wisconsin logging dates to 1839. In *The Wisconsin Logging Book, 1839–1939*, author Malcolm Rosholt wrote that the logging industry of the state owed its significance to the prolific presence of "great white pines." Logging transformed the existence of settlers by providing them with a steady supply of wood, he said, which elevated their standard of living.

"The lumber, laths and shingles from the Wisconsin pinery gave pioneers in the frontier settlements of the Midwest a chance to move from sod huts and log cabins into frame buildings," Rosholt wrote. The pine wood itself he called "a soft, pliable wood, yet sturdy and easy to work with a saw . . . or sculptor's chisel."

In the 1830s and 1840s, the primary crop in Wisconsin, which calls itself the Dairy State, was wheat. Farmers initially cut down the woods in their vicinity to build homes, barns, and other buildings on their property. This limited-scale logging was focused within a few miles of the Wisconsin River. Without a railroad nearby, wholesale logging was impractical. When rail lines were constructed, areas deeper in the forest were opened up for commercial logging, and by 1905 Wisconsin was the leading paper-producing state in the country. Logging was big business in the Heartland.

Blanchard said, "In the old days, logging was the only business going on. Everywhere there was timber." He usually referred to the forest of northwestern Wisconsin as "The Big Woods."

Logging still is big business in Wisconsin, though in a more mechanized and regulated way. In 2002, when Cowley, who is known as the "Jackpine Poet," wrote *There's Daylight in the Swamps*, his foreword was penned by Wisconsin state representative Mary Hubler, who said that year forest products and forest-based recreation contributed more than $23 billion to the state's economy. While "forest-based recreation" was not defined, it seems apparent that Wisconsin is reaping financial gains from trees that were allowed to grow and flourish—from people either simply looking at them on hikes or camping among them.

Wisconsin is still benefiting from its trees, whether they are in the horizontal, cut position or vertical.

Big Timber

The United States was settled from the East Coast to the West, from the original thirteen colonies up and down the Eastern Seaboard from New England to Virginia and on to Georgia, and when Europeans took their arduous seafaring journeys to the New World they were confronted by basically two things—Native American Indians and a stunning, incalculable number of trees.

It was a good many years before new Americans recognized that the Midwest was flat and the Great Plains existed, followed to the west by the Rocky Mountains. A good many years, that is, at least in terms of thinking about farmhouses, settlements, and cities.

The natural bounty, beyond the rich soil that was needed for crops to survive and thrive, consisted of forests, trees as far as the eye could see in many areas. A man with an ax and some muscle in his shoulders could cut down enough trees to build his family a home, protecting it against the harsh New England elements. That was the first step in the relationship of new Americans with their trees. Once a home was built to shelter the family, new settlers cut trees to build common buildings, churches, and courthouses. Then entrepreneurs who wished to make a living by providing goods and services needed wood cut for their buildings, a stable, or a general store.

The path led ever westward, and ever more dramatically in terms of building, into New York and Pennsylvania and then the Midwest. The people who embarked from ships from Europe were seeking new lives, and whatever country they came from, many joined other nationalities in the woods as lumberjacks. Towns and cities continue to grow, and even though brick, concrete, steel, and glass go into modern buildings, wood is still needed in abundance for the ever-expanding appetite for more housing.

Technology to construct skyscrapers and mesh other materials into sturdier structures had not evolved by the mid-1850s when logging became a major American industry. The demand for wood far superseded any other raw building material. It was that hunger to expand cities and build new homes that drove the logging world and provided the impetus for the start-up of remote logging camps in Maine, the north woods, and the Pacific Northwest.

Wherever the white pine reigned, men invaded the woods, working a harvest to fuel the nation. There were other trees that could be felled, but in an era before industrialization transporting lumber from the remote woods presented difficulties. The best way to start the process of turning a tree into a bedroom set was to cut it down in the forest and haul it to a river. Then the river did the transportation work with its natural current. Other kinds of trees might have provided an attraction, but hemlock, basswood, and hardwoods tended to sink, making them a poor alternative.

There were so many million pines to choose from that no one ever foresaw a dearth of them. Although the dissipation of forestland can be compared to the enthusiastic slaughter of the buffalo, which occurred around the same time, no one was inclined to make the comparison. No one took the time to do simple math. If it had taken a hundred years for a tree to grow so tall, why would anyone think it would take less than a hundred years for it to be replaced?

But America was the land of big business, and there were no constraints on a company taking what it wanted from land it owned. There was also no environmental consciousness. The first general stirrings of environmental awareness and the philosophy of leaving things intact or behind for our grandchildren did not take root until Teddy Roosevelt's presidency in the first years of the twentieth century. For the first time, as the National Park System was established and expanded, Americans began looking at a tree as something more than an inanimate object that could simply be destroyed. The appetite for wood was never satiated, but a minority sprung up espousing the notion that maybe it was not a good thing to cut down every tree in the forest all at once. How things looked when loggers abandoned an area did matter to some. Fields of stumps left behind as an area was forgotten appeared unnatural, even offensive to some.

Yet America was schizophrenic. On one hand some wanted to preserve the woods' beauty. On the other hand, many wanted new houses and businesses coming to their towns. It would still be decades, until the 1930s, before logging slowed down. It is estimated that between 1825 and 1880, 63 percent of Wisconsin's forest was denuded. Until then, the piney woods seemed inexhaustible and the lumberjack was the man you wanted to hear stories from while you sat in a saloon, even if you didn't want your daughter marrying one. It has taken a hundred years, through slow-growth restoration and regeneration, but 54 percent of the original Wisconsin forestland has been restored.

Lumberjacks had a certain status in the community as long as you didn't pry for too much detail. Not every job in the forest was created equal (even though they are considered equal today under the umbrella definition of *lumberjack*). The men who wielded axes and saws were the kings of the forest, the strong men of the profession who with their own coiled power cut down gigantic trees. Being a member of the support crew, which included working as a hauler with oxen or horses, or as a swamper who sawed the fallen tree into logs, was seen as a little less prestigious. A timber cruiser was a middleman of sorts. He moved through the woods and chose which trees were to be cut. It was a good job, though not as romantic as that of a sawyer or axman. The job title "river pig" turned people off, but it did not require working with smelly animals and herding them into their pens at the end of the day. Rather, the river pigs herded the logs together in the water and shooed them downriver to sawmills or railroad cars waiting to take them away. These logging groups worked in teams.

Accounts of the early days in logging camps are filled with deaths. Sudden deaths and harsh deaths, because of tumbling trees, but especially careless missteps on a river drive, barely seemed to interrupt the proceedings. The work had to go on. If a river pig fell between the logs and drowned, his body might not turn up for days. Sometimes his only grave marker was draping his boots on a tree limb overhanging the river. Early lumberjack stories made casual mention about these fatalities and always stressed how swiftly life returned to normal.

Camp life could be hard. The accommodations were not five star, and log cabins used as bunkhouses and cookhouses, with their tiny personal spaces, flimsy bunks, and drafty spots, were not constructed for a man's long-term comfort. They provided the food and shelter basics. It was not difficult to fall asleep, despite the crowd surrounding your bunk, because everyone was so tired from the long workdays stretching twelve hours or more. And it was all physical labor, too. Privacy was at a premium, and lumberjacks slept toe-to-toe in the squashed quarters.

Some early accounts of logging camps in Minnesota indicate that the men were not even provided shelter, but camped in a field, outrageous conduct by the operator, especially considering that this was winter in a place that knew winter well. A little later camps were established with large hearths throwing off heat at the center of a room where lumberjacks lay in their sleeping bags. A July 29, 1956, newspaper article from Duluth, Minnesota, indicates that in some camps there weren't even enough blankets to go around and when the temperature dipped a whole work crew slept under a large rug. Not surprisingly, the headline proclaimed, "No Sissies" as its way of informing readers that these were tough guys.

The next step in the care and feeding of lumberjacks was to actually build something stronger to protect them from the weather. Those were cheap structures, shanties. Finally, owners wised up and realized that for a minimum investment they could erect more solid logging camp structures. These buildings came with higher-class cooking and meals and indoor sleeping areas that were tight but better than lying on the cold, cold ground.

Modifying the trees into logs and removing them from the forest was the challenge facing nineteenth-century businessmen. Their costs were high because they needed to invest in labor and equipment that would allow them to move their product great distances.

Lumberjacking was a winter occupation because timber camps had no way to build roads and relied on smoothed-over, hard-packed snow as back-woods highways. They did not have plows to remove drifts, so the workers did their best to flatten spots and freeze them. This transformed the surface into ice. You might say that the loggers were the first ice road truckers.

The logging barons learned that the best available method for shipping logs that would speed them toward export to states in need of lumber was hooking draft animals up to sleighs and coaxing them into hauling. From draft horses to oxen, lumberjacks used the best available labor to load large sleighs—or overload might be the better description since the sixteen-foot logs were piled as high as possible without making the sleigh tip over.

Some logging camps preferred using horses, some oxen. Eventually, the next step in evolution reared up. Draft animals were eliminated by machinery that could haul more, had more strength, and didn't have to be fed fancy meals like hay. The haulers were train engines modified to move forward on treads like tanks. The development of these special trains also aided lumberjack travel immensely. When the camps first sprang up, the only way into the woods was on foot. In order to get to work, the loggers had to walk into the forest. Sometimes they had twenty-five or more miles to traipse. With no train or horses to ride, that made for a very long walk.

Still, lumberjack work in the north woods continued into the twentieth century at a thriving pace. Horses and oxen were replaced by trains, and they were replaced by tractors and trucks. More rugged vehicles conquered the terrain and allowed the loggers to work faster.

The days began early, at sunup, when the call of "R-o-l-l out" was one shout and the men only returned to the cookhouse at dusk. If there was daylight, it was meant to be productively used. Loggers worked six days a week with Sundays off. Booze was not allowed in camp—it was a dry town. And gambling was prohibited, not because the owners cared if a logger was foolish enough to lose his paycheck but because they didn't want fights starting over it or due to allegations of cheating. However, it is hard to believe that when loggers began to hold timber sports competitions there was no betting on the outcome.

It was years before men went after trees alone with saws. For decades they worked in teams, handling crosscut saws together. Two men worked a tree with axes as well. It was not until the advent of the chainsaw that a man could forgo the use of a cutting partner.

Camps meticulously recorded how much wood came out of their work stations and was shipped to market for the company. The statistics were marked down and in Wisconsin, at least, were reported to the state. One list from the 1888–89 season reports that the "Main Chippewa Camp" produced 75 million board feet of wood, with the South Fork camp at 38 million and Couderay at 30 million. Eau Claire, in western Wisconsin, became known as "Sawdust City," and in 1881 more than 203 million board feet of lumber passed through the community. One board foot is a square of wood measuring 12 inches long, 12 inches wide, and 1 inch thick. That's a heap of Lincoln Logs.

As a major logging industry center, Eau Claire was home to Porter's Mills from 1867 to 1893, Sherman Mill from 1888 to 1924, Kaiser Lumber Company from 1913 to 1924, and other enterprises. The business was huge in town.

In a scenario reminiscent of the Old West with arguments over un-branded cattle, lumberjack camps made claims on "stray" logs floating down the river, even if they had not cut them. By 1861, Wisconsin had a law in place requiring companies to stamp their logs with some kind of identification. Whereas tampering with a man's cattle in the West might involve gunplay, the fine for messing with a man's logs was ten dollars.

As romanticized as lumberjack work is now, when fewer people do it or realize how backbreaking some of the tasks were, there is little in popular culture that tells the story of the true logger. It has been left to events such as the Lumberjack World Championships to play a role in preserving the historical sidelights of a rough-and-tumble profession.

There are few movies that celebrate the logger or even portray him in a realistic light. While the logger is not an anachronism—logs still roll down Wisconsin's state highways on trucks—even avid movie fans would be hard-pressed to think of many that show the lumberjack in celluloid.

One exception is the movie *Sometimes a Great Notion*, based on the novel by Ken Kesey. Published in 1964, the story is set in the Pacific Northwest and is a tale of one family's struggle to survive as small-business loggers doing things their own way without extensive modernization. This was no feel-good Paul Bunyan tale but a hard look at modern life and trying to cope with change. Henry Fonda played the hardheaded father and Paul Newman the hardheaded son in the movie, which was released in 1971.

Another movie was *Come and Get It*, based on an Edna Ferber novel. Made in 1936, the show starred Eddy Arnold, Joel McCrea, Frances Farmer, and Walter Brennan and featured the story of a Wisconsin family at the end of the nineteenth century and beginning of the twentieth when logging was at its peak in the state.

Reality TV shows are the rage in the twenty-first century, and television did find its way to the forest, or at least to the lumberjack world. A show entitled *Ax Men* has joined *Ice Road Truckers, Survivor,* and others of their ilk on the air. But it's unlikely that any TV producer would have dreamed up an axman show without exposure to timber sports from the Lumberjack World Championships via ABC's *Wide World of Sports* or ESPN's *Outdoor Games.*

For those at the top of the timber sports world, many likely would have worked in the logging world if they had been born seventy or more years earlier. Some have found their niche and work in wood, from Rick and Penny Halvorson, who own their own small logging company in Alma Center, Wisconsin, to Dave Jewett, who carves animal figures with a chainsaw.

In a very different world that hums along because of high-tech machinery and computers, they know they are fortunate to be able to indulge their passion for handling saws and axes in any manner. But they also have a sense of history and tradition and feel the connection to the old logging days in their hands and hearts and through what they do.

"They were real loggers back then," said Ron Lambert, past president of the Lumberjack World Championships, of the men of the forest from days gone by. "They're athletes now."

There is considerable truth in the observation, but many of the championships' champions have paid their dues as real-life woodsmen in carving, cutting, or sawing endeavors and adapted their work techniques into competitive skills. Matt Bush of Croghan, New York, is a two-time single-buck winner in Hayward. He has shared three double buck titles and won the coveted all-around best lumberjack trophy three times in a row from 1996 to 1998. What does he do for a living? He operates a sawmill.

While the link is strong between timber sports and real-world logging, in Bush's mind in recent years they have drifted farther and farther apart.

"It's slowly separated," Bush said. "This is competition. It's not related to the logging industry anymore. Not how we apply it. It's a sad thing."

Sad thing or not, it is unrealistic to expect timber sports to mimic the current, more mechanized logging world. The Lumberjack World Championships have modified their approach, especially in terms of showmanship over the last half century, and certainly many of the big dudes of power and strength performing so superbly over the years had the wherewithal to work in the forest if they wanted to or if the opportunity was present in a profession of diminished size.

The logging world remains in their minds and in their roots, and is not forgotten, but Bush is correct in stating that the majority of the best timber sports athletes in the world are athletes, not loggers. It is a reflection of the passage of time and if not the passage of a way of life, a major alteration of it.

What was once solely a hard way to make a living has been embroidered and modified. Yet still the axmen cometh, and if someone needs a tree cut down he need look no farther than the Hayward Lumberjack Bowl to find an able candidate.

A Man with a Plan

Tony Wise was a visionary, as well as a wise man.

Born and raised in northern Wisconsin, Wise returned to Hayward after a distinguished army career during World War II brimming with ideas on how to make the community a hotbed of skiing.

His plan to turn Hayward into a mecca for tourism was kindled by his wartime experiences with the Fourteenth Armored Division in Bavaria, where he served as a captain. Watching soldiers ski in the mountains made him wonder if his home area could become an attraction for cross-country skiing. Wise had earned an MBA from Harvard University, and he was determined to mesh his business acumen with his belief that Americans would take to skiing in Wisconsin the way they had in Europe.

Born on March 15, 1921, in Hayward, Wise was part of an established north woods family that had been in Sawyer County since the nineteenth century. A grandfather, Anthony Wise, founded the A. Wise Land Company. After his military service, the enthusiastic and ambitious Tony Wise moved back to Hayward in 1947 with his commitment to revving up the local postwar economy implanted in his mind.

Using five thousand dollars in savings accumulated over the years, Wise made the down payment on a new ski resort, called Telemark, and it opened for business in December of 1947 with an old airplane engine powering the towrope. Over the following years, Wise was also the man behind the creation of the American Birkebeiner, the marathon ski race that is the premier event of its type in the United States, and a tourism park called Historyland. In 1960 he was instrumental in establishing the Lumberjack World Championships in Hayward and promoting them into the dominant event of its kind in the world.

Diane McNamer, the executive director of the championships, said she first met Wise in the mid-1970s and actually worked as a cocktail waitress at the Telemark resort for a while. Wise was not a huge man, standing about 5 feet, 10 inches, and he had light brown thinning hair, the hairline receding from front to back. It was not his physical magnetism that made people listen to his ideas, that sold his schemes, but the passion behind them. Wise could explain his visions in such a way that others saw the value in them, too. He talked fast, and when he was on the go, which was most of the time, he walked fast.

Some in the small community felt it was destined to remain a remote place tucked in the woods at the end of the road. It took persuasion to make them believe otherwise. Wise talked of luring thousands of visitors to town each winter for skiing, each summer to watch lumberjacks, and year-round to visit Historyland. He was right. The ripple effect from those who came to visit Wise's operations was significant. Tourists spent money at restaurants and hotels and bought souvenirs. As long as they could cope with the cars and foot traffic, everyone benefited.

Like his other enterprises, Wise's Historyland attracted attention not only from tourists with money to spend but from reporters with ink to spill. Gareth Hiebert, a columnist for the Saint Paul *Pioneer Press*, in the Minnesota city located about 150 miles southwest of Hayward, made a pilgrimage north in 1965. He couldn't get over the crowds of people in the streets of the little town. Muskie fishing (always a lure), boating and canoeing, and the north woods in general were partly to blame for fifteen-minute waits to reach the counter in a bakery, but the real culprit, Hiebert noted, was Historyland's appeal.

Hiebert called Historyland "a real magnet, with things to do and see, and eat," and a place covering three hundred years of Wisconsin history on sixty acres of land. Hiebert noted that Wise employed one hundred Indians from five tribes at his Native American educational exhibits and village and marveled at an eight-car train and five different restaurants on the premises, observing that Historyland's managers must believe that "a well-fed tourist is a happy tourist."

The reporter read Wise's mind. Not everyone could, or thought like him, either.

"He was a man who said, 'Why not?'" McNamer said of Wise. "It was never, 'We can't.' His thinking was, 'Why can't we bring these people here?'"

With the passage of time, McNamer has reflected on what made Wise tick, so determined to put his town on the map, so driven to organize larger and larger events meant to place the nation's or world's spotlight squarely on Hayward and its most prominent proponent. "Maybe it was from his time growing up through the Depression," McNamer said.

Wise poured his energy and money into making Telemark a success. It was an achievement to get the ski resort up and running in late 1947, but his "if you build it they will come" philosophy was more complex than that. Not only did Wise build it, but he expanded it, grew it, and made Telemark into a palace of a ski resort, not just some halfway decent building where you could change out of your street shoes and lace up ski boots.

Wise constantly made improvements, adding a T-bar lift, snowmaking equipment, townhouses, and a fancier lodge.

By the early 1970s, Wise had expanded Telemark into a much broader based recreation site. It was no longer merely a ski resort, but after the snow melted it offered golfing, horseback riding, canoeing, tennis, bicycling, and swimming and had facilities to host events attracting two thousand people. But, as Wise might have said, "Wait, there's more." In the Rathskeller bar there was a singing waiter. In another room there was a jazz piano. Elsewhere a room featured bands with rock music aimed at teenagers under the legal drinking age. He brought in big-name acts for concerts, though he lost money because older members of the community did not turn out. That disappointment made Wise focus his attention more tightly on luring younger people to the resort, and he added a special New Year's Eve show and extravaganza aimed at people in their twenties.

"This finding made me realize that this is the group to which we've got to gear our business," Wise said. "Older folks have other interests."

Long before Wise turned Telemark into a kind of combined Olympics-Copacabana site, he stretched his brain to think up a complementary summer destination that could pull in crowds, too. In 1954, Wise opened Historyland. In the warmer months, tourists were taken back in time through exhibits on Native American life, the lifestyle of the early fur traders, and logging. From the start there was a strong Native American presence at Historyland, and one featured attraction was a reconstructed Ojibwe village. Not neglecting the bounty of the outdoors, visitors could also take paddle-wheel rides around Lake Hayward.

In an example of forward thinking for the times, Wise not only had a deep respect for the local Native Americans, but he developed a working relationship with tribes and guaranteed that at least 10 percent of his work force would be Native American, with particular thought given to the Ojibwe on the nearby Lac Court Oreilles reservation. That was a nearly unthinkable step in the 1950s and 1960s.

Wise was not one to simply throw open the doors and expect people to come to his attractions. He was manic about making improvements, about keeping up with market changes.

"It isn't enough anymore to offer people hunting and fishing, a place to rest, or even a place to ski," Wise said in 1967. "They want more, and they're going to go where they find more. To my way of thinking, there are three major facets to this leisure-time business. The other two, besides recreation, are low-keyed education and lively entertainment. You've got to combine those three—at least that's what I've been trying to do."

And if none of Wise's existing facilities jump-started tourists' juices sufficiently to provoke them into throwing the kids in the car and taking a drive to Hayward in 1960, his indefatigable energy manufactured the Lumberjack World Championships. Lumberjack games had been played for decades, although for the first thirty years or so of their existence they were pretty much confined to logging camps where the men filled their spare time with competition.

From about 1900 on, timber sports spilled over into mainstream society at county fairs and such events. "Communities near logging operations across the country often treated loggers' work as entertainment, as accounts of crowds gathering to watch log drives and loggers' holidays attest," an article in *Journal of American Folklore* reported. There were occasional gatherings of the clan, more regional than national in nature, and certainly not a showcase of lumberjacks from far-off lands like New Zealand. The arrival of competitive lumberjacks from down under lay years in the future.

If Wise were a human pie chart, his body could be carved into six equal sections with three parts risk-taking entrepreneur, two parts showman, and one part savvy businessman. He overwhelmed people with his devotion to a cause, his persuasive arguments, and his willingness to put everything on the line to make a go of an enterprise. He could be like a runaway truck racing downhill with no brakes, and while he cared about how the end product turned out, and he was intensely proud of his creations, it was possible to see him as perpetually restless, unable to let well enough alone, and always hungry to take on the next challenge rather than stepping back and fine-tuning an operation that might need some care and nurturing.

The skiing came first. Wisconsin has no mountains high enough for a serious alpine ski resort. And until Wise transported his World War II memories to Wisconsin, Hayward wasn't a big cross-country skiing area, either.

"Tony is really the guy who got everybody skiing up here," McNamer said. "He charged the kids twenty-five cents to come after school."

It was good strategy to build support among the locals, four hundred of whom were employed by him at Telemark at its peak, along with an un-known chef named Emeril Lagasse, but the money to be made was in the wallets of the outsiders, tourists looking for a good time. It was an un-tapped market, and at times Telemark was nearly overwhelmed by its own popularity. In the January 22, 1967, issue of the *Duluth Sunday News-Tribune*, writer Walter Eldot reported on a New Year's visit to Telemark. Over the holiday, while older people stayed out of the winter chill, 2,500 "young folks flocked to the Hayward area for skiing and fun."

The community could not handle the deluge of partying visitors. With all accommodations booked to overflowing, some of those young folks spent nights in jail—not as lawbreakers but in lieu of hotel rooms. And Wise, responsible for bringing all of these people to town, put twenty-four tourists in a Pullman railroad car and opened up a building on his property that had been closed for years to sleep twenty-seven. The train car was part of a Historyland exhibit, and the former rooming house was supposed to be preserved as a historical artifact. Business boomed so much that Wise ended up routinely renting space on the train and in the ancient structure.

The historical railroad cars were part of a onetime Soo Line train that cost Wise, always on the lookout for a colorful bargain, twenty thousand dollars. The line was renamed the Hayward Telemark, Bayfield, and Lake Superior Line, which was all well and good, but it didn't carry passengers anywhere. In Wise's mind it was better to have the artifacts on hand and then think of some way to make them more useful or popular for the visiting masses.

Wise never forgot where he came from or where he lived. He did not try to force-feed irrelevantly inane projects to the populace, and he did not try to attract visitors to Hayward for events or to see sites that were out of place. He would never have built a sailing or mountaineering museum in Hayward. Skiing made sense because Hayward received lots of snow. Historyland made sense because its exhibits were all about Wisconsin and the region's past. There were Indians involved because they were native to the territory.

Similarly, the logging industry and the lumberjack lifestyle were linked to Hayward and northern Wisconsin. Local people related. So when Wise brought the Lumberjack World Championships to Hayward for the first time in 1960, it made perfect sense. Fifteen years later, when the championships were established and thriving in Hayward, Wise wrote, "The Lumberjack World Championships were inaugurated in 1960 to perpetuate and glorify the working skills of the American lumberjack. Hayward, Wisconsin came into existence because of the lumber industry. Two of the greatest American lumbermen, Frederick Weyerhaeuser and Edward Hines, had saw mills in this town. Therefore, it was fitting that one of the largest logging competitions should be held here also."

The logic was impeccable. As the Lumberjack World Championships grew and prospered, Wise compared the event to major rodeos and Wild West gatherings, citing its fame alongside that of the Cheyenne Frontier Days, the Calgary Stampede, and the Gallup, New Mexico, Indian Gathering. "Americans have great love for cowboys, Indians and lumberjacks," Wise wrote. "The aforementioned events bring back the flavor of those frontier heroes. The camaraderie and friendship that is so evident among competitors, officials and spectators at the Lumberjack World Championships each year makes this event resemble a grand homecoming."

Wise knew his product. He was right on with his analysis and viewpoint. As McNamer said, the closest cousin of the Lumberjack World Championships is the rodeo, the working lumberjack versus the working cowboy at play.

Lumberjack games in the camps date to at least the 1880s, but it was not until about 1910 that organized competitions conducted by loggers took hold in a public environment where fans watched. Buffalo Bill Cody and his Wild West extravaganza played around the world to standing-room-only audiences, spreading the gospel of the cowboy and Indian with his showmanship, staging, and wildly colorful live shows, but rodeo only gained in popularity later.

Neither animals nor Indians dressed in full regalia were part of lumberjack competition, but gradually shows caught on regionally with fascinated fans. In 1960 Wise, always thinking big, dreamed of staging the biggest lumberjack championships of all. He did not want just another regional showdown. He wanted lumberjacks from all over to come to Hayward.

Yes, Wise wanted to use the word in his advertising, but he wanted to conduct a real "world" championship.

In the parlance of hard-boiled police stories, the chief always announces, "Round up the usual suspects." Wise followed the same path. Through word of mouth, diligent research, and fast talking, he tracked down many of the finest lumberjack athletes in the universe and invited them to Hayward, Wisconsin. It's a good bet many of them consulted a map to see where Hayward was after Wise reached them via telephone, letter, telegram, or perhaps messenger.

"For the first time," McNamer said, "he brought together under one umbrella the best of the best to compete."

Judy Scheer Hoeschler, the seven-time women's logrolling world champion from Hayward, who grew up friends with Wise's children, remembers him making phone calls all over the United States and the world trying to bring together the top lumberjacks. Five decades later, she marveled at how the Lumberjack World Championships had grown, how each summer they bring Hayward together, and how the Lumberjack Bowl serves as the sport's best venue.

"It's all an achievement of Tony Wise's vision," Hoeschler said. "Look at the site. Nothing can compare to it. It's also a testimony to the community. He was ahead of his day. He was bigger than life in a place that's hard to make a living."

Hoeschler's brother, Fred Scheer, another multiple champion, said he got to know Wise well and was impressed with his boldness and what his energy produced for the community with his establishment of Telemark, the lumberjack championships, and the American Birkebeiner.

"Obviously, he founded these world-class events," Scheer said. "Tony was the kind of guy who was, 'Let's do it and we'll figure out how to fund it later.' And that worked for him for a long time. He was a fascinating guy. He was not afraid to take on and do things."

Wise was no millionaire, but his ideas were worth a million bucks. By the end of the 1950s, Telemark was a popular retreat and Historyland was a destination for families. Given Wisconsin's logging history, why not celebrate that era and industry with a new event emblematic of the past? Where better to hold a lumberjack gathering than the north woods? The Lumberjack World Championships, a product of Wise's fertile imagination, were about to become a reality in the summer of 1960. The motto was "Bring your axes and saws and be prepared to use them in pulp friction."

The Biggest Fish Around

When Tony Wise was mulling over his grandiose plans to make Hayward a center of north woods tourism with the Telemark Ski Resort, Historyland, the Lumberjack World Championships, and the American Birkebeiner, he was aided by one simple fact in the community's background.

The Hayward area was already a fishing mecca. It is located in the heart of prime northern Wisconsin muskellunge territory. Since the late 1930s, the lakes and rivers around Hayward had become world renowned for offering anglers the best chance to catch muskie the size of elementary school children.

Those huge fish, choosy on the bite, are hard to catch but provide supreme thrills when hooked. World-record fish are caught and certified in the region and the sport spawned an industry that spurred the area's economic engine. Eventually, the National Fresh Water Fishing Hall of Fame was built in Hayward and its symbol became a kitschy, 140-foot-long, two-story sculpted muskie that has a staircase inside and offers views of the surrounding area by stepping through the big fish's mouth. Hayward may be the home of the Lumberjack World Championships, but it is also the self-proclaimed "Muskie Capital of the World," with good, legitimate reason.

The fishing hall of fame is its own tourist attraction and is located just across a parking lot, less than a quarter mile away, from the Lumberjack Bowl. When timber sports fans come to town, it is easy to take in the other attraction. Some tie in fishing day trips themselves, a cornerstone activity in the Hayward area. They can't resist taking a shot at capturing and releasing such an imposing fish. For anglers used to catching bass, perch, and bluegills, it is like switching from guppies to granddaddies when they pursue muskies that measure more than fifty inches long and, if they sniff the world record, might weigh sixty pounds.

Both Wise and those behind the fishing hall of fame had one major area of common ground. They wanted to see as many people as possible visit Hayward. They didn't care if they came for the fishing, the sawing, or the skiing; once they were in town they hoped they would walk through the doors of their establishments.

Hayward is located more than four hundred miles from Chicago and more than three hundred miles from Milwaukee. A major core of the constituency for Wisconsin recreation is based in those two cities, yet it is not a day trip to fish for muskie or to drop in on the lumberjacks. Wise and the directors of the hall of fame sought any incentive to get solo anglers, couples, or families to take a longer vacation in the north woods.

As of 2009, according to hall of fame executive director Emmett Brown, the hall averaged fifty-four thousand visitors a year. Brown, fifty-nine, is from Chicago, but his family spent summers in Hayward. He was a regular visitor from 1980 until 2004 when he moved north to take the job that combines work and pleasure, intertwining with his fishing hobby.

"It's the number-one tourist attraction in Northwest Wisconsin," Brown said. "When families come, kids catch their first fish in the pond on the grounds. The serious fisherman who is here for muskie comes by on a lousy weather day. We get lots of couples in the fall that come for the area's leaf walking. They're the gazers."

The pond on the premises contains about eighty thousand gallons of water. Sunfish, bluegills, perch, and crappies swim in it for the kids' catch-and-release fishery. The fish come from Lake Hayward, and in late September, as summer is waning and winter is on the horizon, the pond is drained and the fish swim back to the lake.

While the gargantuan muskie building is the showstopper (seen easily from afar), the hall's garden also features eight sculptures of different fish. They range from a coho salmon and walleye to a smallmouth bass and bluegill. These sculptures are a mere six to eight feet long. But no one talks about the other fish. The only topic of conversation (and you can get a postcard) is of the oversized muskie. In theory it is like Jonah stepping into the belly of the whale in the Bible, except that the whale didn't have a staircase lined with framed fishing photographs.

"That is the centerpiece," Brown said of the building, "the landmark. Especially for people who haven't been here before. If you're going to be in Hayward, you've got to see the muskie."

The National Freshwater Fishing Hall of Fame is more than a hall of fame, more than a tourist attraction, and more than a museum. It is also the repository and governing body that reviews world-record applications (three hundred a year) for 125 different freshwater species and the variations of line test records.

Above all, Brown said, "Hayward is a muskie town." He called the Louie Spray and Cal Johnson record-caliber muskies caught in the 1940s "supertankers," a terrific description if you think of the other, smaller species as cabin cruisers, sailboats, and pontoon boats. Brown attempted to craft an explanation of why three fish of such tremendous proportions were caught by Spray and Johnson within a short period of time and why no others of their ilk have been seen since.

"The muskie explosion," Brown said of that era, "was probably a perfect storm. The lakes were really not fished terribly hard. They were not exploited very heavily."

Essentially, that means there weren't hundreds of fishermen fighting for space on the water on a given weekend.

"Tackle was unsophisticated," Brown continued, "and not terribly efficient, and you had fish that had never been caught. At the time if you caught a muskie in Wisconsin that was thirty inches you killed and kept it. That was allowed for. I believe they probably do grow large still. Every once in a while one is found dead. Fifty-pound monsters always have been and continue to be unusual, but I think there are some record fish still around."

Developments in fishing lures, through trial and error, through experience acquired over years, have been dramatic. They also have become extraordinarily expensive, easily topping twenty dollars a lure for some fancier makes. Brown's point about that evolution is well taken, but so is the fact that more fishermen pursued muskie in recent decades and first caught and kept smaller ones, preventing those fish from growing to full size. Muskie once caught and released also become wary of biting on lures in the future. Maybe the fish do not have the same IQ as Albert Einstein, but they do have self-preservation instincts that kick in when they sense danger.

"They don't have intelligence," Brown said, "but they certainly have savvy. They have this tremendous instinct to feel out a situation. It's learned behavior: don't bite. Catch and release does teach fish not to bite."

Depending on who is doing the talking, muskies are said to be the fish of a thousand casts, or ten thousand. They are not so aggressive that they will chomp on just any lure at any time. They are picky to begin with. Yet knowing that the odds are worse than those of the Saint Louis Rams winning the Super Bowl any time soon, a muskie fisherman remains optimistic.

Knowledge and experience gained by a local guide are always helpful on a lake or river, but accidents do happen when a fisherman heaves his heavy lure out as far as he can and it conks a muskie on the head. Voila, the muskie grabs it between its sharp teeth.

"Even a novice fisherman can think, 'This could be the cast,'" Brown said.

The hall of fame recognizes with plaques and enshrinement ceremonies famous guides, anglers, and individuals who have advanced the sport with inventions. It contains about fifty thousand artifacts, Brown said.

As long as anyone can recall, the muskie has been the alpha fish in the region. Research by author and guide John Dettloff, whose family has maintained a lodge in the Hayward area for decades, indicates that five world-record muskies have been caught and verified in the immediate vicinity's bodies of water. There is a postcard reproduction of a photograph showing angler F. J. Swift wearing a snappy three-piece suit while standing next to the record 51-pound muskie caught in Chief Lake. The catch dates to September 13, 1916.

Dettloff, the author of *Three Record Muskies in His Day: The Life and Times of Louie Spray*, is a key supporter of Spray's claim that he caught three record-setting muskies. Spray was a controversial character, some considering him a bit of a con man, others calling him an out-and-out liar and fraud, and still others believing everything he said.

Spray was not a large man, but when he posed for a photograph with his first record catch holding it by the mouth it looked as tall as he was. The weight of the fish taken from Grindstone Lake on July 27, 1939, was 59 pounds, 8 ounces. Spray did not retire and rest on his laurels. He kept fishing the local waters for muskie, and on August 19, 1940, he announced that he had bettered his previous record with a 61-pound, 13-ounce muskie caught on Lac Court Oreilles. It was a beauty.

About nine years later, a local fisherman named Cal Johnson, prowling on Lac Court Oreilles, injected himself into the giant muskie debate.

Johnson hooked a muskie so large he had difficulty holding it up in the air when he posed for his trophy fish picture. Johnson's catch on that lake weighed in at an astounding 67 pounds, 8 ounces. The fish's length was 60$\frac{1}{4}$ inches.

The milestone catch was made on July 24, 1949. Johnson's fish was mounted and placed in a glass case. It resides in the Moccasin Bar in downtown Hayward, except when it makes road trips to outdoor shows. For someone used to catching fish that are a foot long or less using minnows or wax worms, Johnson's muskie resembles a cousin of the Loch Ness monster. *Monster* is the appropriate word. Muskies devour smaller fish in lakes and rivers as part of their diet. If another fish sees a muskie coming it will try to outswim it. If not, it's goodbye, into the gullet.

In some quarters, Johnson's catch is believed to be the true record. He has benefited from the continuing existence of the mount, which has long outlasted him. When Johnson's muskie eclipsed Spray's two massive fish, it was likely believed that the record would safely stand for quite some time. Wrong. Only a few months later, on October 20, 1949, while fishing on the Chippewa Flowage, Spray hooked and landed still another gargantuan muskie. This one weighed 69 pounds, 11 ounces and was 63$\frac{1}{2}$ inches long.

Three times the colorful Spray, who was a deft self-promoter, made once-in-a-lifetime catches. In an era when rules for record recognition were simpler and less formal, and when media attention was limited, particularly in the electronic world, there was less demand for detailed proof of records. Still, there was suspicion that not all of Spray's catches, and their professed sizes, were on the up-and-up.

Questions surrounding the legitimacy of Spray's muskie claims garnered huge amounts of publicity over many years, and to some the matter, despite hall of fame recognition, will never be resolved. The attention lavished on the Spray debates, however, was good for business. Whether his fish hauls were genuine or not, there was little doubt that the muskies he snared were huge. That meant perhaps someone else could come north and better Spray's marks.

Rather remarkably, nearly sixty years after Spray's last record catch, and more than twenty years after his 1984 death, the case was reopened and reinvestigated after a group of Illinois and Wisconsin anglers protested its legitimacy to the hall of fame. In 2005 the hall attempted to put the issue to rest for all time with a ruling that reconfirmed its acceptance of Spray's fish as the world-record muskie. "In retrospect, Louie Spray's world-record muskie is likely the most scrutinized muskie ever caught," a statement from the hall of fame said. "Some may never want to believe in the muskie, and perhaps that goes with the territory whenever one talks about such a fantastic accomplishment or happening. However, the fact remains that Louie Spray's 1949 world-record muskie is exceptionally well-documented and the National Freshwater Fishing Hall of Fame is confident that the fish was as big as claimed."

There were many eyewitnesses when Spray brought the fish to Herman's Landing on the Chippewa Flowage that fateful day, the hall of fame stated, and those people indicated the fish was freshly caught. (There were some arguments advanced that the muskie was previously caught by some local Indians and Spray bought it). However, photographs support Spray's claim. As part of their investigation, the hall's study committee submitted those photos to experts who concluded the fish had to be at least 63 inches long.

Dettloff, nearing fifty, runs the Indian Trail Resort, a longtime family lodge on the outskirts of Hayward on the Chippewa Flowage that got its start in 1955 and is his most special place in the world. He has fished for muskie since 1972, and it is the only fishing he pursues. While still living in Chicago as a youth, he vacationed in Hayward from the time he was ten.

"All's it took was just catching one," Dettloff said of igniting his passion for muskies. "As a kid, I wasn't that interested at first because it took too much effort to catch one." Even though he was a youngster, he was put in charge of keeping the seasonal muskie charts because he had good penmanship. In the 1970s if someone caught a muskie, a siren sounded on the flowage, announcing the good fortune to everyone. Now at Indian Trail Resort a bell is rung to let the nearby world know a muskie has been tamed, if only temporarily.

Before the days of catch-and-release, big muskies were brought ashore and carried to the bar at the resort. Spectators gathered for the weighing and measuring to determine just how impressive the fish was. After two summers of taking notes, when he was twelve, Dettloff's interest in muskies was stoked. He caught his first, brought it to the dock, and had it measured at 33½ inches. "It was so exciting to have that thing on, thrashing around," Dettloff said. "I scooped him up with my bare hands. I ran over to the bar screaming and hollering."

After that thrill, Dettloff wanted to learn everything he could about muskie fishing. A local luminary with experience named Frenchy, he said, "took me under his wing."

Speaking like the guide he is, Dettloff said a Louie Spray catch is one thing, but every muskie caught is special because they are so hard to hook. "In my mind, every muskie is a trophy," he said. "You've conquered the ultimate freshwater sporting fish."

Lodge record keeping over a half-century period tells Dettloff that fishermen have caught something in excess of 160 muskie of at least 30 inches in length on the Chippewa Flowage that have been measured at Indian Trail Resort. "It's a muskie factory," Dettloff said.

Dettloff is a Spray acolyte. He has defended him in print and verbally in meetings. He put thirteen years of part-time research into his Spray book, and when he finished he believed Spray's record muskie catches were legit. Dettloff said Spray was seen as a somewhat shady character who made money from bootlegging and this tarnished his veracity when he talked about fish. "Louie was a wild guy," Dettloff said of the muskie king, who died in Arizona far from the lakes and rivers he loved. "He was a good-time Charlie." Yet despite some of the sketchiness that surrounds the Spray tale, including the fact that his mounts were destroyed in a fire and cannot be examined, Dettloff thinks Spray spoke the truth about the big fish.

Not so, according to a fellow named Eli Singer, a passionate muskie man from Park Falls, Wisconsin, who thinks Spray was a big, fat liar and said so in one of his books, *Musky Chronicles III*.

"Spray was a calculating self-promoter," Singer wrote. "Was Louie Spray the best fisherman who ever lived? Or was he just the best of the frauds?" Singer has called Dettloff "a sneaky guy." Dettloff thinks Singer has rocks in his head. Singer thinks Spray may have put rocks in his fish.

Dettloff believes some level of controversy, simmering on a back burner or argued about publicly, will focus on Spray's catches forever unless someone breaks the record. Whether it is a fanciful notion, the reinforcement of a myth, or he is merely a daydreamer, Dettloff is sure that a world-record muskie still plies the waters of the Chippewa Flowage like a submarine.

"I actually have no doubt," Dettloff said. "In the right structure, in the right habitat, and of course the genes have to be there."

Every year a 40-pound muskie is caught on the flowage. That's a big fish but a far cry from record class. Every few years a bigger fish is caught. Dettloff said for more than three years he has been stalking a muskie that is at least 45 pounds and 55 inches and might be bigger. Each summer he searches for the fish, finds it, and tries to catch it. It always shows up in the same spot, a place he keeps secret.

"I had it on and lost it a couple of times," Dettloff said.

No one has to tell Dettloff that fish might still be growing into record-class consideration. He doesn't believe his mysterious fish is a record now, but someday it could be, and he wants to know how big it truly is.

"You can go twenty years without seeing a fish like that," he said.

Regardless of what really happened long ago, the National Freshwater Fishing Hall of Fame accepts the final major Spray catch as its official muskie record and Hayward's muskie fishery remains a critical element of the local economy. It was one area that Tony Wise didn't touch unless he sent a visitor at his Telemark Resort to a guide in the summer.

Although he had no real hand in the muskie fishery, Wise owned the winter. The Telemark Resort grew and grew, and the always-thinking Wise kept dreaming up ways to attract more visitors. One thing northern Wisconsin has in abundance during the winter is snow. His brain working on all cylinders, Wise imagined a way to make Telemark a premier destination for a huge event. Telemark was located in nearby Cable, just down the trail from Hayward. Business was booming, but Wise reasoned that if given a sexier reason to visit, even more cross-country skiers would patronize the lodge.

From the beginning, as he did in all his ventures, Wise thought big. He wanted to create a cross-country skiing extravaganza that would be both a citizens' and a high-quality competitive race. His goal was to lure five thousand skiers to the trails of Hayward and Cable during a three-day festival that might bring in three times as many people in all if skiers came with families or if spectators were curious enough just to watch.

Transferred from passing thought to paper to ski trail, the first American Birkebeiner was held in 1973. Smoothed by snowmobiles and designed to take advantage of the hilly terrain and the area's natural beauty, the Birkebeiner course is a marathon of 55 kilometers. Wise did not hit his target figure of skiers at first, with just 54 entrants in year one, but before the end of the 1970s he came close, with just shy of 4,500 skiers entered in 1979.

In succeeding years, as the American Birkebeiner morphed into one of the most prestigious long-distance cross-country ski races in the world, participation kept growing. In 2008, some nine thousand skiers entered the Birkebeiner and a shorter companion race. And while almost four decades had passed since its inception, the number of spectators had grown some, too, reaching fifteen thousand. It now takes two thousand volunteers, roughly equal to the population of Hayward, to make sure the "Birkie," as the race is fondly nicknamed, runs smoothly.

Some of the original skiers still live in Hayward and continue to race. One 1973 racer, Ernie St. Germaine, who was then a Wise employee at Telemark, said the boss pretty much told him he had to race if he wanted to hang on to his job. "Tony was one of those people that didn't have to ask me with words," St. Germaine told a Birkebeiner historian. "He more or less asked me with a look that ordered me to be there." St. Germaine was glad he became a race pioneer because he could later say he had competed for the first thirty-five years of the Birkebeiner.

It took just four years for Birkebeiner participation to mushroom from fifty-four race starters to more than two thousand. In 1978 Wise pushed for creation of an international cross-country ski race circuit, which was established with the Birkebeiner as one of fifteen races in which a top-notch skier could accumulate points. The race had already been discovered by Europeans, and the year before four hundred Norwegians crossed the ocean to race. Given that cross-country skiing is the national sport in Norway that was a stamp of approval for Wise's idea.

Tony Wise was right again. The twenty-fifth anniversary American Birkebeiner attracted 7,882 entries in 1997, two years after Wise died, and skiers kept on coming, closing in on an entry high-water mark that was moving toward 10,000. On the American Birkebeiner website—a development with which Wise was unfamiliar but certainly would have embraced—one longtime racer talked about the hold the Birkie has on him. Randy Bates, a Waukesha, Wisconsin, resident, said he named his first dog "Birkebeiner" and brought one of his baby daughters home from the hospital in a Birkebeiner souvenir shirt. "Long live Birkie fever!" Bates said.

Leslie Hamp, the author of a Birkebeiner history article, said Wise may have died, but he is not forgotten by Birkie stalwarts. "Tony Wise, founder of the American Birkebeiner, passed away in the spring of 1995," she wrote, "yet his influence and vision still dominate the American Birkebeiner. Those carrying on his vision see just one thing in the future. They, like Tony Wise, envision the world coming to Northern Wisconsin each year to ski the Birkie."

All of it, the muskie fishery and all of Wise's projects, from the departed Telemark Resort and Historyland exhibits to the American Birkebeiner and the Lumberjack World Championships, has helped Hayward's economy to thrive and put the community, located far from any interstate highway, on the map.

"How do you measure any of this stuff?" said Bill Swintkowski, who was the mayor of Hayward in 2009. "You know it all brings money into the community. The Lumberjack World Championships is a very big deal. They'll put four thousand people in the stands and they have to eat. They stay in hotels. With the economy tougher, they don't spend money like they used to, but there's a certain group that come up for something."

Swintkowski has never caught a muskie in his more than half a century on earth, but he said when he was eighteen he caught a seventeen-pound walleye ice fishing on the fishing line that baseball hall of famer Ted Williams promoted through Sears. In weight the fish should have qualified as a world record, but it didn't make the cut for a technical reason. He also thought of himself as a bit of a lumberjack in his youth.

"Because we needed firewood for the house," he said. "Guess who chopped it?"

Of course, it was understood that every Hayward kid would visit Historyland. Swintkowski remembers statues of an Indian and a lumberjack in front of a downtown store, too, where a nickel could be placed in a slot and they would talk. He is an intense follower of the Lumberjack World Championships, making the Lumberjack Bowl his home for a few days each summer.

"I never missed one of them," he said.

Swintkowski was back at the bowl as he spoke, attending a special dinner recognizing fifty seasons of the lumberjack championships and welcoming people from all over the world. As he gazed around, Swintkowski reflected on the impact Tony Wise made with his entrepreneurial visions for Hayward. "Telemark Resort, Historyland, the Birkebeiner, the lumberjacks," Swintkowski ticked off Wise's contributions. "That's quite a bit. That's one guy that hasn't gotten enough credit. He was a great promoter for the community."

Muscles and Sawdust

Northern Wisconsin was logging country, and Tony Wise knew that very well. In his mind, linking an industry that was one of the most important economic cornerstones of the region with entertainment was an easy leap. Men in plaid were common in the north country. Locals identified with men swinging axes and pulling saws.

The Lumberjack Bowl, best known today as a stage for lumberjack shows and competitions, was already in existence. It was a cul-de-sac of water, a massive holding pond where the North Wisconsin Lumber Company stored its logs after they were cut and before they were sent downriver to buyers.

So the facility was in place, and the only thing Wise needed was lumberjacks to make the venue come to life again. He knew there were plenty of people with lumberjack skills in the immediate Hayward area, throughout Wisconsin, and sprinkled around the Upper Midwest. He was not concerned with reaching out to them. Those nearby would get the word, take a flyer on a new event, and show up. That wasn't good enough for Wise, however. He wanted to be the biggest and best right from the get-go, immediately eclipsing any smaller-scale regional contests of lumberjack skills.

Wise tirelessly researched and came up with a list of lumberjacks he wanted to invite to Hayward for the first Lumberjack World Championships in 1960. He was operating in a different world a half century ago. He had a tight budget. He had a limited number of lumberjack contacts, and there was no Internet to search to compare credentials. He was initiating contact from a small, remote place that many distantly located lumber-jacks might not even have heard of, and, unless they were also enthusiastic about cross-country skiing, they would not have heard of him, either.

For those who can't believe that fifty years have passed since 1960, that was the year John F. Kennedy was elected president, the Pittsburgh Pirates stunned the New York Yankees in the World Series on Bill Mazeroski's famous home run, Marilyn Monroe was the sexiest woman in Hollywood, and a group of men, calling themselves "The Foolish Club," with as much hardcore passion for football as money in their wallets, formed the American Football League.

Wise did not receive nearly as much ink or airtime as any of those other people or sports developments he shared the year's headlines with, although as someone whose businesses thrived on publicity, he would have craved it. He made do, learning on the fly what worked, what appealed to fans, what would entice lumberjacks to Hayward. There was a streak of promotional genius coursing through Tony Wise, and each time he came up with a fresh idea he could call on his experience in making his previous best idea become a reality.

In the same way promoter and circus impresario P. T. Barnum under-stood how to please public ticket buyers, Wise knew how to tap the trait in humans that made them want to come to his Hayward installations for a good time whether it was to enjoy the outdoors in winter on their skis or to relive a part of America's bygone era when lumberjacks were lumberjacks and trees were trees, not sacred objects in nature. Wise knew how to insinuate into the heads of tourists the message that these were the type of men who conquered the frontier and built their homes.

Historyland and lumberjacks. Come on down. Step into the past.

The lumberjacks came, and so did the people. In a land that was just starting to embrace pro football with unprecedented fervor but devoured boxing matches, horse races, college football, and, of course, baseball, the national pastime, timber sports did not have a niche. But they were quirky, they were unusual, and they added a different dimension to the sports menu. America was coming out of the bland 1950s, when families fled from urban environments to the suburbs, when reliance on the automobile exploded, and when inventors more or less between wars (Vietnam had yet to heat up) poured their energy into peacetime projects like bringing the nation's youth what it wanted most—the hula hoop.

Unlike the American Birkebeiner (still to come on Wise's list of creations), an event designed for the masses, the Lumberjack World

Championships was not about participation but elite competition. Undeterred by his lack of contacts in the lumberjack world, Wise started talking and didn't stop until inquires led him to a man named Dave Geer.

Geer, originally a state champion weight lifter from Lisbon, Connecticut, was a lumberjack down to his soul. As late as 2005, at age seventy-nine, after coping with cancer and faltering knees, he still won an ax-throwing contest in a lesser lumberjack competition. When it came to ax throwing, Geer was like a cross between Davy Crockett and Crocodile Dundee—it would have been useless to run from him. During his heyday, starting from day one at the Lumberjack World Championships, Geer won forty-four world titles in various disciplines.

Geer got his start in local lumberjack championships in Oregon around 1956, and somehow Wise heard about him. One day Geer returned home to receive a phone call from this stranger in Wisconsin with big dreams who needed help.

"Tony Wise called me," Geer recalled, "and he said, 'I'm interested in getting a lumberjack championship started.'" Geer committed to coming to Wisconsin in July of 1960, and when he stepped off his plane in Minneapolis, Wise was there, as promised, ready to drive him to Hayward. On the drive, and for days thereafter, Wise picked Geer's brain, asking for advice on how to stage events, how to do things correctly.

"Tony Wise wanted to have the best," Geer said nearly fifty years later. "He told me, 'I want you to get me the best axmen in the world.' This is where the Lumberjack World Championships was king."

It was a seat-of-the-pants operation in the sense that Wise and his minions, with Geer as his sidekick professional consultant, were inventing the championships as they went along. People did flock to the Lumberjack Bowl for the grand opening of the championships in 1960, and, without strict seating rules, Geer remembers fans flocking to the individual competition sites, forming crowds in circles close to the sawyers, pole climbers, and axmen. They were all lucky that no one was hurt by flying debris or sawdust or, in the case of the 90-foot pole climb (included to simulate the challenge of tree trimming at the crown of a tree), that no competitor landed on a spectator's head.

Showmanship was always a Wise consideration, and in the early days of the lumberjack championships, he made use of water for reasons that went far beyond floating logs. A glittery, on-the-water parade inaugurated the championships with gusto. The *Namekagon Queen* sternwheeler, Native Americans wearing spectacular headdresses and paddling birchbark canoes, and voyageur-like fur traders paddling their own canoes put on a spell-bindingly colorful show. And that was just the introduction.

When Lumberjack World Championships executive director Diane McNamer was researching a 2009 pictorial history of the event, she became more impressed with Tony Wise than ever. "Someone once called Tony Wise second only to Mother Nature in putting Hayward on the map," she wrote. "Mother Nature gave Hayward lakes, rivers, and pines, and Tony took advantage of all these natural resources when he created an event that had the unmistakable flavor of the Olympics. From national flags flying, to the boom of Indian drums, to the high-pitched whine of the hot saw, Tony created an event that was just that, an event. He always had a gimmick, from cars to bands, and under his practiced eye the Lumberjack World Championships truly became the Olympics of the forest."

Tony Wise might have developed winning concepts that provided appropriate value for the tourist dollar, but one could never be too under-stated. He definitely believed in the ability of pageantry to sell his wares. It got the folks in the right frame of mind.

Young Dave Geer probably slew the ladies, or at least made them blink. He had dark hair full of waves, broad shoulders, and impressive biceps. Geer figures he competed in the first twenty lumberjack championships in a row and won woodchopping titles nine times, the all-around crown four times (in 1964, 1965, 1966, and 1973), the underhand chop (he won the first one contested), and the springboard chop. When he was seventy-four, Geer broke his ankle in a competition. Did that send the message that his bones were giving out and it was time to retire? "I retire every year," Geer said in 2009 when he was eighty-three.

Way back when, decades ago, when Johnny Carson was the king of late-night TV, Geer was a guest. He remembers sharing the guest couch with actress Lauren Bacall and Dr. Benjamin Spock, the baby advice doctor. Since he didn't sing or dance Geer was supposed to entertain the studio audience with his accuracy throwing an ax.

"He [Carson] wanted me to take a cigarette out of his mouth from twenty feet away," Geer said. Geer mulled the prospect over and said, "If I miss, you're a dead duck." What happened? Well, nobody died.

Forty to fifty years ago, Geer said, the world was a very different place, with fewer rules and regulations governing acts like that. "They didn't care if you did kill somebody," Geer said with slight exaggeration.

Once, at a Milwaukee outdoors show, a guy who performed death-defying acts such as putting his head into a crocodile's mouth did get killed, Geer said. But no humans or animals were killed in the making of his ax-throwing career, one that escalated into a surprising level of popularity. During one public event, he drew a larger crowd signing autographs than a Detroit Lions fullback. And that was when the Lions weren't a horrible team.

When he made his annual trek to Hayward, Geer said he hung out with Wise, visiting him at home, staying up till all hours talking about the Lumberjack World Championships, always trying to think up ways to make it a better event. What could be added? Should something be subtracted from the program? Did it move along too slowly? Were the best lumberjacks coming to town or should they seek them out?

"Tony was striving for perfection," Geer said. "He wanted to make this the best. We had some happy times. He was a great promoter. He wouldn't spare any expense to get the best in the world to Hayward."

It was one thing for a promoter to call on the phone from a small town and try to woo lumberjacks to northern Wisconsin. It was quite another for the Dave Geers of the world to place the calls and say something like "Hey, you really want to be in Hayward in late July." Word spread that if a timber sports guy wanted to show his stuff, Hayward was the place. The fans were loud, the competition was keen, and the hosts took good care of you.

The men who came to Hayward in the beginning, in 1960 and the years immediately following, were pioneers in lumberjack sports, and now those still living are grandfathers. They are septuagenarians or older, but they still seem to have more sawdust than blood in their veins.

Arden Cogar Sr. was another early star, a real-life logger from Webster Springs, West Virginia. Cogar became all-around champ in 1962, making him king of the lumberjacks for a year, and he won his first double buck sawing title with his brother Benny in 1961. Although none of these early lumberjack heroes was as tall as the supposed eight-foot skyscraping Paul Bunyan, with their bulging muscles they did seem to possess his strength and each was a mountain of a man in his own right.

Cogar, whose son, Arden Jr., joined him at the lumberjack championships over the years, said he started logging in West Virginia in 1956 and was a regular in Hayward from 1960 to 1999. He dropped by for the 2009 championships, partly because the old-timers were going to have some seniors events. "I'm still chopping," Cogar said. "I can't do too much. I can still cut one off [the neat slices of wood required], but it takes a while. Meaning the old bones creak. But then, who is at their physical peak in their mid-seventies?"

Cogar gives the credit to Wise for starting something special. "He was a great man," he said. "He's the one who made the show."

Sometimes, Wise, wearing a distinctive Jeff cap that seemed an odd chapeau in a lumberjack environment, would grab the microphone and say a few words to the fans. Wise liked wearing the flat caps with the stiff brims that are more commonly seen in the golf world. He was no lumberjack, but he did relish putting on a show that would leave the fans buzzing—and anxious to return the next year.

Wise did not dish out cash payments as appearance money that would make anyone rich, Cogar said, but what he did do when talking to one of the top lumberjacks ahead of time is make certain he could afford the transportation to Hayward. "He said, 'Do you need any help to get to the show?'" And Wise did not stagnate, did not sit back in self-satisfaction once he got the championships from the drawing board to the Lumberjack Bowl. "He was always thinking about next year," Cogar said. "Like I said, he was a great man."

Like just about everything else in the world, the tools of the trade of loggers have been updated. Better axes and saws are made. Cogar has followed those developments closely because he was always a logger, always a woodsman. But he is not jealous and does not denigrate those who participate in sawing and chopping but are not professional loggers. He thinks it's great that someone who works in another field can develop the talent to reach the top rung in timber sports.

"You can be a barber or a doctor," Cogar said.

You can be, but you probably won't win.

In the championships' early days, timber competition was viewed as a quirky sport with a limited following. But as each year passed the championships got more and more attention from Wisconsin newspapers and television stations, then from magazines and national newspapers. *Look* magazine came to Hayward in the early 1960s. The publicity helped establish legitimacy outside the subculture of loggers and lumberjacks and introduced the games to new fans.

"I think it gives us great exposure," Cogar said of the media. "This is our (Hayward's) national sport."

Sons used to follow their fathers into the family business, whether it was running the corner grocery store or studying to be a lawyer. It is less common now, but enough time has passed for the Lumberjack World Championships to have seen multiple generations of competitors in several events. Arden Cogar Jr., of Hamline, West Virginia, is definitely a chip off the old block. In 2006, forty-four years after his dad's all-around championship, and thirty-two years after his father's last standing block chop victory, Junior won the title.

Then there are three generations of French Canadian Merciers from Sainte Etienne, Quebec. Grandpa Napoleon is seventy-eight, dad J. P. is fifty-three, and grandson Maxime is twenty-eight. Max, a plumber, first visited Hayward in 1991 as a nine year old. He said that given his genes and family commitment to summer pilgrimages to Hayward, it was probably preordained that he would flex his muscles in Wisconsin sooner or later.

Napoleon's primary language is French, and he uses his son and grandson as interpreters when making lumberjack talk. Max said he learned English by attending lumberjack competitions in Wisconsin watching his father compete. Grandpa is a saw maker, the operator of Mercier Racing Saws, and that influenced the clan. They watched the utensils being handmade, and they wanted to use them.

"I grew up with the saws," said Max. "It's kind of an advantage for me. I always traveled to see the show [in Hayward]. It's kind of weird. You've always been watching and now I'm in it."

J. P. made his first trip to Hayward in 1991, with Max tagging along. He and a cousin had formed a double-buck-sawing team in Canada, and they wanted to test themselves at the Lumberjack World Championships against elite sawyers. "We wanted to see how we could do," Napoleon Mercier said. They made the finals.

J. P. said he won a double-buck-sawing title in a Vancouver competition with his father in the 1990s, one of his greatest memories. But he made a breakthrough in Hayward with a major win in his specialty with teammate Dennis Daun of Round Lake, Illinois, in 1997. That year, J. P. and Daun made music with their saws, defeating all comers on the regional circuit wherever they competed in the United States. With a new partner, the much-admired, powerful sawyer Dave Jewett from Pittsford, New York, J. P. claimed the world title at Hayward in 2000, 2001, 2002, 2004, and 2006.

Although Grandpa was an artisan first and a timber sports competitor second, he, too, made the journey to Hayward in his old age, not only to see his saws in action but to compete. In 2000 and 2002 Napoleon won the masters underhand chop. He made his first saw in 1986 and has been making the equipment full time for twelve years.

Napoleon's connections with wood run deep. As a younger man he worked for a paper mill in northern Ontario. In the forest he was expected to lift trees off the ground at times and help remove stones. The lumberjacks of earlier eras were probably stronger than the young bucks competing now, he feels. As someone in his eighth decade, Napoleon is amazed at the speed with which sawyers rip through wood these days. Athletes in every sport evolve, but Napoleon doesn't want to underemphasize the credit due the younger generation.

"Competition is way, way faster," the elder Mercier said, "but the tools improve, too."

Napoleon was too old to do too much damage to wood too quickly. J. P. was past his prime. Novice Max was feeling his way. The odds weren't very good that the Merciers would collect much hardware in Hayward in 2009, but J. P. didn't care. What mattered most was that all three of them were together, taking part in the world championships in front of the thousands of fans at the Lumberjack Bowl.

"Three generations," J. P. Mercier said. "It's a big thrill."

Anyone speaking the word *thrill* in connection with the Lumberjack World Championships would have thrilled Tony Wise.

Hercules Bares His Chest

When Ron Hartill peeled off his shirt, the Lumberjack World Championships entered uncharted territory—the lumberjack as sex symbol. The massively powerful Hartill had the type of torso that made women swoon and men gasp in admiration. If a Hollywood casting director was at the Lumberjack Bowl, Hartill might have been signed to play Superman in a movie.

Some compared Hartill to Hercules, even though he was a down-to-earth fellow from Sooke, British Columbia, who just happened to have muscles growing on top of muscles, all of which rippled when he swung an ax or pulled on a saw.

Those were traits he shared with other men who were at the top of the heap in lumberjack events like the springboard chop, double bucking, and single bucking. What set Hartill apart was his physique and his willingness to show it off. When he posed for a photograph standing atop the remnants of a log, ax in hand dropped low, naked above the waist, it made female hearts go pitter-patter. It also, to Tony Wise's delight, crossed an ill-defined line transporting timber sports into show business.

Hartill was another lumberjack luminary Wise recruited. After Hartill won a regional lumberjack contest in Albany, Oregon, in 1972, Wise telephoned Hartill and asked him to come to Hayward.

"He wanted the big guys," Hartill said of Wise's never-ending efforts to find new talent for the championships. "He was a great guy, a fun guy, but just try to tie him down to one spot for more than five minutes. He was going nonstop. He put Hayward on the map. He really did. He put me in front of the world, too."

Going shirtless was not a gimmick, really, just the fact that Hartill was more comfortable chopping with his torso bare. Any publicity bonuses were gravy. Wise relished Hartill's he-man appearance—if the fans liked it, he liked it—and recognized that the uniqueness could become a Hartill trademark. At 6 feet, 5 inches and 225 pounds, Hartill possessed the statuesque build of an NFL linebacker. And Hartill's bright blonde hair, a mix of curls and waves, contributed to his image as a male model type who might be pictured on the cover of a romance novel. But it was going shirtless that became his signature look.

"They still talk about that," a much older Hartill, then seventy-three and white-haired, said in 2009 as he reminisced about his 1970s lumberjack prime. He was wearing a shirt as he spoke and had no plans to remove it outside of the privacy of his own bedroom. "The people in the bleachers fell in love with it."

Longtime former competitor Dave Geer agreed.

"That was really something," Geer said.

The phenomenon started innocuously. During the 1972 championships, the sun beat down and the temperature soared. Although lumberjacks generally wore bare-armed competition singlets anyway, Hartill was still uncomfortable. So he pulled off his shirt and went topless. He didn't think much about it.

"It was hot and muggy," he recalled.

Well, the wolf whistles and cheers and oohs and aahs began. For the most part Hartill just smiled or ignored most of the commentary. But Wise didn't. It turned out that when Hartill went home people still talked about his half-naked body as much as his lumberjack prowess. Wise is the one who got the feedback and took note of it. The next year, when Hartill returned for the competition, Wise took him aside, informed him that he had caused an ongoing sensation, and asked him to continue competing without a shirt. So Hartill literally donated the shirt off his back to the lumberjack cause.

Although these things are difficult to assess, it probably made a difference that Hartill was also very good at what he did, winning championships in several disciplines. If he was an also-ran entrant, competing without a shirt might have worked against him in the fans' minds, regardless of how he looked. He might have been dismissed as a dilettante. However, being a winner with his own shtick gave the fans another reason to like Hartill and remember him. He stood out. Naturally, Wise encouraged developments that began accidentally and innocuously if they added to the common good, and anything that got spectators talking and buying tickets was very good indeed.

But the publicity worked both ways. Hartill gained fame that transcended the sport. Not only was he a seven-time all-around winner as the best lumberjack in Hayward, but his reputation spread. He took a job working for Wise doing lumberjack sports demonstrations at Telemark for the ski patrons. Wise pretty much billed Hartill as a real-life Paul Bunyan. Hartill was tall and chiseled and could strike a hero pose on demand.

Hartill got his start in lumberjack sports in 1968 when someone gazed at his body and said, "I'm going to teach you to chop." That may have sounded like an off-the-wall suggestion, but it changed Hartill's life. He has been a logger and truck driver and worked with helicopter pilots, but his fame in the lumberjack world translated into a long-term gig traveling the world selling chainsaws.

Hartill's wife Kathy worked for Wise at Telemark, and they served Cokes to Wise because he didn't drink alcohol. When Hartill was able to parlay his lumberjack performances into the chainsaw rep job he had the clout to add a clause to his contract that has paid dividends many times over.

"When I got the chainsaw endorsement," Hartill said, "I put in the contract that she [Kathy] goes with me. You know, it's been a hell of a life."

Translating an idea from brain to reality involves faith and risk for any entrepreneur. Wise knew he had stumbled on a good thing as soon as the Lumberjack World Championships became a reality in 1960. His instinct that it was critical to bring the best athletes to Hayward rather than conduct a faux "world" championship was also an important one. Wise didn't want lumberjacks elsewhere to criticize his baby on the basis that its title was misleading, or, heaven help him, fraudulent.

By rounding up the leading suspects, Wise immediately turned Hayward into a key destination on the calendar. Through the quality of the competitors, right from the start, Wise made the championships matter in the lumberjack world. Instead of having stars of the sport dotted around the country showing their stuff only in regional competitions, they all came to

Wisconsin. Instead of a timber sports athlete being able to say Hayward was not a real championship because he wasn't there, the question was turned around and posed, "Why weren't you there?" Wise's initial premise, to bring the best in the world to Hayward, was crucial for long-term credibility. He spiked theoretical challenges before they could be mounted.

Once Wise provided the venue in which the best could compete, it was up to them to come to Hayward to answer their own questions about how good they were. And once Wise could advertise that the best of the best came to Hayward, he was certain the ticket-buying public, essentially those living in the north woods, would want to see the show. Wise's faith in his product was well placed.

Still, he had to keep on hustling, keep on working, keep on fretting and sweating to make the Lumberjack World Championships better known and more seriously respected outside of the logging culture and lumberjack world. He was aided in his quest because he had something worthwhile to sell. The more newspaper and magazine reporters that came around each summer, the more attention and publicity the Lumberjack World Championships received in distant corners of the country, and in other countries.

It is safe to say that the audience reached by these feature stories and news reports can be summarized in a single-word reaction: "Cool." That's what people thought when they saw timber sports action, or read about it, for the first time. You can pay a Madison Avenue advertising agency millions of dollars to craft an image, but it is so much better, so much more authentic, when the product is flat out cool to start with. Those involved in the logging industry were an easy sell. Timber sports were in their wheelhouse.

The frontier/western/cowboy romanticists were right at home with the link to American history. And those with fresh eyes, who had never seen anything like two husky men bent over a log sawing for all they were worth with sawdust spraying in every direction, just liked the look of the whole thing. They couldn't imagine doing it, they couldn't put their finger on what appealed to them, but it was just . . . well . . . cool. It was like the time when the country seemingly spontaneously was caught up in the America's Cup because of the mesmerizing blue ocean, the white sails cruising along the horizon, and close-ups of straining men working as teams to defend the honor of the USA. Nobody knew the first thing about jibs and halyards, and they didn't know anything about saws with teeth the size of an African lion's, but the average Joe decided he liked what he saw in both sailing and lumberjack sports.

In the early 1960s *Life* magazine ran a few pictures of lumberjacks with references to the championships. *Life* was read in important places, and as a result of the lumberjack article Wise found himself fielding questions from ABC-TV, which wanted to televise the championships. On Saturdays, ABC had this little gem of a show that just grew and grew in fame. It was called *Wide World of Sports*. In another era, years before the existence of ESPN and other round-the-clock cable networks, there were only a few TV stations in each city's market—the three major networks, ABC, CBS, and NBC, and maybe a Public Broadcasting System station. Unlike today, when it is almost impossible to escape coverage of a local sports team, in the 1960s only major league teams such as the Red Sox, Patriots, Bruins, and Celtics would regularly find their way into the homes of Boston sports fans. If a sports fan lived in a National League city, he or she would never see an American League team play on the tube until the World Series in October. Pro football was just beginning to become a weekly Sunday program, especially with the advent of the American Football League to challenge the National Football League. The other sports had their local fan bases.

The truly big sporting events, the ones that could attract a national audience without a specific team allegiance—the Kentucky Derby, Indianapolis 500, World Series, and NFL title game—were on the calendar. What was missing was niche sports. College basketball was ranked below the pros. The same was true for college baseball, World Cup ski racing, and hockey involving teams outside your neighborhood. There was just no outlet for these types of sports viewing.

It was the genius of ABC to recognize that fans wanted more than meat and potatoes for dinner, that even if the audience was not in the multi-millions, a significant number of sports fans were interested in stock car racing, hunting, and fishing and were hungry to watch a show that provided at least a glimpse of their favorite activities. Begun as a summer show, *Wide World of Sports* was an immediate hit. It showed everything from rodeo to demolition derby and was actually the early television home of NASCAR.

Hosted by Jim McKay, *Wide World of Sports*, which was on the air from 1961 to 1998, broke its ninety-minute program into two or three segments. The opening credits and fanfare music were accompanied by a little ditty welcoming viewers to a program that was "Spanning the globe to bring you the constant variety of sport . . . the thrill of victory and the agony of defeat." The phrase entered American lexicon, applied to not only sporting situations but other circumstances. The show's opening included dramatic film footage of a ski jumper crashing at the end of his leap. That was example A of the agony of defeat.

The television sports universe has changed beyond belief over the last forty-plus years. In the 1960s, almost nothing was on. Now almost everything is on. When *Wide World of Sports* contacted Wise he was likely amazed. Imagine, an out-of-the-way enterprise trying to build its core base of support being offered national exposure. "Getting *Wide World of Sports* to come to Hayward was huge," said Lumberjack World Championships executive director Diane McNamer.

The days of big money payouts for sporting event rights lay in the future, but *Wide World of Sports* contributed to the Lumberjack World Championships' coffers starting in 1967. Just like the scene in *Casablanca* when Humphrey Bogart and Claude Rains walk into the fog with the closing line, "I think this is the beginning of a beautiful friendship," the Wise–ABC alliance was noteworthy. In many ways, *Wide World of Sports* was Wise's new best friend.

Once the TV people came to Hayward they were hooked. The relationship went on for more than two decades. Millions of TV viewers were introduced to timber sports through *Wide World of Sports*. Although the earliest paperwork between Wise and ABC is not available, one contract, signed in 1979, likely illustrates the two sides' connection during the heyday of the partnership.

The contract was addressed to Wise care of "Historyland, Inc." and confirmed ABC's decision to televise the next four years of the Lumberjack World Championships (1979–82). It was stressed that the four-year contract provided ABC with options for the broadcast rights and if the network did not like the way things were going, it had the power to cancel an individual year of coverage with sixty-days notice.

What this "sports event" would consist of, the contract stipulated, "shall include or comprise, but shall not be limited to, the following events: Men's log rolling, women's log rolling, trick and fancy log rolling, tree topping, speed climbing, two-man sawing, horizontal cut chop, standing cut chop, power sawing, ax throwing, All-Around Lumberjack. Each Sports Event shall be staged with the overall quality of prior years."

In return for the exclusive rights to show the lumberjack championships, Wise agreed to rights fees of $11,500 for 1979, $12,500 for 1980, $13,750 for 1981, and $15,000 for 1982. By current standards that amounts to very little, but at the time, when there was no competition for the rights and virtually no other forum on which to see the events on the air, it was a hard-to-top arrangement.

The relationship held together even longer. According to paperwork in a Tony Wise file housed at the Wisconsin Historical Society, ABC sent by Federal Express a check for $18,150 to cover its obligation in filming the 1984 Lumberjack World Championships, conducted roughly two weeks earlier in July. Visitors to Hayward for the lumberjack championships who bought an event program were liable to see a message reading, "As seen on ABC's *Wide World of Sports.*" The affiliation was a point of pride.

It was also a connection of incalculable value. Free publicity is free publicity, and when just about all of it is good publicity, it's a windfall. The Lumberjack World Championships combined many television-friendly attributes. It was G-rated before there was a rating system, programming that no parent would worry about his or her child watching. It featured intense competition. The disciplines were familiar in the sense that everyone knew who Paul Bunyan was and that the logging industry played a large role in American history. And again, there was a coolness factor.

While the competitors generally were supersized, the events they excelled at didn't look all that complicated. They were visually understandable without the need for expert commentary and chalkboard talks. How many people around the country chopped wood in their backyards? Maybe not quite so swiftly, but those folks understood the rudiments of the game.

The increased attention also paid off for the lumberjacks. Television helped make some into personalities. Hartill got his chainsaw endorsement contract. Peter Haupt, a Hayward lumberjack, auditioned for a Miller Lite beer commercial in the 1970s with fishing legend Grits Grisham at a time when the brewing company was writing witty skits for athletes in a multitude of sports.

Haupt had some choice tales to tell about flying to New York and being put up in a pricey hotel. He said he was a fish out of water, coming from backwoods Wisconsin, and wore blue jeans into fancy places. He checked into his Hyatt carrying a duffel bag rather than more conventional luggage, too. Strangely, Haupt said the advertising people told him they auditioned eighteen other actors for the lumberjack role before finding him and they were about to give up when he was scouted and invited to try out.

Instead of packing up, the crew gave Haupt a shot to play a tall-tale-telling lumberjack. While in a bar, the lumberjack and the fisherman begin talking. Haupt tells Grisham that he once "birled a log over a hundred-foot waterfall and came up still holding [his] Lite beer from Miller. It's a good thing Lite is less filling." You've got to love the implication that Haupt might have drowned if he hadn't been drinking diet beer.

Grits replies that he "once hooked into a large-mouth bass that pulled [him] up a hundred-foot waterfall." Of course, that's just the type of an exaggerated story a fisherman would tell. Ironically, Haupt was also a fishing guide, but the audience didn't need to know that.

Haupt answers, "Well, it's Lite's great taste that kept me going when I was felling all of those trees in the great Sahara Forest."

Gresham's turn: "But the Sahara is a desert,"

Haupt: "Yeah, it is now."

For whatever reason, the commercial never ran. Haupt said he got to keep all of the lumberjack attire the company bought for him. Presumably, some of it was plaid.

Matchmakers in certain cultures that still rely on experts to put young men and women together in arranged marriages should be as lucky as *Wide World of Sports* and the Lumberjack World Championships. It was a perfect match for television hungry for offbeat programming and an event eager to grow and embrace attention. Ideal fit.

One thing the annual exposure on *Wide World of Sports* did was help create a new generation of lumberjack competitors. Granted, anyone living in or near Hayward, or another hotbed of logging and regional competition, had a built-in advantage, but TV has a way of planting suggestions in youngsters' minds, and there was no telling if some tyke in Oklahoma watching hot saw cutting in Wisconsin might be a future lumberjack.

With Telemark Resort, the Lumberjack World Championships, and the American Birkebeiner, Tony Wise was on his way to promoting and supervising his personal wide world of sports.

Stay on Your Feet, Stay Dry

Judy Scheer Hoeschler was born in 1956 and grew up in Hayward with Tony Wise's six children as her playmates. From the time she was in elementary school, Hoeschler was fascinated with logrolling. She entered the Lumberjack World Championships' companion amateur competition at thirteen, and the lady was a champ.

"Now I'm really hooked," she said. "I'm getting a trophy."

A year later, in 1970, Hoeschler entered the open championships competition. This was the elite division. The big guns were not from Wisconsin but visitors from West Coast logging havens.

"We were intimidated by them," Hoeschler said.

It was no surprise that Hoeschler lost in the first round of her first competition. She took a dunking. The top women at the time were Cindy Cook, a four-time winner; Phoebe Morgan, champ in 1971; and Penni McCall, champ in 1972. Hoeschler gradually made gains, reaching the semifinals.

Just from observing and studying the best men and women, Hoeschler realized that the men were far more aggressive, working hard to dump the other guy rather than just fending off moves in order to stay atop the log.

"Most women rolled defensively," Hoeschler said.

She adopted a no-guts, no-glory attitude, being proactive and trying to put foes away rather than just reacting to what the competition did. There are tricks in the arsenal of good logrollers that can sway a match. Some of the best can maintain balance as they dip one foot into the water and kick upward in an attempt to spray water in an opponent's face. Once regarded as a dirty move, now such aggressive tactics are routine.

In 1973, Hoeschler was seventeen, and she won the title. A newspaper headline proclaimed "Hayward Girl Wins!" From 1973 to 1977, five years in a row, Hoeschler was unbeatable. She was a celebrity in Hayward and within the timber sports community.

"Logrolling was the premier event," Hoeschler said.

Calling Tony Wise a visionary for seeing the possibilities in creating the championships and holding them in Hayward, Hoeschler said she was intrigued by the games from the first moment she saw them. She and her friend Liz Wise played, worked, and appeared (in one guise or another) at Historyland. In 1969, Hoeschler was queen of the Indian village on the banks of the Namekagon River. Meanwhile, logs were floating in the water, and when she had time Hoeschler drifted over to the holding pond and practiced her rolling, imitating what she saw competitors do. No one instructed her.

"I was just trying to figure it out on my own," Hoeschler said. "I remember being obsessed. 'How do I stay on?'"

Another friend, Mailys Hodde, who had been the local Muskie Queen, learned logrolling from Billy Hopinka, a local Native American, and she performed in logrolling exhibitions for tourists at a pancake house located adjacent to the Lumberjack Bowl. Patrons could pour their maple syrup on their breakfasts and watch logrolling for amusement. Hodde was very entertaining, said Hoeschler, who also was a Wise logrolling exhibition hire once she became a star.

Logrolling was a skill needed in the logging industry when lumberjacks were forced to break up logjams and start logs floating downriver. Logrolling in the championships is sport, but logrolling in the camps was part of the job.

Much of American society was still chauvinist in 1960 when the Lumberjack World Championships began, so the prevailing thought was that homemaker women were too weak, too dainty, and too much at risk to cope with the heavy equipment needed to chop wood or reduce logs to pulp. But it was thought possible that ladies could balance on a floating log and topple another lady into the water. In the context of the championships that was not an unseemly prospect. There was no physical strength necessary and no physical contact. So logrolling became the first women's sport in the championships. Women did not compete against men—and still don't—but they do compete in logrolling in addition to men.

Another name for logrolling is birling, and birling was one of earliest popular lumberjack sports. The U.S. Log Rolling Association was formed in the 1920s, and when Tony Wise began the Lumberjack World Championships it was the only timber sport that had its own governing body and a recognized world champ. Evidence suggests that Eau Claire, Wisconsin, conducted a public birling contest in 1888.

Jimmy Murray of Eau Claire was in the forefront of a traveling group of birlers during the early decades of the twentieth century. The group gave exhibitions at state and county fairs, which included trick and fancy logrolling, a more showy style than simply trying to knock someone off a log.

A regular champ between 1914 and 1933 was Eau Claire's Wilbur Marx. Reports indicate that four thousand spectators watched Marx win his first title. After repeat wins his exploits made it into newsreels shown in movie theaters, and he gained a national following. Marx, too, made barnstorming logrolling appearances around the country.

By the time Hoeschler became a logrolling titleholder, the event was the anchor of the games. Tall and thin, and active in individual sports like alpine skiing and tennis, Hoeschler was politically aware enough to realize that federal Title IX legislation was shaking up the schools and would make a long-term difference in the lives of girls. Under the act, passed by Congress in 1972, any educational entity that received federal funds had to provide equal opportunity for males and females. Translated into the world of sports, that meant there had to be equality of opportunity for high school girls and college women to participate on school sports teams. Title IX dramatically altered the nation's sports landscape, igniting a revolution the results of which continue to be visible today.

"I was a very athletic kid," Hoeschler said. She used a word that has fallen out of favor to describe her childhood sports interest. "I was a tomboy. I really loved sports, and Title IX was changing things."

It is doubtful that Tony Wise or any other organizer imagined logrolling capturing the attention of so many so quickly. Maybe it was in the genes, but the Hoelscher-Scheer family seemed to produce ridiculously resourceful, well-balanced kids with just the right touch of killer instinct to wipe out all comers. They were local, too, adding a nice touch for Hayward fans.

Unforeseen was just how taken Hayward would be with logrolling, to the point of starting schools for youngsters. If you lived in Hayward there was a half-decent chance you would immerse yourself in logrolling instead of Little League. By 1969, Hayward was offering logrolling classes, and

Hoeschler took them. By 1972, she was teaching such classes herself. Logrolling champions are objects of public pride in Hayward. There is a proprietary interest in the Lumberjack World Championships, but there is a special connection to logrolling that extends beyond a feeling of ownership. When someone from Hayward wins (as frequently occurs), it's almost as if a member of the family has won.

Long before the Lumberjack World Championships got their start, there was a World Log Rolling Association. Not linked to any overall timber sports event, from the 1920s on, the group hosted its own championships to crown the finest logrollers in the world. Even earlier, a World Log Rolling Championship was contested in 1898 in Omaha, Nebraska.

"Logrolling was the only sanctioned event," Hoeschler said of the 1960 start-up of the Lumberjack World Championships. "It put the 'world' in Lumberjack World Championships. That's why he [Wise] featured it. In those days [the 1970s] it built up to the final event. All eyes were on the logrolling."

That meant that the attention of four thousand pairs of eyes, as well as the cheers of the fans, had to be blocked out. Focus was a Hoeschler strength, but it did not come as easily to her as many thought.

"There's so much tension in it," she said. "The adrenaline is really serious. It was really, really hard for me to control my nerves."

Hoeschler helped develop that sense of drama as she brushed away all the competition during her five-year span as queen of the logs. She was only twenty-one, and it seemed as if she had many good years left in those feet encased in spiked shoes. But in training, preparing for the 1978 championships, Hoeschler took a fall and landed hard on a log, injuring her back so badly that she developed sciatica. The doctors told her that she could not continue logrolling, that it was too dangerous for her to compete.

Instead she became Professor Judy. She started a kids' logrolling program called the La Crosse Rug Rollers in which the children learned logrolling on a carpeted surface wearing tennis shoes rather than spiked shoes. At one point Hoeschler and her husband Jay lived in Colorado, and there she taught logrolling in a pool.

One thing she noticed: kids were fascinated by logrolling. Some had seen it on television, but others were attracted by its offbeat nature or as something neat to do.

Hoeschler was hardly the only one in her family to succumb to the siren song of logrolling. That's hardly unusual in Hayward. Families that logroll together compete together. Periodically, matches pit siblings against each other for the right to win gold, silver, or bronze. Lumberjack sports in general attract families. Sometimes competitors are brother and brother, sometimes brother and sister, sometimes husband and wife, and sometimes father and daughter or father and son.

Fred Scheer, Hoeschler's brother, also emerged as a logrolling stalwart, starting in 1969. Siblings are often influenced by older brothers or sisters. They see someone having fun and think, "I can do that." Sometimes the next in line following the role model even eclipses the older sibling's achievements. Judy Hoeschler was sidetracked by injury, but brother Fred faced no such impediment.

When Scheer broke into the sport, it was dominated by Phil Scott from Barrington, Nova Scotia. Scott won his first title in 1968, then two in a row in 1970 and 1971 and added six more crowns between 1973 and 1980, almost always going head-to-head with Scheer. Scott was a logger and said he loved competing in logrolling at the Lumberjack World Championships because it reminded him of his youth working in the forest.

"Logrolling was the highlight of my life," Scott said. "It brought back memories [of] when I was a young child when I left school for a few weeks to work on the river drives. It was really the last of a great way of life, one I took great pride [in] and placed great effort into. I loved coming to the Lumberjack World Championships—here I could both remember and revisit my past."

Sometimes Scott competed wearing a checked shirt and a baseball cap. In those days, Scheer was just a kid, the young pup in the group, with curly hair so thick it looked as if its sheer weight might pull him off the log. For five years in a row, as Scheer gained experience and learned the tricks of the trade, the finals match at Hayward ended the same way, with Scheer being thrown into the water as Scott spun the log. No matter what Scheer tried, Scott had the answer. Their duels were legendary and pitted one generation against another. Scott always found a way to beat Scheer.

"He was Tiger Woods," Scheer said years later.

Being the Tiger Woods of logrolling meant Scott was pretty much un-beatable and also projected an aura of invincibility. Highly motivated, always seeking to find the edge against his nemesis, Scheer trained exceptionally hard for the 1978 championships. By then he was twenty and no longer wet behind the ears.

"I was pretty determined," Scheer recalled. "He hadn't ever been standing in the water. I'm local and I'm the crowd favorite."

At last it was Scheer's turn. Scheer and Scott stared at one another on the log. They shifted feet. They did a little dance to send the log into a controlled spin. There was a little foot splashing aimed at distracting Scott.

"It was gamesmanship," Scheer said. "It was a pretty serious match."

Ultimately, Scheer made one move Scott couldn't counter and Scott tumbled into the water. Game, set, match to Scheer. He did it. Fans erupted with cheers. Some three hundred spectators poured out of the grandstand to mob Scheer and dive into the water.

"It was bedlam," Scheer said of the memory. "It became a throw-everybody-in-the-water party. My dad got thrown in. My mom got thrown in. People who were dressed up got thrown into the mud. The next year I beat him again."

The strategy of splashing water in a guy's face with your foot was new. Taking it a step beyond, Scheer was surprised when Scott spit on him. Scheer said he thought Scott was just trying to think up a fresh way to knock him off his game.

"I don't know if he felt confident kicking water," Scheer said. "I didn't hold it against him. It was just gamesmanship."

When Scheer ended Scott's streak at five wins in a row, he said Scott told everyone that he took the second-place trophy and chopped it up.

"He was really an intense competitor," Scheer said of Scott. "He hadn't been challenged in ten years. So when you've been the man, and all of a sudden a twenty-year-old kid beats you decisively . . ."

Scheer captured the rematch a year later, but Scott reclaimed the title one last time two years after Scheer's breakthrough.

"He kept coming," Scheer said. "And he beat me. He shouldn't have. I choked. I got my attention diverted, but he did it. Logrolling is a gift really. Logrolling is like putting in golf. You'd better have your head on straight. A lot of guys miss 3-foot putts to lose the Masters. They sink that putt a hundred times in a row and yet they miss a 3 footer to lose the Masters. Once in a while, they miss. With log rolling, it's the same thing. It doesn't matter who you're rolling. You're always one step from the water. But things happen really fast, especially at the top level."

An innate sense of balance is needed to excel at logrolling. Lifting weights won't help. Running miles won't help. The mental pressure is also intense, and the ability to cope with that aspect of the game is critical.

"There are a lot of guys over the years that were certainly world-caliber logrollers that were good enough to win the world championships that just never do," Scheer said. "They just couldn't win the big match. I see it all the time."

The biggest evolution in logrolling competition is the number of entrants who have the foot-splash move down pat. In the late 1970s almost no one employed it. But as in so many other sports, added difficulty, added trickery, became commonplace. There is risk in employing the maneuver since it requires removing one foot from the log.

"You're turning yourself sideways and going on one foot while the log is moving and reaching out and kicking water," Scheer said. "A lot of guys fall in. More guys fall in doing it than make the other guy fall in."

When Scheer was emboldened enough to try the kick splash it surprised his foe and boosted his confidence.

"You're trying to get water in his eyes," Scheer said. "It can totally screw somebody up."

Scheer won the title twice more, in 1982 and 1983, and then younger men, notably Dan McDonough, who claimed nine titles, and Brian Duffy, five titles, came along.

Scheer's success made him a celebrity in his hometown, something he admits would likely not have occurred if he had been from somewhere besides Hayward.

"It's a novelty sport," he said. "There just aren't that many places where people have access to logrolling. Parents got a logrolling school going, and it turns out a lot of kids. Around here it [his win] was a big deal. It made the front page of the paper. Full pictorial. That was before the Internet. That was before cable television. That was when we got all of our news from the local newspaper or watched the six o'clock news. It was a really big deal for me. It was extremely exciting. How often do you get to say you're the best in the world at anything? Even though, and I don't kid myself, it's a novelty sport."

Meanwhile, although Judy Hoeschler had been warned away from logrolling because of her back injury, she didn't travel far from the sport. Always a logrolling teacher wherever she moved, Hoeschler also raised a houseful of logrollers. In 2004, her daughter Liz won the women's logrolling championship in Hayward for the first time and daughter Abby became a boom run champ.

Teaching was fun, but it was not enough for Hoeschler. Playing sports, much more than instructing or watching them, energized her. Years passed without another attempt at logrolling, but eventually she couldn't resist trying for a comeback. Hoeschler was a five-time titlist in 1977 when doctors issued their proclamation. She sat on the sidelines at the games, watching her brother's battles with Scott. But after a two-year break, during which time daughter Katie was born, Hoeschler wanted to get back up on the log.

In 1981, three months after her first child was born, Hoeschler regained her crown. She won again in 1982, nine years after her first triumph. The last time Hoeschler entered a competitive logrolling event was not in Hayward but in Lake Placid, New York, where ESPN was hosting its Outdoor Games.

By then Hoeschler's competitive fire had dimmed. In the summer of 2000 in Hayward daughters Katie and Liz were entered in the women's logrolling and that shook her up.

"I never thought I'd still be rolling when they got into the elite division," Hoeschler said. "I had to roll head-to-head against Lizzie."

Advancing through opposite sides of the draw, the competition led Hoeschler to a semifinal match with Liz, and Judy didn't want to go through with the face-off. Nursing a small injury, Judy was completely psyched out.

"I was crying," Hoeschler said. "I was thinking, 'I don't want to do this.' There was something so unnatural about it to me. I didn't want to be in that position. On the log I'm pushing, and I remember getting pushed back, and I went, 'Oh,' and went into the water. I lost, and I lost pathetically. I was already practicing my retirement speech."

When Hoeschler did retire from competitive logrolling, something she had been doing since she was a little girl, she cried. But when the tears dried, "It was a relief" that she was done, she said.

It was time. The next generation of young people, many of them taught to logroll by Hoeschler or inspired by her winning ways on the log, was taking over.

Tony Wise, founder of the Lumberjack World Championships in Hayward, Wisconsin. An innovator and creative businessman, Wise wanted to put his hometown on the tourist map. (photo from Sheila Wise, courtesy of Lumberjack World Championships)

Tony Wise on the microphone, speaking to his guests who have come from all over the world to attend the Lumberjack World Championships. (Lumberjack World Championships Archives, Fred Morgan Photography)

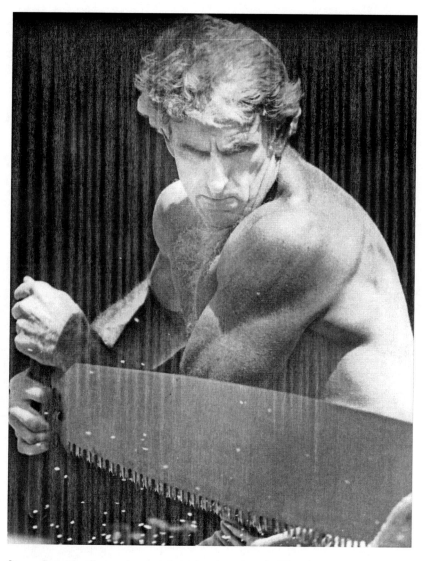

Sawyer Ron Hartill caused a sensation when he stripped off his shirt to compete at the Lumberjack World Championships and displayed a Hercules-like upper body. (Lumberjack World Championships Archives, Fred Morgan Photography)

Left: A young Dave Geer, former Lumberjack World Championships all-around champion and an early aide to Tony Wise in rounding up the best timber sports athletes. (Lumberjack World Championships Archives, Fred Morgan Photography)

Rick Halvorson of Alma Center, Wisconsin, an all-around king of competition, waves to the crowd at the Lumberjack Bowl as he is introduced before the hot saw competition. (Lumberjack World Championships Archives, Brett Morgan Photography)

Right: Ron Hartill demonstrates how it's done in the springboard chop, slicing the top hunk of wood cleanly off after working his way up the log. (Lumberjack World Championships Archives, Brett Morgan Photography)

Penny Halvorson, a Jack & Jill sawing star with husband Rick, argued for the expansion of women's events in the Lumberjack World Championships and became a four-time all-around winner. (Lumberjack World Championships Archives)

Right: Young Fred Scheer (*right*) going up against many-time champ Phil Scott in the men's log rolling. It took many tries, but Scheer dunked Scott in the water to become world champion. (Lumberjack World Championships Archives)

Judy Scheer Hoeschler (*right*) tries to spin opponent Bonnie Pendleton into the water during the women's log rolling. (Lumberjack World Championships Archives)

Right: Arden Cogar of West Virginia axes a hunk of wood in half during the standing block chop. (Lumberjack World Championships Archives)

How *Yo-ho!* Became
a Household Word

Will wore red plaid and khaki pants that stopped short of his ankles and were held up by suspenders, and every other phrase out of his mouth included the word *Yo-ho!* It served as a wake-up call to patrons, an audience participation rallying cry, and even punctuation and an end-of-chapter marker.

Whenever Will could fit in a "Yo-ho!" he did so, as if reporting that the only word a real lumberjack or logger needed to survive in the forest was that short comment that started with *Y.*

The "Yo-ho!" chants and plaid-clad Will are not part of the Hayward championships. They are part of a family-friendly lumberjack show that takes place at the Lumberjack Bowl to provide tourists with a sense of timber sports when the world championships are not going on.

Although it was not mentioned in the course of an hour-and-ten-minute show, it would have been appropriate to issue a shout of "Yo-ho!" to Fred Scheer. Long after he made his local reputation in his title-winning years as a competitor in the Lumberjack World Championships, Scheer is a pivotal figure in the making of timber sports popularity.

Whereas the championships are about serious competition, Fred Scheer's Lumberjack Show of Champions is about entertainment. Woven into the show, however, is a considerable amount of educational information.

"Yo-ho," that's an old lumberjack call," said Will, the master of ceremonies for a Scheer show in Hayward. "Logging history around here goes back to the mid-1800s. What they were looking for was the great white pine."

In 1981, Fred Scheer and his brother Rob dreamed up the idea of putting together a lumberjack show for tourists that would be more about fun and games than competition. They sold the idea to Tony Wise, who backed them. The first shows, Fred recalls, were a little bit rough around the edges. He started to call them a joke, but backed off, saying that the audiences enjoyed them. With practice came sophistication and smoothness.

"It just grew and got really big really fast," Scheer said.

In 1983, the show hit the road, and within a few years the Scheer brothers had five touring lumberjack units. Fred bought Rob out, and Rob went to Alaska to start a new version of the show in Ketchikan in the southeastern part of the state. Fred became a tourism entrepreneur. He built a miniature golf course and Lumberjack Lodge in Hayward. He thinks the lumberjack show has made at least one appearance in every state in the union. Scheer was on the go. He organized everything and participated in the lumberjack events from logrolling to chopping.

"Who doesn't like having people ask for your autograph?" he said. "How many people get to do that with their job?"

After a while, Scheer tired of the logistics of the road, sold the touring component of his business, and retrenched, staging lumberjack shows only in Hayward and elsewhere in Wisconsin. Rob Scheer still runs his independent operation in Alaska, and sister Tina has her own lumberjills operation in Maine.

"I didn't like the travel, but it was fun. Rob is geared a little bit more to entertainment than to competition," Fred Scheer said. "Ours is a little more tongue-in-cheek. It's all still entertainment."

The lumberjack show's stage in Hayward is the Lumberjack Bowl, which Scheer bought in 1988 through a bankruptcy sale, and he also owns the adjacent pancake house.

In some ways, Scheer's make-believe shows have spread the gospel of timber sports more dramatically and efficiently than actual competition. If you come to Hayward in the summer to fish at a time other than championships week, you can still get a flavor of the lumberjack lifestyle by attending Scheer's show.

Scheer shares the nationwide limelight with Tina and Rob. The timber sports shows, with individual variations, are a coast-to-coast enterprise. Tina adopted the nickname "Timber Tina" and bills her crew as "Timber Tina's World Champion Lumberjills." The show got its start in Trenton, Maine, more than a decade ago.

Like others in the family, Tina Scheer made her mark in Hayward first. She is passionate about timber sports and loves the championships and the shows she orchestrates. Her nickname is not on Tina's birth certificate, but it might as well have been bestowed on her in the cradle.

There is little doubt that Tina is all lumberjill. The Wisconsin license plate on her truck reads "Lumbrjil." A portion of her e-mail address contains the term *axewoman*. The Lumberjills have a Maine-based Bar Harbor summer home, but they also travel to county and state fairs in the Northeast and wherever they are welcome. What vacationers wouldn't want to watch Timber Tina, with her long, blonde, flowing tresses, try to balance on a log or pulverize wood with a saw?

Tina's revolving lineup (the same as any sports team, really) can be found on a lumberjills website along with their first names, photos, and short biographies. At one point, Taylor was attending the University of Wisconsin–Superior majoring in exercise science and minoring in health. She also played college basketball. Being a lumberjill was a neat summer job.

Alison was a budding television personality, appearing on *Life Moments*, a show about women performing firsts. She was filmed during her first competitive woodchopping effort. She also was featured on *Park Raving Mad*, an Outdoor Life Network show, where she was filmed ax throwing.

Denise, who posed cradling an ax, was director of a logrolling school and traveled to Australia with Tina for timber sports exhibitions several times.

Tina finds it hard to believe that something she began as a lark, logrolling at age ten, turned into a lifetime of excitement, fun, pleasure, and a livelihood. Once when she was flying into the island community of Kodiak, Alaska, she allowed herself a passing thought as she looked out the window. "You're getting paid to go logrolling," she said to herself. "You are so lucky."

The first time Scheer was invited to give a timber sports exhibition in Australia was 1985. There was only one problem. She couldn't afford to go. But she was a Hayward gal, where timber sports are not just part of the summer agenda but a way of life. The community raised the money to send her. What seemed likely to be a onetime thing mushroomed. Over the years, Timber Tina has been to Australia (many times), New Zealand, and Africa for timber sports exhibitions.

Who else gets to live such a life through timber sports? Not many people, male or female. Not many people at all.

As he approaches his goal of retiring at age fifty-five to spend his free time fishing, Fred Scheer could be one of those lumberjack world travelers if he wanted to take his show on distant roads. But he is content where he is. One thing Fred is proud of is his show's enthusiastic acceptance by audiences. He certainly does not observe every show, but like a Broadway producer who sneaks into the back of the theater to see and hear if his show is a hit, Scheer does occasionally watch to see if things are going smoothly. His track record, at this point, speaks for itself and is reassuring. Times have changed, time has passed, but the lumberjack show still resonates with the public.

"It's a good way to expose people to lumberjacks," Scheer said. "There's been logging here. There's historical commentary in the show. It's education for people who would otherwise never hear it."

During his twenty-eight years of supervising the lumberjack show, Scheer said his actors, most of whom are skilled in the lumberjack arts and some of whom compete, have played to 750,000 people.

"I cannot seriously remember in that entire time getting more than one or two complaints," Scheer said. "That's a pretty outstanding record. If I can get through a week at the pancake house without a complaint, that's unusual. It's nice to have a product that leaves people with a smile on their face."

"Yo-ho!" There is no denying how frequently the word is employed during a single lumberjack show. Sometimes Will Hoeschler, the master of ceremonies, shouts it. Sometimes, he asks the audience in the grandstand to shout it. When he is at a loss for words, for no apparent reason, he shouts it. It's a catchall term. Also, there is something unique, friendly, cuddly, and just plan silly about a group of strangers yelling "Yo-ho!" together that makes them giggle. Just saying "Yo-ho" tends to make spectators, kids included, feel good.

Will's introductory narrative involves lumberjack history. It's a short but sweet way of letting people know that what they are about to see has roots in an authentic era of American history. His version of how timber sports began is simple: the guys in the logging camps had free time, and they started challenging one another to see who was the strongest and fastest at different tasks. The competitions spread from there.

"Then they wanted to find out who was the best in the whole north woods," Will says.

In the show a group of lumberjacks are split into two teams, one wearing green plaid shirts, the other wearing red. They served as uniforms of the forest, although, unlike baseball players, no last names or numbers were stitched onto the back of the shirts.

Will is a man with a keen sense of showmanship. Many times when he made a comment it was unclear if he was telling the truth or making a joke with show business license. So when he introduced Sam as a man "who grew up with an ax in his hands and was nicknamed 'The Bull of the Woods,'" no one had the slightest idea if it was an accurate assessment. For all anyone watching knew, Sam was someone who grew up in midtown Manhattan, went to University of Michigan, and never touched an ax until he chopped wood one weekend on a getaway in Vermont.

Not that it really mattered. The audience was not going to be talking about Sam's ax-swinging prowess when it left. The success of the show was measured, as Scheer said, by the smiles on faces as it exited.

The show offers a little bit of wit, a little bit of slapstick, and genuine skill with axes and saws. Will informed the crowd somberly that Sam really shouldn't start his chainsaw between his legs. "No, no, Sam," he said. "You'll ruin a perfectly good pair of pants." Or do worse damage than that, a point that was noted with guffaws from the audience even before Will warned that if Sam were not careful he would never have children.

Again, as a form of audience participation, Will, the overseer of the five-man show, split the audience of several hundred into two groups to cheer for the green and red sides. As watchers laughed, clapped, and issued the periodic shouts of "Yo-ho" on command, there were definite links to the lumberjack world to be gleaned from the entertainment. The sound of a chainsaw revving reminded everyone how loud logging work can be. Once the guys pulled the chains on their saws the air was filled with a noise akin to revving automobile engines with no mufflers.

Whether such equipment was dictated by the Occupational Safety and Health Association or just good sense, Sam, Dave, Brodie, and Charlie wore goggles to protect their eyes from flying sawdust and wood chips and wore extra large, over-the-head earphones to muffle the incredibly loud sounds of blade slicing wood.

Sam, it turned out, had a special talent. He could take a big, clunky chainsaw and shape sculptures with it. His event, which was solo, turned out to be speed carving.

"I'm the best," Sam said. "I've never been beaten. That's because I'm the only one in it."

Sam played to the children in the crowd, who watched him sculpt with the same rapt intensity they might watch *Sesame Street* on television. Sam attacked a block of wood with his roaring utensil and a few minutes later held up what was very obviously a carved rabbit. "Yo-ho!"

Sam glanced at his adoring audience and announced, "Prepare to be amazed!"

His next carving was Mr. Potato Head. Then, without being asked, he returned to his rabbit and slashed in some whiskers.

"What did you do?" asked Will. "You gave the rabbit a mustache."

Not so, Sam pointed out. "It's a booger." Sophomoric humor, indeed, but when you are playing to seven year olds on vacation, you've got to aim some of the show at their funny bones.

Dave hopped onto a log floating in the pond just off the dock to attempt a move he called a "double whammy two-foot water kick." Whatever it was or was supposed to be, Dave pitched forward and landed straddling the log. Will asked what happened, and Dave said, "It was just nuts." The adults felt his pain. Dave looked at Will with innocence in his eyes and said, "I hit my elbow."

As veterans, the guys knew what was hitting and missing with the audience and they knew the timetable, so they brought the show in on time. Will wrapped up his monologue after the last wood chips flew. "You folks have fun today," he said. "Yo-ho!"

One last "Yo-ho" for the road, of course.

When the show ended, several audience members, most pulled along by kids, approached the lumberjacks for autographs. They signed some of the largest remaining pieces of wood and talked about lumberjack show life. Most of the actors were younger than they looked, mostly holding summer jobs during their time off from high school or college. They also had long family ties to timber sports or had grown up watching the championships each July in Hayward.

Brodie Orton, just sixteen, from Hayward, said playing the lumberjack role is a kick.

"I love it," he said. "It's pretty fun."

Sam was Sam Fenton, age twenty-one. He was two years into his show participation and had advanced to manager. As if sitting at the same poker table as Orton, he raised his stake in the show. "It's a lot of fun," he said. Fenton had his own lumberjack experience cutting down trees with his father. He was five years old when he first wielded some kind of blade as he helped his dad clear a lot for the family house.

"I've been coming to the shows since I was born," he said, referring to Fred Scheer as "Uncle Fred."

The actors, including Dave Sievert, Charlie Fenton (Sam's brother), and Shane Sabin, are friends. They sometimes do more than one show in a day, performing in the afternoon in Hayward, next door to headquarters, otherwise known as Scheer's office, and then piling into a car and driving fifty miles to another town in Wisconsin for a night show.

Master of ceremonies Will Hoeschler is Judy Hoeschler's son and Fred Scheer's nephew, and at eighteen he knows his lumberjack jargon. Growing up in La Crosse, Wisconsin, really just down the street from his mother's hometown, and with his mom and sisters competing, there was no way he was going to avoid a Lumberjack World Championships education. Not surprisingly, logrolling is one of his personal interests.

"From the time I was four years old I trained with my sisters at home," he said. "My whole life."

When Hoeschler says he's been aware of timber sports his whole life he isn't exaggerating. His mother took the time to educate him on the logging history of northern Wisconsin and informed him of logrolling's origins, and when he joined the show that came in handy. Scheer wanted him to weave more history into his monologues. Clearly, given all of his relatives' connections, the Lumberjack World Championships and the lumberjack show are in Hoeschler's blood.

There is some debate, real or teasing, about whether the first word Hoeschler uttered was "Mom" or maybe "Dad," but, as the joke goes, it was "Yo-ho!" It's hard to bet against "Yo-ho." When it came to memorizing lines for the show, it was not difficult to remember how important it was to toss in the judicious use of "Yo-ho" to keep things moving along. Actually, nothing was difficult for Hoeschler to remember about the show because it was harder for him to forget the script than recall it.

"I've seen the show hundreds of times," he said. "I know the routine."

Hoeschler had a starlike contract, too. He didn't travel, only doing Hayward shows.

"It's good to be here," he said. "I'm doing what I like to do, too."

And apparently it's what everyone else likes, as well. More than 750,000 people can't be wrong.

Fred Scheer can't count how many times he has been part of or seen his lumberjack show. He rarely attends for more than a few minutes. But his office is in a building adjacent to the holding pond and chopping dock, and he can hear the audience clapping and cheering.

"I can open the window in my office and hear the whole show," Scheer said. "That almost tells me more than watching it. I can listen and know how the announcer is doing. It's got to keep rolling. If there's gaps, I'll talk to the boys."

As for Will Hoeschler, whether he is in college, in the business world, or just observing the annual Lumberjack World Championships in Hayward each summer, the word *Yo-ho* is imprinted on his brain for a lifetime.

Family Affair

The Jack & Jill Saw event turned into a pain for Dennis Daun. Literally. As he strained his upper body pushing a gigantic saw back and forth on a log he also planted his feet wide and pushed with his haunches. Boing! And that was not the saw whipsawing out of his hands. That was his ample gluteus maximus twanging. Nothing like a pulled muscle that leaves you hurting when you sit down.

Injuries are part of the landscape in every sport, and getting hurt is just one of the hazards of the trade in the several events that combine speed and power at the Lumberjack World Championships. It is not uncommon to see competitors icing their arms or some other portion of their bodies, which are easily strained due to the repetitive motion of chopping and sawing. It takes energy to turn wood to pulp, to transform sturdy logs into sawdust.

The real-life logging profession, back when trees were harvested in great numbers for home and furniture making, and currently, too, is much more dangerous than timber sports. In the real world of logging a tree may fall on you and make you one with the forest floor. It is more likely in the woods that an ax or saw will hit a rough spot, spin out of control, and cut off a finger or hit someone nearby who is not paying attention.

There is little bloodshed in timber sports competition, but it is an ever-present threat. Rarely do small cuts sidetrack entrants, if they even acknowledge them. More likely than not, muscle fatigue may interfere with top performance. It's tiring to keep on sawing, cutting, or chopping, especially when the effort is measured against the clock. There is no time to pause, wipe one's brow, and resume cutting at your own pace.

Certainly there are risks, but danger is not a specific byproduct of timber sports. That's one reason why, to a surprising extent, the Lumberjack World Championships is a family affair. It is typical for an entire household to embrace certain sports if the parents are heavily engaged. The sport may be long-distance running, hiking, fishing, or playing soccer. So it does happen with frequency that one member of a family getting involved in timber sports leads to other members doing likewise, and that leads to a continuum of generational involvement.

The Scheers/Hoelschers are hardly unique in sending several members of the same family to the starting line of an event. One would think participating in timber sports is a hereditary trait, even though it is learned behavior.

From the time the north woods in Wisconsin was first logged in the 1830s, the job of lumberjack was pretty much a man's profession. The lumber camps were set up for men in the remote wilds, and sleeping and showering in communal quarters was a one-sex operation. Not to mention that women were not expected to have the strength and wherewithal to hack down trees. The lumber camps were definitely a man's domain, and society would have frowned on any respectable lady venturing into the workplace.

But just as society at large has changed and men and women work side by side in many professions formerly closed to women, lumberjack competition has expanded its outlook and opened its doors to women, too. The Jack & Jill Saw is the only co-ed event at the Lumberjack World Championships. Many other events offer separate competition for men and women. Some events bring together more than one generation from the same family. Lumberjacking is no longer just a bunch of guys wearing plaid flannel shirts. It can be guys and gals wearing plaid flannel shirts—and their offspring in the same attire.

Dennis and Lindsay Daun are a rare father-and-daughter sawing team from Round Lake, Illinois, a suburb of Chicago. Dennis's physique has all of the makings of a lineman for the Green Bay Packers, with broad shoulders, wide bottom, thighs as big around as the logs he cuts, and calf muscles that seem bigger than baby calves. Lindsay inherited some of the same traits. She is big boned and 6 feet tall, though not at all heavyset. It appears her body contains the power of an Olympic rower, but she prefers working in wood.

At the time Dennis complained of his aching rear end ("my right butt"), as he described the locus of his injury, he was fifty-one. That's what you get if you are a card-carrying AARP member and you pretend that you are still as spry as you were in college. Indeed, a few years later Daun was retired, reduced to cheering on his daughter. Daun the younger was still college aged when she teamed with her dad, and the difference was that she would not have even the slightest muscle strain the next morning.

Dennis Daun began competing in timber sports in 1990 after three years of attending the championships as a spectator. As his build suggests, he had been a college football lineman, his measurements at 6 feet, 4 inches and 265 pounds, although at one point he weighed 100 pounds more. Daun was a top-three placer in sawing events, but in 1997 he and J. P. Mercier were gold-medal winners in the men's double buck competition.

While Lindsay has seen many of the greatest timber sports athletes up close, when asked who is the best lumberjack competitor, she was loyal. "My dad," she said.

At twenty-two in 2009, Lindsay was nearing completion of her college career. She majored in sociology at the University of Wisconsin–La Crosse. Lindsay has often joked that it was so easy to practice timber sports the way her dad had set things up at the house that she could "roll out of bed" and chop wood.

Her father did not browbeat her into joining him at timber sports. For a while, as a little girl, she just watched him practice. But the older she got, the more intrigued she became, and soon she wanted to start competing, too.

"At the beginning he was just giving me encouragement," the younger Daun said. "He'd be practicing all of the time, and you would want to try it. He gave me a little bit of a push, but once I got into it and started meeting people and doing better at it, it was fun."

Lindsay has traveled to Australia and New Zealand six times for international timber sports competitions, not something with which most of the students wandering around the La Crosse campus can identify. More humorously, when she tells other students what she does when she is not attending class, they don't all believe her. "Some of them," she said, "go 'Yeah, whatever.' I have to show them that I'm a wood chopper. At least they ask me."

When some guys find out that the tall blonde is a lumberjill they go macho on her.

"A lot of guys want to arm wrestle," Lindsay said. She looks them in the eye and responds, "I don't want to hurt you."

The travel and reciprocity with all of the down under timber sports athletes who visit the United States during the North American summer is enlightening, but it is not easy being a lumberjill on the road with your own equipment in this post–9/11 era of heightened alerts about terrorists. Explaining to airlines why you need to transport your own ax and crosscut saw in your luggage can be as daunting as frontline competition at the championships.

The discussion might start with an airline agent looking at her bulky saw bag and asking Lindsay, "What's in there, skis?" Um, no. Once the airline people figure out it's a hot saw, they ask if the alcohol-based fuel has been drained from the motor. Put it this way, no matter how devoted Lindsay is to her personal competition utensils, they are not flying carry-on.

Dennis Daun's body did wear out, and after undergoing hand surgery, he retired from timber sports in 2008.

"As you get older, it takes a lot to stay on top of your game," he said. "I miss the competition. I miss being out there on the dock in front of the fans. I don't miss the backstage stuff, pacing and getting ready, and working out."

But Daun still has a vested interest. When Lindsay travels to competitions, Dennis fidgets, frequently glancing at his watch. Then he waits for a report on how she did.

"It's all Lindsay now," Dennis said. "She competes, and I keep looking at the time. I wait for a text." Then he either sighs or smiles. "She did OK," he says to himself.

Timber sports create an unusual type of father-daughter bonding. There are few couples like the Dauns in the sports world. For the Dauns, sawing wood together is more satisfying than hitting a movie at the local multiplex, though if polled, their neighbors might vote for them attending the latest Academy Award nominee over roaring, buzzing, backyard shared time.

Actually, the Dauns alternate practice locations at their Round Lake home. When it's sunny and clear they fire up the hot saw, a gas-powered saw with the teeth of a white shark, and churn logs into toothpicks in the backyard. This is not as placid or quiet an activity as contemplating a pond's stillness. Truth be told, when a sawyer yanks the cord on a hot saw to rev it up, the sound approximates Danica Patrick hitting the accelerator at the Indianapolis 500. The best advice is to jam in the earplugs. When it's colder, the Dauns work at the chopping-block setup they've arranged in the basement. Some homes have pool or Ping-Pong tables; the Dauns think outside the box. They can't hang laundry to dry at the same time the wood is flying.

"We never run out of firewood," joked Lindsay.

Sawing and chopping can be common ground in families. If more than one member of the clan participates, they understand what it takes to excel in terms of time and effort. It doesn't really matter if the events involve sawing, wielding the ax, or doing the boom run. It takes one to know one, and if an athlete is going to succeed at an event it helps to have a supportive spouse.

Given that premise, when the lineups for each individual event at the Lumberjack World Championships are reviewed, it makes perfect sense that there are many identical last names. Over time there have been Dennis and Lindsay Daun; Fred Scheer and Judy Scheer Hoeschler (and her daughters and son); Jason Wynyard and his wife Karmyn, who in 2009 competed while pregnant; husband and wife Arden and Kristi Cogar, plus Arden Cogar Jr.; and Rick Halvorson and his wife Penny. Rick is a past men's all-around champion, and Penny is a past women's all-around champion.

It's clear that lumberjacking for Jacks and Jills both is in the blood. That's probably what officials look for in the blood tests before their weddings.

Rick Halvorson of Alma Center, Wisconsin, just past sixty, has won world titles in double buck sawing and the hot saw, as well as being the all-around point getter. Put a saw in his hands and Halvorson is as proficient as a hair stylist with scissors.

"When I started," Halvorson recalled of his fumbling beginnings in timber sports, "my goal was to someday be good enough to make the finals of one event."

Not only did he far surpass that modest ambition, but Rick and Penny combined for five Jack & Jill Saw crowns. Now that's sharing.

Kids who grow up in northwest Wisconsin, either in Hayward or in the vicinity, are indoctrinated into timber sports from an early age. Chances are they checked out the sport as entertainment with their families if they lived in town, or the area, by the time they were in elementary school. By the time they reached junior high school age they likely were curious enough to try an event that made sense for their body type. The lighter-weight boys and girls would gravitate to logrolling or the boom run. The heavier, bulkier kids might try chopping or sawing. By high school, some of the locals become among the best in the world at their specialty.

Tina Salzman Bosworth was one of those Hayward lumberjack children.

"When I was younger, I used to think that everyone over here was a god," she said in adulthood.

Bosworth, older sister of JR Salzman, practiced and improved and the next thing she knew she was a goddess herself in logrolling, winning ten world titles. A slender woman, she was ill-suited to the power events that required ax swinging and sawing. The logrolling—essentially tap dancing on a moving surface—requires excellent balance, which she had.

Salzman has balance in everyday life, too.

"I'm good on a pair of ice skates," she said. "I'm not a klutz."

Neither is JR, who followed her into the logrolling arena and also became a star. Once again, a combination of genes and environment might have something to do with that.

Jason Wynyard is one of a significant number of New Zealanders who spend a good chunk of each summer in the United States looking for timber sports battles culminating in the Lumberjack World Championships in late July. There are plenty of trees in New Zealand, so these lumberjacks can identify with the Wisconsin site and they have much in common with their American counterparts. While no lumberjacks from Maine, Wisconsin, or Michigan would have given much thought to loggers on the other side of the world in the nineteenth century, it turns out they are kindred spirits of the woods.

Wynyard has been a regular at the Lumberjack World Championships since he was eighteen in 1996. He loves his annual visits to Hayward and not only because he has won so many titles that his name comes up in any talk about the greatest timber sports athlete of all time.

"This is probably my favorite competition," Wynyard said. "I have a very strong following. We have the same heritage where the sport evolved down under through logging."

Wynyard definitely has a following in Hayward. The fans know his name because he has been coming to town for years, and they like him because his performances often awe them. When Wynyard's name is announced as he steps up to a block of wood, he is greeted with a roar. Spectators know he is going to produce, that he might well be a gold-medal winner, and that he could set a world speed record.

When Wynyard comes to Hayward, he brings his wife, children, and a complex pile of luggage that dwarfs Lindsay Daun's airline planning. Hayward and the championships have become a huge part of Wynyard's life, and his victories have become a huge part of lumberjack sport lore.

Few names are as well known to Hayward Lumberjack World Championships aficionados as Scheer and Hoeschler, given the family's long history with the sport. Fred Scheer's competitive heyday is past, but his involvement with timber sports lives on in his lumberjack show, another family operation given how many actors, lumberjacks, and relatives he employs. He gets a lot of mileage out of the undeniable fact that you can still enjoy timber sports even if you can't participate in them.

"There are not a ton of people who have the skills," Scheer said. "But people like to watch it."

When Dennis Daun was young he wondered if Lindsay's fascination with his sawing would translate into another timber sports competitor in the family or if she would be a full-time spectator.

"My dream was that she would wake up one day and she'd be sawing," Dennis said.

As part of his subtle propaganda campaign, he began taking Lindsay to the games in Hayward when she was a baby. It gave her a chance to soak up a more exciting atmosphere than she got watching Dad practice in the basement or yard. Lindsay started her athletic career as a basketball and volleyball player, but she made Daddy's day the first time she asked if she could help him saw. He was as pleased as a poppa could be when she suggested training as a lumberjill. Lindsay was twelve, and once she started, she kept it up.

Dennis's second dream was that he would be able to coax enough competitive years out of his aging body to compete in the Jack & Jill Saw with his daughter. He held on, and they had several good, fun years together on the saw, although they didn't win. They just weren't quite fast enough.

Dennis is definitely undergoing some withdrawal pains, and he very much wants his daughter to succeed. If she is competing miles away she can count on him checking up on her frequently.

"I carry on the legacy," Lindsay said. "He calls me every ten minutes. 'How are you doing?'" Usually, she is doing fine.

Lindsay understands that her dad is past his prime, and with the aches and pains that come with being a longtime athlete in his mid-fifties, he is better off on the sidelines in retirement.

"He's done," she said.

Whether it was being back at the championships in the old environment, whether he was teasing, or whether there still is a spark of competitiveness left in Dennis Daun's soul, he immediately responded, "I've got my ax."

Putting the World
in World Championships

Tony Wise's first step in making the Lumberjack World Championships into a first-class event was to round up the best lumberjacks in the United States and lure them to Hayward each July.

The second step was figuring out how to add legitimacy to the event by making it live up to its title. Wise was not content to call the event a world championship without meaning it. He did not want the "world" part of his event's name to be all talk and no action. He wanted to see competitors from around the globe traveling to Wisconsin and entering.

Without a serious budget it was difficult to make financial guarantees to lumberjacks located halfway around the world. The best thing Wise had going for him was word of mouth. When one guy ran into another at an event in Oregon, they would talk about what was new, and one would tell the other that he had to go, if only once, to Hayward, Wisconsin.

It worked. Many of the best competitors from thousands of miles away began marking Hayward on their maps and calendars. Wise, of course, with his sense of promotion, nudged things along with supplemental ideas. Jubiel Wickheim, from Sooke, British Columbia, won the first Lumberjack World Championships logrolling title in 1960 and seven of the first ten world titles (his brother Ardiel won in 1961 and 1967). The Wickheims apparently had birling in their genes.

Acting as a representative of the Canadian government at a trade convention in Japan in early 1965, Wickheim gave a logrolling exhibition. It attracted considerable attention and resulted in a delegation from Japan heading to Hayward for the 1965 championships.

The team of Japanese logrollers came to Hayward under the auspices of the Japanese Lumber Association and tried to balance on American logs under championship rules. Until a couple of months before, they had never used the short-spiked shoes employed by Hayward rollers, and they did not fare well in the early rounds. The three men competed in traditional logrolling against the usual field and added a new dimension to the games in an exhibition.

Dressed in traditional Japanese headscarves and waist-length kimono-type jackets, the logrollers performed a wide variety of acts. One spun a log as quickly as possible and stayed upright while holding a parasol. Another trick involved two men balancing on parallel logs as they held up a young woman in a basket by resting a pole across their shoulders over the water. It was showtime more than competition time.

Hitoshi Adashi and Tsutomu Itoh were the national trick and fancy logrolling champions of Japan. The Japanese style of logrolling was a far different animal than the "knock the other birler off the log" way of doing things. One newspaperman who wrote about the doings at the time said the duo's efforts "could be likened to the movements of a ballet atop the water."

The performance earned whistles and cheers, and there is no doubt that there was skill involved in balancing on the logs. Although it was more Broadway than sport, if the spectators were happy, Wise was happy.

Graham Pocock was a fresh face from a different forest when he entered the 1983 world championships. He made the journey from Papua New Guinea and admitted it was a wearying trip. "It's a bloody long way from Papua New Guinea to Hayward, I'll tell you," said Pocock as he figured out how to get his jet lag under control.

Pocock was actually a native of New Zealand, but he supervised a logging company in Papua New Guinea on a contract let by a company in Singapore. His passport was probably still rippling from the stamps by the time he hit U.S. shores. Pocock was an all-around wood guy, training loggers, working in plywood manufacturing, and even making chopsticks. There was plenty of wood to go around in Papua New Guinea, including, as Pocock reported at the time, pines stretching 260 feet skyward and measuring 8 feet across. A popular activity among residents, he said, was climbing 80-foot-tall coconut trees using just their hands.

At the time, more than twenty-five years ago, Pocock said lumberjack events in New Zealand and Australia were limited mostly to exhibitions rather than events that ranked athletes and paid prize money. A previous competitor in U.S. West Coast events, Pocock was blown away by his Hayward experience.

"People are very friendly," Pocock said. "It's a good thing for the timber industry. There should be more of it. We don't have anything in New Zealand or Australia to any degree." In Papua New Guinea, he said, the smaller physical stature of the residents would inhibit them in chopping and sawing events that require brawn.

Jim Wass, Pocock's friend from New Zealand, accompanied him to Hayward but had already made his mark in Wisconsin, winning the underhand block chop in 1980.

Papua New Guinea never did become a major player in timber sports, but almost from the beginning in Hayward there was a special relationship with the lumberjacks from down under. Tom Kirk and Bill Johnson of New South Wales were already old-timers in the woods by the time the Lumberjack World Championships were created, but in the early 1960s, they made the long-distance pilgrimage from Australia to Hayward, where they not only showed that veterans could compete, but they planted a flag of sorts on Wisconsin soil.

In 1961, Johnson won the men's underhand block chop. In 1963, Kirk won that title but also teamed with Johnson to take the double buck competition, won the standing block chop, and was proclaimed the all-around champion. They definitely showed that Australia could be famous for more than kangaroos and vegemite sandwiches.

That duo was in the first wave of down under entrants, the earliest in a long line of Australian and New Zealand lumberjacks who worked in wood or made their living in the forest and whose sense of competition was piqued once they learned of the Lumberjack World Championships.

Merv Jensen of New Plymouth, New Zealand, was a larger-than-life figure. He was a huge man, weighing about 285 pounds and standing 6 feet, 2 inches. In his prime his body was thick with muscles, and his speech was loud and colorful. He liked making jokes, despite some saying he was bashful at heart and had covered up his shyness by becoming outgoing. He was usually the center of attention when he walked into a room. He was also an expert with a saw.

In the late 1970s, Jensen and partner Ron Hartill, he of the bare chest, combined for two double buck sawing titles. In the early 1980s, Jensen teamed with Cliff Hughes of Auckland, New Zealand, and won two more titles, for four in all. Hughes, in fact, won another title, with another partner, Brian Trow. Jensen also won the single buck competition in 1982 and set a world record for slicing and dicing of 21.70 seconds. As in all sports, records are made to be broken, but in timber sports advances in equipment manufacture have greatly aided speed. In the single buck the combination of faster sawyers and better equipment has halved Jensen's record.

Jensen, who owned a dairy and sheep farm in New Zealand, was also a saw builder and set his Hayward record when he was sixty-seven.

In 1983, Jensen was sixty-eight but still entering lumberjack events. He even spent entire summers touring the United States. In late March of that year, Jensen and Mel Lentz, a legendary lumberjack figure in Hayward, were giving an exhibition on the two-man saw in Sydney, Australia. Jensen stopped, saying he felt as if he were going to faint. He was loaded into an ambulance but died en route to the hospital. The diagnosis was a heart attack.

To those who saw Jensen compete, that came as less than a shock because he was addicted to cigarette smoking, puffing before and after individual events. But fans took note that Jensen literally died doing what he loved.

The success of earlier generations of down under sawyers and choppers in Hayward has motivated new groups of younger timber sport athletes to travel north. It has become a tradition for the best to make the trek to Wisconsin each July, and each new wave of Australians, and lately more Kiwis than ever, has distinguished itself.

There is ample proof that visitors from far, far away can swiftly and powerfully cut wood to pulp. Bill Youd of Tasmania, Australia, was the 1985 springboard chop winner. Martin O'Toole, another Australian, won the springboard crown in 1986, 1987, and 1989; won the standing block competition in 1986, 1989, and 1992; and was the 1992 underhand chopping champ.

But they were practically warm-up acts for Dave Bolstad of Taumaruni, New Zealand, an eight-time springboard chop winner whose hometown sounds quite exotic.

The wood used at Hayward is to the liking of New Zealand and Australian choppers because it is softer than the wood back home. That means it can be cut faster. White pine, from Menominee Indian tribal lands (Wise always had a good rapport with the Wisconsin Indians), was used for the sawing events. Aspen was used in the other cutting events.

Bolstad was an artist with an ax. In the underhand chop event, in which the contestants stand on top of the hunk of wood they are assigned to reconfigure, Bolstad seemed to miss his toes by inches as he smashed the block to smithereens. During the 2001 competition, Bolstad set a world record, his third of four world records in the event over the years, and his style and speed so entranced public address announcer John Hughes that he blurted out, "That was a beautiful piece of wood you tore apart!"

Bolstad was good at that. Standing 6 feet, 4 inches and weighing over 250 pounds, he was as chiseled as the wood he worked on and his short-cropped hair looked as if it had been trimmed by a very sharp blade itself. Bolstad seemed to lower the underhand chop record each time he contested it, and between 1997 and 2003 he took more than twenty seconds off the mark. The huge drop of one-third in a record that is clocked in hundredths of a second was amazing. That is Usain Bolt territory, akin to breaking a record by a huge margin the way the Jamaican sprinter did at the 2008 Olympics.

All evidence indicates that Bolstad just excelled at pulverizing wood. It's a gift. "I've lived and breathed woodchopping my whole life," said Bolstad, who was in his early thirties when he made the statement.

David Foster, of Tasmania, will go anywhere to talk, and he will go anywhere to chop. He came to Hayward in the mid-1980s and brought a standing block chop world title home to Australia in 1985. While Foster never became a regular in Hayward, he at least made a cameo appearance, and in some quarters he is considered to be the best timber sports athlete of all time.

Dennis Daun votes for Foster. "He is the most decorated," Daun said. "He busted a saw handle. He was weighing close to five hundred pounds." Apparently, it should surprise no one given his size that Foster's nickname was "Big Dave." Big Dave is very large by human standards. "He's got shoulders like the back end of a Clydesdale," Daun said.

Thinking back to a visit to Foster's lumberjack competition museum, which is housed in a shed about 30 by 40 feet and decorated with his ribbons and trophies, Daun said, "He's probably the best ever."

Foster has won 163 world titles (though not many of them in Hayward), 140 Australian titles, and more than 2,000 state, club, and overseas championships. That is, indeed, a lot of hardware. He has won the Australian Axeman of the Year award nine times. Just how it rates on a world scale of competition cannot easily be determined, but there is no doubt that the annual Sydney Royal Easter Show is wildly popular. Attendance tops one million.

In 2000, as part of that event, the Australians invited an American team to compete. The American squad featured many names familiar to Hayward fans, including Arden Cogar Jr., Dave Jewett, Mel Lentz, Carson Bosworth, and Dennis Daun. The U.S. team was sponsored by chainsaw manufacturer Stihl, Inc., one of the regular sponsors of the Lumberjack World Championships and sponsor of its own American timber sports circuit.

The featured event was the international relay, for which points accumulated by the U.S., Australian, and New Zealand teams were tabulated. Daun wrote a website article about the experience, saying that "two of the three challenge matches were held on the infield of the 45,000-seat baseball stadium that was built for the Sydney 2000 Olympics. The baseball stadium was filled to capacity with screaming spectators there to watch the event. I am sure that this was the first time anyone from America ever competed in front of a live audience of that number. Everyone on the U.S. Team was in awe of the electrifying effect of the crowd."

Foster's biography says that he began woodchopping in 1976 at the Royal Melbourne Show and won "an Australian hard hitting championship." Advertising himself as a motivational speaker, Foster's theme is "The Boy Next Door Is a World Champion." He also wrote a book entitled *The Power of Two*. Foster's story, according to his website, "is an inspirational one, showing how it's done, that no matter where you come from you can reach the pinnacle of a chosen career."

Foster was twenty-one in 1978 when he began woodchopping with his father, George. The duo won double buck sawing championships for eleven years in a row. When his dad retired, David sawed with his brother Peter, and they won ten additional titles. All of those victories are billed as world championships, but they were not recorded at the Lumberjack World Championships in Hayward. Eventually, David Foster's son Stephen became his sawing partner.

David Foster may be the best ever timber sports athlete, with a laudable, praiseworthy record of achievement, but in Hayward his numbers do not stack up against the best from the Lumberjack World Championships. Whether Foster could have matched the others' accomplishments is moot because he didn't try. Because of that, Foster is merely a footnote in Hayward.

With the passage of time a new generation of first-class competitors from down under, led by Jason Wynyard, has eclipsed Foster's name recognition as an all-timer except among old-timers.

Real Life Paul Bunyans

Whether they were conscious of it or not, the kings of timber sports were real-life manifestations of Paul Bunyan. The Paul Bunyan legend is pervasive in American society when the average Joe thinks of logging.

Baseball players of more than a century ago, pitcher Cy Young and hitter Ty Cobb, for example, are well known to acolytes of the sport. Football players of the 1920s like Red Grange and Bronko Nagurski are well known to their sport's fans. Fans of 1950s and 1960s pro basketball can tell you all about the Boston Celtics dynasty with Bob Cousy and the duels between Bill Russell and Wilt Chamberlain.

But try to name a single old-time lumberjack. There are no heroes celebrated through generational memories and storytelling. There are no well-known timber sports athletes that predate the start of the Lumberjack World Championships. There is only the fictional Paul Bunyan.

Although his height, weight, and exploits vary depending on the tall tale told, it is Paul Bunyan whom everyone knows, not a genuine Babe Ruth of logging. Daniel Boone and Davy Crockett were flesh-and-blood human beings and became fabled representatives of the American frontier whether or not they truly did the things for which they are credited.

If there was a person named Paul Bunyan working the forests in the nineteenth century, it has never been proven. "Paul Bunyan, whoever may have actually borne that name, had by the turn of the [twentieth] century become in story the prototype of the powerful logger." That is how author

Daniel Hoffman describes things in his book *Paul Bunyan: Last of the Frontier Demigods*, published in 1952.

Tracking down the origins and history of the Paul Bunyan story requires a decent sized budget or at least access to many frequent-flier miles. There is the Paul Bunyan of Maine. There is the Paul Bunyan of Wisconsin. And there is the Paul Bunyan of Oregon. Paul apparently popped up in California, too. Either he really got around or there were many Pauls, adopted by loggers in their stories.

What began as a verbal tradition escalated into print. Even today, there are new Paul Bunyan stories being published, freshly illustrated with a modern-day artist's image of the giant among loggers and his sidekick, the resourceful and monstrous-sized Babe the Blue Ox.

Paul Bunyan was the focus of the best lumberjack stories in the logging camps because he was an unbeaten kingpin of the forest who stood up for the little guy. He represented good in the good and evil equation and in essence was the patron saint of loggers. When he wasn't busy making the world safe for democracy, so to speak, Bunyan was either indulging in awe-inspiring feats of strength or simply using his prodigious talents in a way that intimidated louses and raised the spirits of the weak.

In short, at least by the 1920s, Paul Bunyan was sort of a superhero, minus a cape, in the guise of a protector and was multitalented enough to do just about anything. He was a romanticized image of the real-life logger. And real-life loggers carried a swagger in their step developed from their own self-confidence and prowess in the forest and the sense of romanticism that was attached to their profession.

Baseball, basketball, and football players have become heroes through their highly publicized abilities in their sports. Loggers of the past did not perform in stadiums, arenas, or county fairs. Most of the witnesses to their feats of skill were other loggers. Theirs was a compact world, and nobody on the streets of New York would say of a flannel-shirted gent walking through Times Square, "There goes the greatest sawyer who ever lived."

Call it star power or hero making, Tony Wise knew that the best thing he had going for him at the Lumberjack World Championships when he started the event in 1960 was its collection of characters. There are no official odds on such a thing, but Wise had to know that it was a fifty-fifty proposition how the average lumberjack sports fan would react to his show. They might say, "These guys are all crazy and what they do is crazier." Or they might say, "Wow, that looks hard to do, but it's pretty impressive."

Fortunately for Wise and the lumberjacks, public opinion tilted to the impressive side.

Whether it is lifting stumps out of the ground or barbells up to the chin, there has long been an American fascination with strongmen. Strength and speed are admired, and timber sports athletes compete in events that require both. That sets them apart from the mainstream. Once seen at the top of their game, lumberjacks leave little doubt about how they would do against the average spectator. They would pulverize them as they do the wood. Timber sports generally do not provoke fans into spontaneous thoughts of "I could do that." Most couldn't, and few would pretend.

Whether or not he knew it (and given his promotional history, there is every chance he did), Tony Wise was into the hero-building business as deeply as he was the lumberjack competition business. Wise could count a house, and he knew that sports need stars. He spent the time and effort to find the top lumberjacks competing in small events around the country and wooed them to Hayward. After that it was up to them to show who had the right stuff.

Going head-to-head would sort out the gold-, silver-, and bronze-medal winners. Everyone loves winners. But fans especially love winners with big personalities and unusual traits even more. Wise could play only a minimal role in boosting top athletes. They had to make themselves into something more if they were going to become crowd favorites.

The Ron Hartill gimmick of competing without his shirt on, his Tarzan look, happened by accident at first but was nurtured into a calling card. From the start, fun-loving as they were, and bringing young children to the shows, adults in Hayward made up a knowledgeable audience. It was one thing to attend a show with laughs built in, like Fred Scheer's tourism-oriented production, but another thing altogether to promote the Lumberjack World Championships. The Wisconsin crowd knew its stuff, and the athletes had better be the genuine article.

They were. Wise's recruiting was savvy, and from the beginning the door was wide open to welcome men who competed and excelled in small regional shows. They were all given equal chances to solidify and embellish their reputations. You had to perform. You had to win. If you did, pretty soon you had a Hayward following.

Dave Geer, one of Wise's original lumberjack advisers, came from Lisbon, Connecticut, and he now lives in Griswold, Connecticut, where he grows Christmas trees. Geer was good enough to win the world crown in the underhand block chop in the first championships. He also shared a double buck title with Cliff Pitaim in 1969 and with partner Rudy Dettmer in 1975 and 1976. He picked up a single buck title in 1970. More significant, Geer competed well in most disciplines, and he became the Lumberjack World Championships' first true star by capturing the all-around title in 1964, 1965, 1966, and 1973. The man who wins the all-around title is akin to being seen as the most valuable player in a major team sport and is viewed as the king of the lumberjacks. Geer said he once signed an autograph for a pro football player, a definite role reversal.

By virtue of his organizational acumen, his constant presence at the championships, and his world championships, Geer was one of the most popular early Hayward figures. It was a time when anything seemed possible, and the quick success of the championships made the annual trip to Hayward exciting.

"It was front-page news in the papers," Geer recalled. "You couldn't find a place to park around the bowl. There were more fans than seats. People would be up close." They were so close during the sawing, he said, that when slabs of wood and grainy sawdust went flying during a cut "it was a very dangerous business."

Maybe so, but people loved it. They wanted to be up close and personal.

Geer had so much fun, felt so appreciated and rewarded for his efforts, that he traveled to Hayward about twenty years in a row to compete and he has rarely missed a summer visit to Wisconsin. And he never really retired from timber sports, staying in the best shape he could by frequently playing racquetball. Competing in a chopping event at age seventy-four, Geer broke his right ankle. That may have been a message telling him that it was time to holster the ax and hang up the saw, but Geer had trouble picturing himself living outside of the timber sports world.

"I retire every year," said Geer, who not only appeared with Johnny Carson on the *Tonight Show*, but made a guest appearance on *What's My Line?* as well. Then he promptly announced that for the fiftieth Lumberjack World Championships competition in 2009, he was going to enter the masters underhand chop. "I hope they give me a lot of a head start. What once took me fifteen seconds to do takes me a minute to do now."

Masters events in Hayward are mainly a way for old champions to take curtain calls in front of their long-time fans. Like Greer, nobody harbors any expectation that they will do as well as they did when they were younger. Still prideful, the competitors take the events seriously, but fans applaud names more than performances.

The addition of masters events was a creative way to allow popular athletes to keep returning to Hayward and stay connected to timber sports even as younger athletes came along and took over the more serious business of winning world titles.

Even from the start, given a limited budget, Wise did what he could to make the top athletes feel special. He did not have a big bank account, but he talked a fast game to sponsors and one year convinced a local car dealer to loan him a fleet of white convertibles. When a lumberjack star flew into the Minneapolis airport, he was given the use of a convertible—with his name on it. Millionaire baseball players can afford to purchase their own car dealerships as a sidelight business, but it takes only minimal stroking to make a timber sport athlete feel wanted.

It is impossible to quantify just how much the 1960s lumberjack competitions benefited from the exposure in national magazines and on *Wide World of Sports*, but it was good publicity at a time when it was sorely needed, and it laid the foundation for the future attention lavished on the sport. If Geer didn't think it was wise to try to knock a cigarette out of Carson's mouth with a thrown ax, former baseball player Bob Uecker, a renowned humorist and broadcaster, went through with being shaved with a large ax. That close shave was a gimmick, of course, but it was memorable theater.

Competition times have become faster, and age slows down competitors in timber sports just as it does in others. Geer may be an older man by societal standards, but he stays young on the chopping block. He won the masters underhand chop in 1992, 1994, 1998, and 2001. He was sixty-five when he won his most recent world title.

There has pretty much always been a Cogar from West Virginia at the Lumberjack World Championships, starting with Arden Cogar and including relatives Benny, Katie, Arden Jr., Kristy, and Matt. Arden Sr., like Geer, was one of the first outstanding lumberjack competitors. Powerfully built, with quick reflexes, he had an immediate impact in the 1960s.

Arden Sr. won the double buck sawing title in 1964, the standing block chop in 1970, 1972, 1973, and 1974 (Arden Jr. won in 2006), the underhand block chop in 1970, 1974, and 1977, the first masters underhand chop in 1991, and the first all-around title in 1962. Cogar was in his seventies, but like the other competitors in the masters chop—also known as the old folks event—he still looked muscular enough to chop down a cherry tree for George Washington.

Arden Cogar Sr., who started his own annual woodchopping festival in his hometown of Webster Springs, West Virginia, was called "a legend in the sport" by ESPN, and his son, Arden Jr., also called Jamie, is a unique competitor. Arden Jr. is a full-time civil defense attorney in West Virginia, a job that leaves him minimal time to train. But woodchopping is in his soul, and he somehow makes time to ready himself for journeys to Hayward each summer.

"I was born into a logging family in Webster County," the younger Cogar said. "My family has been involved in lumberjack sports for three generations. I started competing while in elementary school. What I learned from splitting firewood, cutting timber, and setting chokers has carried over into my adult life: work hard and persevere."

Cogars of every age and sex were busy competitors at the 2009 Lumberjack World Championships. Arden Jr. placed second in the springboard chop, fourth in the standing chop, sixth in the single buck, fourth in the double buck with partner Chris Bradshaw, and fifth with wife Kristy Cogar in the Jack & Jill. Arden Sr. placed fifth with partner Dave Stadler in the masters double buck. Just ahead of Bradshaw and Arden Jr. in the double buck was the team of Matt Cogar and Mel Lentz.

It was a rare appearance for Lentz, now fifty and onetime king of the games. Some years ago he was severely injured in a logging accident, and that, along with increasing age, cut short his lumberjack activities. When he attended the fiftieth-anniversary celebration in 2009 he had only been to Hayward once since 2000.

Another West Virginian, Lentz followed in the footsteps and eventually in the lead of his father, Merv. Merv Lentz won the all-around title in 1967, 1968, 1969, and 1971, but who imagined son Mel would be ever better? Youthful, with a strong background in logging, in his early twenties and into his thirties, Mel Lentz won nine all-around crowns, an astonishing and legendary mark. He was the best of the best in 1981, 1982, 1983, 1986, 1988, 1989, 1990, 1991, and 1994.

Now in his early fifties, Lentz was eighteen years old when he first competed in Hayward in 1977, and it took a few years for him to hone his skills in the competitive realm. Even as a teenager, Lentz performed in exhibitions. An expert chopper, Jim Alexander, took him under his wing, gave him tips, and helped transform him from a hopeful to a contender. Of course, with his father an outstanding timber sports athlete, going to Hayward for the world championships was always on Mel's mind. He just didn't know how he would fare.

"You hear about Hayward," Lentz said. "I wanted to come. It kind of grew on me. You don't really know how good you'll be."

Lentz marveled at the changes in the championships, how it had become a smoothly running operation, how word of timber sports had spread, and how competitors from New Zealand and Australia had made such a big impact. Lentz was a great admirer of Tony Wise and what the promoter put into the creation and expansion of the Lumberjack World Championships.

"He was a great guy," Lentz said. "He'd be really pleased with what it has become. He had a vision like this."

Others appreciate the Wise vision, too, even if they are not competitors. Bob Pendleton Sr., in his mid-eighties, is a Hayward man who owns a 400-acre ranch. White haired, with blue eyes, he aspired to become a logger after quitting high school in Saint Joseph, Missouri, and hopped a Union Pacific train, sleeping in a boxcar.

He climbed off in Meachem, Oregon, walked across the street to something he remembers was called the Chuckwagon Café, and ordered a cup of coffee. The waitress didn't even have a clean cup for Pendleton. So he washed his own and got a job as a cleanup guy.

Serving some state troopers, Pendleton overheard them say that loggers were coming to town soon. Sure enough, a couple of days later a few men came into the café and Pendleton sold his skills to them.

"Are you loggers?" he said. "Do you need any help? I can run a bulldozer."

"Good," they replied. "That's what we need, a cat skinner."

He did it for two years, leading up to World War II, when he served in the Merchant Marine. In 1971 he visited Hayward. A decade later he settled in the town. He quickly became friends with Tony Wise and said he loved it when Wise pushed to make the area home to the lumberjack championships.

"He was a man of great commitment," Pendleton said. "When he decided to get something done, it was going to get done. He was very, very persuasive. No one could get more volunteers together on this earth than Tony Wise."

When Historyland introduced logging history to the public, Pendleton took his five kids to see it. He wanted them to understand what he did as a youth. "They were looking forward to canoeing," Pendleton joked.

For ten summers, before he moved to Hayward, Pendleton mostly watched the lumberjack championships, although he did some logrolling, chopping, and sawing. As a resident, Pendleton still keenly appreciates that the Lumberjack World Championships made its home in Hayward.

"It's getting together with other loggers," Pendleton said. "It's a homecoming."

And for him, it's a pleasant journey back to a time when he was young and strong, full of vigor, and one of the princes of the forest who made his living doing what Paul Bunyan did.

And the Wood Chips Fly

The chopping dock was filled with men and their muscles. Lumberjacks stood in a row, poised to fire up their "hot saws" that could carve a turkey in seconds. Both the men and the saws were bulky, and they could slice three neat, round circles of wood from white pine logs in under seven seconds.

The hot saw, or chainsaw, is potentially the most dangerous event in timber sports. The contestants wear goggles to protect their eyes from the sawdust erupting in the air, or from wood chips shooting up in the case of the saw snagging on a knot of wood. There are mesh fences to protect officials and fans. And none of that even takes into account the key utensil, the saw itself. Noise should also be mentioned. The men wear ear protection. Big ear protection, like the type formerly used when listening to your home stereo cranked all of the way up. When fully roaring, the saws sound as if the field of the Daytona 500 is coming around the bend right at you.

As each athlete settled into his starting position during the 2009 competition, master of ceremonies John Hughes provided biographical details with great enthusiasm. Appropriately clad in flannel shirt and talking like a backwoodsman, Hughes, the son of former competitor and world champion Cliff Hughes, added to the flavor of the event.

When pausing to make a transition between topics or briefly at a loss for words, Hughes belted out a "Yo-ho!" Audience members chanted it right back, a full-throated "Yo-ho!" yourself of sorts.

Actually, there were two masters of ceremonies working the crowd, although they wore the same uniform of a kind. The other was Eric Maki, and he took charge of "the loony bin," as the area around the tree climbing was called. Perhaps because many people are scared of heights, whether it is in the Fred Scheer show or during the championships, those sections at timber sports layouts are always termed the loony bin.

Maki plays a role as he announces, but there isn't much room for ad-libbing because the championships are on a tight schedule. He must provide the basic information about each competitor—regardless of which side of the pond he works, the chopping dock or the loony bin. And while show business is welcome at the Lumberjack World Championships, it must be remembered that it is a contested sporting event, not to be confused with the lumberjack exhibition shows.

"I always have fun," said Maki, who has been performing at lumberjack shows since 1989 and began handling world championship duties in 1990.

Maki is of Finnish heritage, and he tries to play his character like a Finnish woodsman might. "It's my takeoff of a Finnish immigrant accent," he said. The role is patterned after an old Fred Scheer character called the Pinery Boy. Maki enhances his man of the forest image with a reddish-blonde beard and mustache.

Maki, who has acted in a couple of plays and says he can sing, said he is not proficient in any of the timber sports and could never compete at the Hayward level. He knows he must impart the basic information about a competitor, but otherwise he must work at keeping the mood of the crowd happy and providing some lumberjack history and background.

"Most of the time random interaction is good for the show," Maki said. "Once in a while there's a jerk."

With a twinkle in his eye, Maki said the best remedy for a heckler is to throw him into the pond. Not that anyone would do such a thing. Of course if someone exhibits rude behavior at the Lumberjack World Championships, he could just be turned over to one of the hot saw or chopping behemoths. A heckler might be sliced into his own pile of wood.

Powerful, heavy, and snaggletoothed, the hot saws are not exactly what a customer who wants to clear brush behind his home is seeking when window-shopping for chainsaws. Started by yanking a cord, gas-powered saws came along decades after loggers worked the forest with single hand-saws and two-man, crosscut saws. They did more of the work than the lumberjack, whose responsibility was more to steer the saw than put the full power of his back into the cut.

The best cutters in timber sports have modified the original chainsaws, converting snowmobile engines for greater horsepower, and by the time they have fixed them up to compete for a thousand dollars worth of prize money here and five hundred there, they might have ten thousand invested.

The hot saw is a melding of man and machine to cut wood into nice, neat stacks. The discs of wood cut during the competition measure roughly twenty inches across and are coveted souvenirs of the championships. Fans can't wait to obtain game-used wood, and if they can do so they generally traipse around the lumberjack grounds seeking autographs from timber sports veterans. Even some of the competitors, especially young ones just starting out, collect the discs and ask fellow athletes to sign them. Just bring a sharpie. The wood is surprisingly easy to write on.

The hot saw is a big-boy event. It helps to be large and powerful. It's almost a job requirement. First of all, you have to be able to pick up the chainsaw, no easy feat when they can weigh thirty or even fifty pounds. Then you have to aim it and cut cleanly.

Hot saw competition lasts no longer than the 50-meter dash. The event starts, and before you can turn your head, one guy's done, three round slabs of pine lying on the dock at his feet. It once took more than twelve seconds for a lumberjack to cut the wood. Now the winners stop the clock in less than six. Slice down, slice up, slice down. Event over.

Over the years, since the event was introduced in 1961, many of the biggest names and biggest men in timber sports have excelled at the hot saw. Sven Johnson from Utah was the early dominating figure, winning ten world titles between 1967 and 1987. Dave Geer won four times. Mel Lentz won three times. Rick Halvorson won three times. Dave Bolstad took away two titles, and Dave Jewett won once. Bolstad, from the melodically named community of Taumarunai, in New Zealand, has diced a log in 5.55 seconds during hot saw competition.

Jewett, who is from Pittsford, a tiny town in upstate New York, is taller and lankier than the others. He possesses wiry rather than big-boned muscle, but he works with what he has. Jewett excels with a teammate, winning gold in the men's double buck five times with J. P. Mercier. He and Sheree Taylor of TeAroha, New Zealand, have won the Jack & Jill, and Jewett and Lindsay Daun have formed a partnership for that event now that Dennis Daun has retired. Taylor, a three-time women's all-around champ, runs a family-owned chicken farm and raises 750,000 broilers a year. Lumberjill events are her release.

Just as mixed-doubles tennis players shift allegiances, so can Jack & Jill sawyers. Jewett went after Daun.

"Lindsay was floating around without a partner," Jewett said. "Lindsay was available."

A year into the arrangement, the duo was still trying to develop a cutting rhythm, and even leading up to the 2009 Lumberjack World Championships, they were trying to smooth out the kinks. "We had a few hiccups in practice the other day," he said.

Practice made perfect, however, and in 2010 the Jewett-Daun tandem not only won gold but set a new world speed record for the event.

Jewett is past forty now, and he began competing in Hayward when he was twenty-two. He was just finishing school at Finger Lakes Community College, also located in upstate New York, when Mike Slingerland, another lumberjack world champion, invited him to test his skill in Wisconsin. He's been coming back ever since. Actually, Jewett began as a spectator and then tested his speed and strength in smaller events elsewhere.

"I was a novice, at first," he said of coming to Hayward in 1992. "It was not knowing how good I was. I had bad equipment. I didn't think I would be a professional woodchopper. But I wasn't going to settle for an everyday thing as a career. I was able to lead a single life and was able to travel."

Jewett has led an intriguing life. When he is not competing in lumberjack events during the summer he works in wood. He grows Christmas trees and is a chainsaw carver, making log furniture with the hot saw. He carves wooden bears with his chainsaw, too, selling them in sizes ranging from eight inches to eight feet tall. "I do a really good bear," Jewett said. "They're cute."

Jewett has also become a television commentator for lumberjack sports. A fan clicking through the channels on his or her cable package might well alight on Jewett's voice describing the action for the Canadian Timber Sports series or for ESPN's collegiate lumberjack series.

Having been everywhere and done everything in the timber sports world, however, Jewett has no hesitation in naming the Hayward event the most important.

"It's definitely considered the most prestigious event in the United States," he said. "It holds a lot of weight. It's bragging rights for a year."

Sometimes the bragging can last much longer given that small groups of lumberjacks have established near monopolies in their specialties over the last half century.

The men who excel at the hot saw also seem to have an aptitude for ax swinging. They are power personified. Their names dot the championship results of years gone by, whether it is in the hot saw, the single buck, the double buck, the underhand chop, or the standing block chop. Sometimes there are keen rivalries. Sometimes relatives alternate championships. Sometimes one guy dominates all comers over a period of years.

Almost from the moment he arrived on the scene in Wisconsin in 1996 as an eighteen year old, Jason Wynyard has been a lumberjack to be reckoned with. A native of New Zealand, where he began working in the forest years ago, Wynyard promptly established himself with other competitors and the Hayward fans, who recognized him as the real deal almost immediately.

That first year Wynyard, 6 feet, 4 inches tall, 300 pounds, and not an ounce of fat on him, won both the standing and underhand block chop. It was foreshadowing. Soon enough, Wynyard was winning every men's event that put emphasis on strength and power. And fifteen years into his annual odyssey from New Zealand to Wisconsin, now bringing a wife and kids, Wynyard is being mentioned as potentially the greatest timber sports athlete of all time. At the very least, he is in the picture.

It is no surprise that Wynyard married into a New Zealand logging and timber sports family. His wife Karmyn is a former University of Alaska–Anchorage college basketball player whose maiden name is Lane. Her father, Gil, took up timber sports while Karmyn was matriculating in the mid-1980s. When she returned from Alaska, her dad prevailed on her to join him in Jack & Jill sawing. She did pretty well and enjoyed competing. Her brother Dion became a crackerjack timber sports star, and his name is all over the Hayward record book.

Dion Lane won five men's single buck sawing events, and for a period of time in the 2000s Lane and Wynyard kept the title in the family, going back and forth with championships. Then Lane and Wynyard teamed up in the double buck sawing, winning three of those titles together. Lane also won a Jack & Jill championship with Sheree Taylor, while Jason and Karmyn have won five of those championships. The family that slices wood together definitely stays together.

The offspring of Jason and Karmyn have had a head start in timber sports. By the time oldest son Toutoko was eight years old, he was cutting the family's wood. Tai, one and a half at the time, didn't truly know what was going on when he was brought to a timber sports competition, but he played lumberjack the way American youngsters of the 1950s and 1960s played cowboys and Indians.

"He gets out there with a wooden ax," Karmyn said.

On the final day of the 2009 championships, as the games were winding down and Wynyard was collecting more than his share of trophies, a chant went up from the grandstand. "Wynyard, Wynyard, chop that tree!"

The voices were traced to a group of youngsters, aged around ten, who had bussed from a Wisconsin overnight camp to watch the sports. Wynyard had earlier visited the camp to talk about his life and the origins of "Yo-ho!" It piqued some interest in lumberjack events, so the campers were taken to the games.

"He came to our camp and he told us how to chop things," ten-year-old Max Goldstein of Highland Park, Illinois, said.

Another trio of campers walked up to the fence separating the competitors from the fans and debated tying to get Wynyard to autograph their ticket stubs. Was this going to be a special treat, meeting their hero in the flesh and watching him win another gold medal in a sawing or ax event? Not exactly.

"Do you think we can get eight dollars for them?" one boy asked aloud. "I want to put it on eBay."

Hero worship has its limits apparently. The boy was asked if it wouldn't be better to obtain the autograph on the stub, hang on to it, and then someday reminisce about how he got it.

"Nah," he said.

Among Wynyard's character traits is an ability to stay cool and relaxed. If he overheard any of the kids' discussion he would have laughed. Wynyard represents the new breed of timber sports competitor, but he is also a throwback.

Wynyard worked chopping wood when he was a teenager. So he has that in common with most of the early competitors. The older guys from the 1960s let their brawn do their talking and let their natural muscles earned in the forests do it on the chopping dock. However—and here's where Wynyard represents a new generation—he still gets nervous. But he is as prepared as he can be, training by lifting weights to supplement his innate power.

It is part of the gig now. Although no one would say it is impossible, Wynyard doesn't want to count on his conditioning being at peak form solely due to chopping. In his case that is particularly important because he spends most of his time on the lumberjack circuit. Forget staying at home clearing the trees instead of following a physical fitness preparedness regimen.

Each year Wynyard travels to the United States and stays on American soil for months at a time traveling to Stihl timber sports series shows. But his summer is always focused around the Lumberjack World Championships. "I love this sport," Wynyard said. "I've devoted my life to it. It's my passion. This [Hayward] is one of my favorite places to be in the world."

As Wynyard stepped in front of his assigned block of wood on the chopping dock, ax carried loosely, fans in the stands erupted again. "Wynyard, Wynyard, chop that tree!"

He did so, making mincemeat of solid wood in seconds. Although Wynyard did not acknowledge the group yelling for him, there really was only one appropriate response beyond the simplest of waves. He could have shouted, "Yo-ho!"

His and Her Saws

Rick Halvorson's hair and beard are turning white, and in his early sixties he cannot wield a saw or ax with quite the same speed as he did in 1992 when he was the all-around titleholder at the Lumberjack World Championships. But he is still a regular in Hayward, and his wife Penny is, too. The trip from Alma Center, Wisconsin, is an easy one, just a couple of hours' drive, but it is the lure of the sawdust more than driving the asphalt that brings them back to Hayward every year.

It should have surprised no one that Rick won three hot saw titles, and two double buck sawing championships, in addition to his all-around crown. That's because Halvorson works in wood full time. He is not a logger in the sense of going off to the forest to live in the camps the way his forebears did a hundred years ago, but wood is his medium.

Rick Halvorson began competing in Hayward in 1984. Penny began competing in 1985. The attraction was mutual.

"For our first date he asked me to be his sawing partner," said Penny, who won four all-around lumberjill titles in 1998, 1999, 2000, and 2002.

Rick's father owned a sawmill, and so Rick began skinning logs when he was eight years old. The sawmill used horses, and whatever power they supplied for hauling logs far exceeded anything little Rick could bring to the table at the time. When he stirred up memories after getting to know Penny, he recalled that his father would haunt a local tavern and share beers with her grandfather.

"If I got to go along at all, I got to have a soda," Rick remembers. "I had a Sundrop, a lemon and lime drink."

As Halvorson aged, the woodworking business became more automated. While he retained many of the skills early lumberjacks used, from ax chopping to saw slicing, he said that Halvorson Forest Products is 70 percent automated. Not Rick, though. He has always put a lot of his personal power into his work. Even to start his business in 1969, he borrowed $170 to buy a chainsaw.

In 1971, after hearing about what was going on in Hayward, Halvorson jumped in his car and drove to the Lumberjack Bowl. He sat in the stands that year and was impressed enough to kick-start a lumberjack show of his own in Alma Center.

"I was pretty awed by it," he said.

Halvorson's expertise was in sawing, and he didn't even own an ax until 1983. He practiced with it and hoped his lumberjack background would pay off when he entered his first event in 1984. Halvorson tried the spring-board chop, and it didn't go well. "I didn't have the experience," he said. "But the only way I was going to learn was to go where the best people were."

Meanwhile, Penny competed in smaller lumberjack events in Minnesota and across the Midwest and won titles and trophies. When she arrived in Hayward she expected to win the single buck competition. She placed third.

"I was just devastated," she said. She believed she had let Rick down. That was a quarter century ago, and Penny still remembers the unhappy feeling of losing. She has also greatly improved since.

About that first date. It did not actually play out on the chopping dock. The couple went dancing, and after imbibing a few beers, Rick asked Penny to be his Jack & Jill sawing partner.

"I'll give it a try," she said.

The Halvorsons have been fixtures in the event ever since, winning for the first time in 1990, and adding titles in 1995, 1996, 1998, 1999, and 2002. They are both large humans, and they know how to harness the power in their biceps. They have outlasted most of their original competition and find themselves going head-to-head with younger athletes who are bound to have more toned muscle groups.

"I've seen a lot of them come and go," Penny said of the changing of the guard. "I thank Rick for being a good coach now, but at first I couldn't get used to him." It did take six years to win that inaugural Jack & Jill title. "Once we got together, though," she said, "it was an instant before we decided, 'We're going to do that.'"

The lumberjack world works in mysterious ways. Rick and Penny were meant for each other and meant for timber sports. However, there is always going to be a question of where the new generation of athletes comes from since neither Fred Scheer nor Judy Hoeschler is going to have enough children to stock an entire sport. And not even counting on every father or couple that competed over the years producing offspring that will someday compete in Hayward will be enough to keep the championships going.

Although the Lumberjack World Championships are an invitational event bringing in only the finest athletes, and there are no teams to be drafted by, people must get their training somewhere. Stihl, the saw manufacturer, is a key sponsor of the Hayward events, but Stihl Timbersports also supports a collegiate championship. These athletes are not the children of Rick and Penny Halvorson, but they are the spiritual descendants of their endeavors. Because people like the Halvorsons have been big-name competitors for years, they help to inspire future generations to try timber sports. Each year young athletes who might not qualify for the top tier of open competition in sawing and chopping represent their schools in competition.

The Intercollegiate Series, which had more than fifty schools entered in 2009, broke up the nation into sections, with the top finishers advancing to a finals event. Although athletes represent their schools, the assault of wood with a deadly weapon is not a sanctioned college sport. In 2009 there was considerable drama. Logan Scarborough of North Carolina State, a muscular giant of a young man, overpowered the competition in the regular season Southern Conclave events but almost fell short of qualifying for the championships because of a disqualification.

Scarborough, a junior in forest management, was so good in the underhand chop that he won the event by about thirty seconds, a monumental time differential. But he crossed over a line on his up cut, missing a mark. He was saved because of his other top scores and the fact that several other axmen were disqualified for the same reason. Scarborough made it into the six-man championship field as a wild-card selection.

Among the athletes in the field was Matt Slingerland, son of Mike Slingerland, of Rockwell, North Carolina, a veteran Hayward competitor and past world champ. There was some irony in this. Mike Slingerland had offered to personally coach an NC State athlete in the standing block chop because it was a new event. The athlete who earned the services of Slingerland's coaching acumen was Scarborough, who was going to try to beat the coach's own son. And even more unusual, Matt helped coach Scarborough, too.

"I drove to his home to train two times before the Southern Conclave," Scarborough said, "and that small amount of guidance from Mike and his son Matt helped me tremendously. This is still very new to me. I can get much better. This sport is not something that can be learned overnight. It takes years of practice and experience."

The finals were conducted in Columbus, Georgia. The event was scored on a combination of performances in the standing block chop, underhand chop, single buck sawing competition, and stock saw, and it was Matt Slingerland, of Montgomery Community College, not Scarborough, who advanced to a showdown against Adam LaSalle of the University of Wisconsin–Stevens Point. Things went wrong for Slingerland in the standing block chop, and LaSalle built a large lead.

"Oh, my god, everything happened," Slingerland said. "I wasn't using an ax I was used to and I suck. I need to practice. My other one broke [during the semifinals], so I used the new one, and it was a little bit longer handle and I wasn't ready for it."

The collegiate championships garnered ESPN coverage, which helped spread the word about timber sports. It was a show that whetted appetites for more, and it built some curiosity in spectators, who might want to make the journey to Hayward to see even better timber sports athletes.

Stihl has long been a major supporter of the Lumberjack World Championships, yet it has also sponsored its own timber sports series since 1985. Spawned by the annual Hayward championships, the Stihl series provides competitive outlets for top-level athletes and also something very critical to timber sports competitors—a chance to make more money. The athletes from down under who travel to Hayward typically come for weeks, or the entire summer, and enter Stihl tournaments in other towns. The Stihl series helps make Jason Wynyard's trip from New Zealand worthwhile.

Wisconsin was the site of the first Stihl events, and they slowly expanded over a twenty-year period until many of the best timber sports competitors in the world became regulars. Each of the Stihl competitions includes the same list of events. Not surprisingly, given the company's interest in promoting sales of its specialty products, the events all involve cutting and sawing. The program consists of springboard, standing and underhand chops, hot saw, and single buck. One event not held in Hayward is the stock saw. This is a speed and accuracy event. In the stock saw the competitors start with both hands placed on a log. When the event starts, they grab for identical chainsaws and must quickly make two cuts of no more than four inches into the wood.

As an illustration of the kinship between the Stihl series and Hayward, world records in all six events are held by veterans of the Lumberjack World Championships, with Wynyard holding three of them, David Bolstad claiming two, and Matt Bush, another former Hayward champ, holding one.

Between 1985 and 2009, Wynyard won the series championship eight times, Bolstad four times, and another Hayward icon, Mel Lentz, six times. But that hardly does justice to the roster of Hayward competitors who also joined the Stihl circuit. In 2009, it was a who's who of Hayward, including such stalwarts as Arden Cogar Jr., Dave Jewett, Dion Lane, Australian Laurence O'Toole, Mike Sullivan, Cassidy Scheer (Fred's son), Guy German, and Sean Duffy.

The Stihl series gave lumberjacks a chance to earn more money, but from a Hayward perspective, the series, like the collegiate championships, helped identify new talent. Longtime entrants like Jason Wynyard someday will cease making the long journey across the ocean. That is one advantage the Halvorsons have over most of the other longtime regulars. The short journey by car will not prevent them from at least watching the games for as long as they can.

Like Rick Halvorson, his wife Penny came to lumberjack work at an early age. She is a fourth-generation Wisconsin resident and said she bucked timber with a chainsaw as a kid. Familiarity with saws made it a natural for Rick and Penny to team up for a sawing event. Rick said he was nervous the first couple of years he entered Hayward events, but those jitters went away long ago.

Penny doesn't flinch from the moment the swift event begins.

"You hear that whistle, and your body takes over," she said.

Growing up in the north woods, Rick Halvorson said all of the neighbors had a chainsaw to cut wood. "You could go house to house and there was a chainsaw at every one of them," he said. "They cut wood in some fashion. People today can relate to it, but they don't have the skills to do it so much. But that gives the athletes respect from the general populace. They can see the difference between wielding their own ax in the backyard and watching experts chop wood for speed."

"Cutting firewood," Rick said of the everyday guy who might have a cabin in the woods he visits once in a while, "they're going at a pace they can sustain. You [the athlete] have to be able to tell yourself to go as strong as you can whether you want to or not."

But your arm muscles ache, and you run short of breath. Once in a great while over the years of a long career, Rick could not go on. It was disappointing but also a reality of sports. "I had to stop," Rick said. "I pushed myself too far. I could feel myself starting to black out."

Then he gathered himself and turned to partner Cliff Hughes. "I suppose we better finish," he said. "Everybody's watching."

That's one motivation that so many people share in public. They don't want to make themselves the object of discussion so they keep going.

Rick and Penny are past their primes in Lumberjack World Championships competition, and they know it. Rick is a couple of years past his sixtieth birthday, and Penny is in her early fifties. She has also had two knee replacement surgeries. Still, they keep coming to Hayward, and they plan to continue, even if things come full circle and all they can do is watch. If at all possible, especially in the Jack & Jill sawing, and even with the aches and pains produced by age, they still want their names to be listed on the roster of entrants.

"It's the history of the show and just being out on that dock," Penny said. "The whole competition thing. I love great competition."

Very Tall Trees

Standing at the base of the 90-foot climbing pole in the loony bin inside the Lumberjack Bowl, looking straight up to the top can give one a stiff neck.

Speed climbing the 90- and 60-foot poles is the object of the game, which in a general way imitates forestry efforts. Loggers did not have to ascend to the treetops because they could trim branches after the tree was felled. In some areas where trees were arrayed on hillsides, however, lumbermen climbed trees and attached cables to help guide a cut tree to more level ground.

At the Lumberjack World Championships, the event has evolved to emphasize the speed aspect of going up and down, and tree trimming has been eliminated (although it once was its own separate event). In the way the 100-meter dash is a highlight event at a track meet, measuring the fastest humans against the clock, the speed climbs stress pure quickness: how fast can you go up and touch the top of the pole and how fast can you come down afterward and touch the cushioned pillows on the ground.

In his heyday (although that specific part of his career is difficult to quantify), Guy German was the fastest. Introduced in Hayward as the "godfather" of speed climbing, German, now in his fifties, competes head-to-head with athletes young enough to be his children.

German won his first world titles in the 90-foot climb in 1988 and 1990 and he won again in 2002. Before tree topping was discontinued, German won titles in 1997, 1998, and 2000. German sparked a revolution in tree climbing by introducing specialized shoes with better grips. In 1990, when

German captured the 90-foot climb, his time of 20.05 lowered the eight-year-old former record by 6.5 seconds. In the twenty years since, the record has only been improved by 1 second. That's how dominant German was.

It was a hot and sunny day in Hayward for the 2009 90-foot speed climb preliminaries. German, then fifty-five, was still game, going against younger recent champs like the all-conquering Brian Bartow, an eight-time champion and son of late 1970s era three-time champ Clarence Bartow.

Lean and muscular, with a soccer player's thighs, German wrapped his sturdy rope around the pole, slipped on gloves for better gripping, and added elbow and shin guards. The padding made him look like a warrior readying for battle. All German needed to complete the ensemble was a helmet, but no one was going to imitate Darth Vader for the climb.

At the end of the 3-2-1-go countdown, the climbers leapt upward, almost like monkeys grabbing onto a tree. Their spiked shoes clacked as they virtually ran up the wooden pole, hauling themselves through leg and shoulder power. Two climbers raced one at a time on adjacent poles, but there was barely time to notice the other competitor. Fans screamed louder the higher the climbers got. Twice German tried to dig in a foot that didn't take, and he lost time because those missteps threw his rhythm off. The climbers descended so swiftly, barely touching the pole, that it almost seemed as if they were in free fall. By the time German landed, his opponent was already down.

"I had two slips," German said. "I don't know why. On the first slip I went back two feet and my race was pretty much over. I'm in pretty good shape. I was doing some pretty good stuff at the top." Between preliminary heats, German munched on popcorn and sipped a beer, not everyone's idea of a health food breakfast.

German was visiting Alaska in 1984 when he attended his first lumberjack show as a spectator in Sitka, a city of Russian American heritage surrounded by massive trees and forest. Something about the climbing events touched German. Maybe it was because he had grown up on a farm in Nebraska with the surrounding land flat for miles. German's athletic background consisted of playing high school football and running track. He asked a lot of questions, bought some equipment, and decided to compete against the professional loggers who made up the field in the event. He even lived in Alaska for a while.

"They were mostly loggers," German recalled of his foes. "There were five local guys. It got me going. Here I was, this farm boy from Nebraska. I was really determined to make a good showing."

Sitka is located next to the Tongass National Forest, so there is a multitude of trees around to practice on, including Sitka spruce. The climbing poles were 30 and 75 feet in height in the southeastern Alaska competition.

German's family did not identify with his passion. When he told someone in the family what he was up to, "they thought I was a little bit kookie," he said. It didn't matter that he was successful and could compete against the best climbers in the world in Hayward. So after a while German didn't bother to tell friends and relatives what he did when he wasn't pursuing his construction career. "I just didn't tell anybody," he said of his closet career. "My dad didn't think I should be messing around."

The first time German competed in the Lumberjack World Championships it was 1986 and he was an outsider, an unknown, although he said he was familiar with a lot of the names in the championships. Two years later he won his first 90-foot climbing title.

German has taken breaks from climbing. He has quit climbing and announced his retirement. But although he has skipped annual visits to Hayward for the championships, he always comes back and resumes where he left off. Sometimes German had no intention of competing in a given year and didn't train. Then, at the last minute, as late July approached, he changed his mind "on a whim," jumped in his car, and drove to Wisconsin. He does admit it's more difficult to train in Omaha, or Columbus, Nebraska, where he currently lives, than it was in Southeast Alaska. The tall buildings downtown just don't serve as a suitable substitute.

"I'll stick with trees," German said.

German is still good enough, strong enough to pick off a third-place showing here and there in the climbing events, and he is amused when teenage girls screech like groupies as the men clamber to the top, although he is pretty sure they are yelling mostly for his twenty-something opponents.

One of those younger opponents who is an admirer of German's longevity is Dustin Beckwith. Beckwith, who is from Hayward, won the 60-foot pole climb in 1993 and 1996 and the 90-foot climb in 2001.

"Guy's the godfather of the sport," Beckwith said. "He's been fortunate to compete at a high level for a long time. It's very cool. In any sport you're going to have your veteran guys. He has such dedication and love for the sport and he competed a little bit more wisely in maybe not going for wins at all costs. He's always finished in the top four."

Growing up in Hayward, Beckwith was exposed to the Lumberjack World Championships early. As the youngest of five children, he was exposed to logrolling by age eight. He had cousins in the sport, and his siblings, everyone it seemed, dabbled in logrolling.

Following his senior year of high school, Beckwith signed on with Fred Scheer's lumberjack show for a summer job. Right away he was thrown into pole climbing. He was far from a natural.

"I hated it," he said.

Beckwith's first day was unseasonably hot. At the time the loony bin was located at the other side of the grounds, next to the Pancake House where dozens of people were eating. Beckwith was strapped into his rope and told to climb. Melting from the sun, and embarrassed by his inexperience in front of so many witnesses, he made it all of fifteen feet off the ground.

"It was way harder than I thought," Beckwith said. He tried again and didn't get beyond fifteen feet that time either. Then he practically ran into a nearby men's room and threw up. "I was initiated, I guess. I kept practicing and practicing and gradually and slowly got better."

Beckwith never got used to climbing upward, but it bothered him less going up sixty feet than ninety. "There was only a rope and two little spikes on the shoes holding me up," he said.

Although Beckwith's last title came in the 2001 90-foot climb, he was still a contender in 2005 when he suffered the accident that ended his pole-climbing career. Beckwith was in the finals, competing against the reigning champion, Brian Bartow. He was trailing slightly at the top of the pole and knew it.

"A few seconds is hard to gain," Beckwith said. "So I just cut loose. We pretty much come down out of control, anyway. But when I landed I shattered my L1 vertebra. I don't know exactly what happened. There was padding around the pole, but I hit a seam. It happened so fast. I could tell there was something wrong. I was in pain."

Officials rushed to his assistance, but Beckwith knew he should not be moved and shouted, "Strap me down and get me out of here!" This was not Beckwith's first serious pole-climbing injury. He had broken both of his legs on other descents that didn't go as well as hoped. Looney bin, indeed.

Beckwith was thirty-one at the time, and he was not giving thought to retirement. The doctors never told him to give up pole climbing, but there was a body of opinion being voiced that he should. Beckwith's father Bill was proactive on that front.

"My dad actually hid my gear for about a year," Beckwith said.

Beckwith did his own soul-searching and made a decision. "It was time for me to go," he said. He retired from pole climbing, went into real estate sales, is married, and has two children. Yet he does go to the Lumberjack World Championships to watch each summer and has been increasing his participation on the off-field side.

"The first year was very tough being there," he said. "But now I'm on to the next chapter in life."

Beckwith's untimely demise in the event took away Bartow's top rival.

Brian Bartow, with his seven world titles between 1999 and 2008, had long before eclipsed even German on paper, although he was aware that on any given Sunday German might still pose a threat with a late-career performance.

Bartow started climbing poles the way youngsters in other cities start climbing trees. He was six years old and got as high as twenty feet.

"Not too high," he said.

Bartow's father and uncle were loggers. He listened to them tell stories about the forest and the timber sports events they entered.

"I was just always around the stuff," Bartow said.

Bartow, who has passed his thirtieth birthday and spent a good portion of his life perched higher than the average house, albeit for only seconds at a time, has brown hair, a thin dark beard, and a mustache. There is a bit of the daredevil in his eyes. Besides Wisconsin, Bartow has traveled extensively, entering speed climbs in Georgia, Utah, Washington, and Oregon, among other states.

"There's always a good pool of competitors," said Bartow, whose biggest payout in competition was $2,200.

After one of his speediest climbs against German, Bartow landed on the life-saving cushion and was quickly mobbed by groupies. He posed for pictures with seven girls, arm in arm. Then he looked up and grinned. "There's a shortage of that," he said of pole-climbing adulation.

Bartow, who has been a high school track coach in Canby, near Portland, Oregon, during the cooler months of the year, finds it somewhat mind blowing that he is competing against German. When Bartow was a first grader, one of the first speed climbers he saw competing was German.

"He was the one I was watching when I was six," Bartow said of the old man of speed climbing. "He's pretty young at heart."

Bartow views his participation in the Lumberjack World Championships and other speed-climbing events as doing his part to help keep the nation's lumberjack history alive and fresh. Sure, he admits, there is a romantic aspect to the public's notions of what lumberjacking is and was, but it's better that they think about it imperfectly than not think about it at all.

"It should always be kept alive," Bartow said of the country's logging past. "It's our American heritage. It should always be kept around to a certain extent. There are a few shows out there, and a lot of those guys in them don't log. Among the fans, somebody might think it's not so hard to do, but then some people ask, 'Why do you do that?'"

Once some of Bartow's friends locked themselves into climbing harnesses for safety and attempted to climb the 90-foot pole. The best made it fifty feet up. Speed climbing on 60- or 90-foot poles is not for anyone scared of heights. Don't look down would be the first piece of advice. Perhaps not thinking about how high off the ground you are would be the second piece of advice.

"They had a hard time with it," Bartow said," and they knew they were safe."

Unless something goes dramatically wrong, pole climbing should be safe. The climbers are strapped in, holding a rope and wearing gloves and gripping shoes, and can protect elbows and shins from serious bruising with pads. Much of the competition is mental, though, the mind convincing the body that this is a good idea and that everything will be OK even if it is dangling far above the ground.

Derek Knutson, in his early twenties, represents the younger generation of pole climbing. He is from Hayward and grew up a short distance from the Lumberjack Bowl. His first job was working for Fred Scheer's lumberjack show, and that led him from exhibition showmanship to more serious competition. In 2007, Knutson placed third in the 90- and 60-foot events. In 2008, at age twenty-two, he placed second in both. He had the makings of a rising star.

In his official Lumberjack World Championships biography, it is pointed out that when he was once asked to describe what speed pole climbing is all about in three words, Knutson said, "Escape from reality."

Knutson is a fixture at the world championships, but he is a larger presence on the Stihl series tour. He is deeply into timber sports and spends his summers on the go, doing whatever he can in the sport to stay busy. One thing that distinguishes Knutson from the average man on the street, or even his other lumberjack sports competitors, is the striking tattoo imprinted on his left arm. It reads, "MAN OF STIHL."

"I travel around and do lumberjack exhibitions," Knutson said. "All of the cool things I've gotten to do have been because of Stihl. I wanted something to show my connection to the sport."

Knutson did not tell Stihl officials that he was going to obtain the tattoo in advance but showed up at an event in Louisville, Kentucky, and displayed it. He raised his arm in the air. Stihl officials saw the tattoo and started laughing. Knutson figures the tattoo could become useful when Stihl inevitably calls to place him in company magazine ads. His marketing and promotional services have not been sought in any big way yet, but he is certain his devotion to Stihl will be rewarded.

For German, as he ages toward the best deals on the menu at Denny's, his finest reward is coming to Hayward once a year and seeing old friends as he squeezes in his last days of competition. He believes he is ahead of the game just by finishing his prelims unscathed. Unless he gets very lucky, he knows that he is unlikely to win another title in Hayward. But that doesn't overrule the fun he is still having or the fact that there are other timber sports competitions down the road.

In 2009 German picked off a second-place finish in the 90-foot pole climb, and the result was energizing.

"I still had something left in my legs," German said. "But it was very hard. It's fun running with the young kids. I can still give most of them a scare."

Although the field is always the toughest in Hayward, German has participated in other series or exhibitions all over the country, from the ESPN Great Outdoor Games to a new timber sports series with an event in Virginia Beach, Virginia. When he heard about that one he thought, "What the heck," and signed up. "I'm always making a little bit of money and I get great vacations."

When he traveled to the West Coast for an event, he climbed 100-foot poles, made a thousand dollars, and had a free place to stay. "It was absolutely a blast," German said.

German has learned that he should not contemplate taking breaks from Hayward unless he truly is going to retire. He would miss the camaraderie of the week too much if he couldn't head to Wisconsin each July and try to speed climb the giant poles looming over the Lumberjack Bowl grounds.

"It's so ingrained in my psyche," German said. "It fills a void in my summer. I would really feel empty without it."

A Festival of Sawdust

For a guy with sawdust in his blood and showing his years through the white in his hair and beard, Rick Halvorson was feeling pretty good.

His muscles weren't quite as hardened as they once were, but his competitive attitude was just as fierce. So when Halvorson teamed up with Alastair Taylor in a masters event in 2009 he was happy they placed well as he was closing in on the opportunity to qualify for Medicare. Not bad for a guy with two heart surgeries on his résumé.

"I feel young," Halvorson said. "I met a lot of my friends."

Halvorson was no longer considered a prime contender in the open sawing events, but when you pass sixty and you have undergone more delicate slicing by a surgeon than you ever performed with a hot saw, your attitude changes. Halvorson looked comfortable sitting in a lightweight chair under an awning as action paused at the Lumberjack World Championships' fiftieth-anniversary gathering in 2009.

Halvorson had every right to feel proud following the two-man masters competition with Taylor. "We hadn't sawed together," he said. "To win the master's category, boy, any time you can win anything here it's pretty tough."

Halvorson and Taylor completed sawing the discs off their logs in 7.84 seconds. Pretty good for old guys. In comparison, the team of Dave Jewett and J. P. Mercier won the open class in 5.54 seconds, three-tenths of a second ahead of the duo of Jason Wynyard and Mike Slingerland.

Mostly, the masters competition was a Hayward blast from the past with such names as Napoleon Mercier, Arden Cogar Sr., and Laurence O'Toole Sr. sprinkled among the entrants.

"I haven't been here in twenty-three years," said O'Toole, of Australia, who did indeed win the standing block chop in 1987. Laurence O'Toole Jr. joined him in the 2009 competition.

Besides being a world championship, the Hayward competition is in some ways a three-ring circus. Over the years organizers have fine-tuned the schedule to eradicate lulls for spectators. Yes, they want the visitors to eat cotton candy and hot dogs and drink the local beer, but they don't want to bore them. The competition is tightly packaged now, with finals following semifinals in quick order and the preliminaries taking place in daytime sessions.

For three days solid, the activity hardly ever ceases, and subplots play out at times when fans are not even in the house. The athletes doomed to finish back in the pack might not perform in front of the biggest crowds. The prime-time athletes get the prime-time audience.

Old-timers who starred in the Lumberjack World Championships in the 1960s have stayed with the sport, even into their seventies in the case of Dave Geer, if only to enter masters events for the fun of it. They are not in awe of the younger generations that have followed them, but they are pretty impressed with the advancements made in technology.

"Power saws get better and better," Geer said of the incredible power harnessed in the new handheld saws, which cut wood like a hot knife cuts butter. But that doesn't mean he and others from the start-up days believe all current athletes are better than they were. "I've done some winning," he said.

Napoleon Mercier, one of three generations of Merciers competing, said it's natural for equipment to evolve. After all, he is from a family that tries to build a better mousetrap, or chainsaw, for a living. Testing it in high-level competition is one way to learn how good a new piece of equipment is. "The tools improve," he said.

The tools that slice and dice logs are sharp edged and require caution when carrying them about. Just as a baseball player does not want an interloper handling his favorite glove and bat, a sawyer doesn't want anyone messing with his saw and an axman doesn't want anyone touching his cutting tool. Lack of care around the implements of wood destruction can result in loss of blood.

Yet the lumberjack championships are a family-friendly event. The snack booths smack of a county fair. There are some sponsor booths promoting Stihl products, but kids can also pose for pictures with their faces in cutouts showing them as lumberjacks or lumberjills. Many senior citizens, a surprising number of them women, pause for the pose, too.

The thousands that descend on Hayward for the championships each year constitute an educated audience. Many are locals or from nearby in Wisconsin. Many travel great distances. Many are repeat customers who trek to the north woods every year. They know their timber sports, not only the rules and what makes for a good performance, but who's who in most events. There are sentimental favorites who have become adopted sons and daughters of Hayward and always get a cheer. There are locals, true sons and daughters of Hayward, and there are stars of the sport from far away whose exploits have made them familiar.

Wynyard might be a relative unknown walking down a street in Milwaukee, but he can't take a step past the Moccasin Bar or the giant muskie at the Fishing Hall of Fame without being recognized and stopped for an autograph. In a clever adaptation of the general autograph approach, in which athletes are asked to sign a picture, a trading card, or another piece of memorabilia related to their sport, fans of all ages and even other athletes create their own "scrapbook" of signatures by seeking autographs on discs of cut wood. It is not uncommon at the championships to see spectators walking around trying to spy competitors between events and then thrusting a hunk of wood at them.

In late July the northern Wisconsin sun can generate sweat. If anyone believes that retreating to the north woods automatically means summer disappears, they are mistaken. Not even being surrounded by tall trees keeps Hayward chilled. It is frequently in the mid-eighties during championships week. The heat makes it easier for athletes to warm up before events, and it invites spectators to swill lemonade. The Lumberjack Bowl is also a haven for barbecue, popcorn, and the Wisconsin delicacy cheese curds. So-called cheese castles are as ubiquitous in Wisconsin as McDonald's are elsewhere.

In addition to the usual food booths at the 2009 championships, there was a small trailer parked on the grounds behind the largest segment of the grandstand. It contained memorabilia and photos touting the lumberjack way of life and represented the National Lumberjack Hall of Fame of Cortland, New York. Some of the stars of Hayward were included in pictures on the inner walls.

It would be a mistake to conclude that the biggest, brawniest guys are the biggest heroes because they cut wood faster than their foes. While the average fan knows he or she can't saw or chop nearly as fast as one of the 250-to-300-pound pros who have the muscles of Mike Tyson, they delude themselves into thinking they could, with a little bit of luck, survive a round or two of logrolling.

Probably not.

Maybe because it is the slender, slightly built girls and women who excel, and the average-sized guys who do well, but it's unlikely that the fans in the grandstand would last more than three seconds on a log once an accomplished opponent began splashing or spinning the log. There is collective breath held sometimes waiting for the big fall.

The road to championship gold is arduous. It takes three days of preliminary heats for a logroller to work his or her way into the finals. While a sawyer completes the single buck in a day and then goes on to other events, the logroller competes Friday, Saturday, and Sunday, sometimes only hours apart, and to eliminate an opponent requires three out of five falls.

As usual, in 2009 there was a Hoeschler in the hunt for a logrolling title, not Judy Hoeschler, who was a nervous spectator, but Katie Hoeschler, one of the old master's daughters. One by one, the female logrollers put one another underwater. No one was going to escape at least one fall into the pond at one time or another.

Of the eight top finishers, seven were from Wisconsin, including three from Hayward and three from La Crosse. The three from La Crosse were either Hoeschlers or competitors trained at Judy Hoeschler's logrolling school. The wild card in the top bunch was Jenny Anderson Atkinson from Stillwater, Minnesota. Atkinson, an elementary school teacher, was a twenty-six-year logrolling competitor who won in 2005, 2006, and 2007. She won the women's boom run in 2007 as well. Shana Martin of Madison was the defending logrolling champion, so the field was loaded. One by one, Katie Hoeschler and Emily Christopherson of La Crosse polished off the contenders, including Abby Hoeschler, Katie's sister, who placed third. Martin was fifth, Atkinson sixth. It was Katie Hoeschler who survived all of Christopherson's tricks as the last woman standing.

Involvement from an early age, having a compatible, lightweight body, learning technique, and being inspired by an older sibling seem to be aspects of various logrollers' success.

"I'm just excited to enjoy the ranks of champions," Katie Hoeschler said. "Everyone in my family has a world title. It's mental preparation. I've trained at the bowl all summer."

Now maybe Hoeschler will get her pick of drumsticks or wings at Thanksgiving as a fellow family champ with new status. Judy, Liz, and Katie have all triumphed in logrolling, but the retired woman with the most crowns is Tina Salzman Bosworth, a ten-time winner between 1990 and 2003. Blessed with strongly muscled calves, Tina, sister of perennial men's winner JR Salzman, often wore a cap when she was balancing on the log. Once again, it was a case of a single family making hay in one event.

Tina Salzman Bosworth, now in her mid-thirties, started logrolling when she was eleven. She and her Hayward friends grew up watching the Lumberjack World Championships, and the Bowl was there year-round with logs in the water. Bosworth and her pals developed their own techniques for staying on the logs as they floated. They loved what they were doing, and, just as a young basketball player cannot be pulled away from the backyard hoop, they played and trained and got serious about logrolling.

"We all kind of started at the same time," Bosworth said. "We spent our days on the logs. You get good at it doing something six hours a day. We practically lived down there from the ages of thirteen to sixteen. It's probably just like any other sports skills. If you have fast-twitch muscle fiber you're able to train it. It's also being able to concentrate in order to exploit your opponent's mistake."

Logrolling can be like chess on your feet. If an opponent is shifting her weight, that moment provides the opportunity to hit her when she is most vulnerable to losing her balance. It is about having a killer instinct, going for the jugular.

"There's probably levels to that," Bosworth said, referring to the hunger to succeed. "You definitely have to have some tenacity and grit."

Although she might be able to give the new crop of contenders a good match, Bosworth insisted her logrolling competition days are behind her. She is the principal of a school in Elkhorn, Wisconsin, and working on a PhD in educational policy analysis, so her days are full. It's not like it was when she was a carefree kid with long days of summer and nothing to do with them. It has something to do with having balance in life.

"Life takes you in other directions," Bosworth said. "I don't want to do it unless I can be the best at it."

What Bosworth learned is that being a successful athlete can pay dividends in other walks of life. As a competitor she let it all hang out, taking risks, giving her all, steeling her nerves to perform in front of a crowd and yet trying to stay calm and make intelligent decisions.

"Absolutely, my logrolling experience has paid off in life," Bosworth said. "It has given me the ability to perform under pressure, to have the stick-to-itiveness to do things in life. I've been in the position of having to listen to that internal voice of reason that you trust, of having that calm."

It is not as if Bosworth is completely retired from sports, either. She's running long distances now, starting with 13.1-mile half marathons and working up to a 26.2-mile marathon.

Even if she no longer has the passion to train for logrolling, Bosworth makes the short trip to Hayward's championships to watch, especially if brother JR is entered. Appropriately, since she is just about the most successful one-event athlete of all, she wanted to be present for the fiftieth games in 2009.

Not even being up close and watching gave Bosworth any pangs about retirement. She didn't miss it enough to get out in front of the crowd again. "I'm good," she said of her mind-set.

Tina got as close to the water as she could when JR competed, watching intently, coaching him when asked for advice, providing body English in empathy with his moves on the log, and groaning when a foe's move sent JR into the holding pond for a major splash.

She so wanted him to succeed. So did just about everyone in the bowl. Salzman's return to competition the year before was something he classified as a disaster even if it was good for him mentally. Now he was another year closer to wellness, to adapting to his physical diminishment and losses, and was making the most of his skills. It took some commitment to convince himself that despite what war had handed him he could be as good as he ever was at his special passion.

Each time Salzman climbed on a log, the eyes in the grandstands followed him. Those close to Salzman may have uttered little prayers under their breaths. Or they just were so happy to see him safely out of a war zone that they didn't care how he did as long as he satisfied himself.

In 2009, Salzman was no longer defending champion. He had a distinguished record of six titles, but sport is very much a "what have you done for me lately" business. One can be a World Series hero one October and be out of the sport with a ruined pitching arm the following May. The games go on. They are still played. And new champions are crowned. Since Salzman had become a solider, and a wounded soldier, there had been three Lumberjack World Championships. His most recent logrolling title had come in 2005. But Jamie Fischer of Stillwater, Minnesota, had claimed the 2006 title and Darren Hudson, a limber, dexterous roller from Barrington, Nova Scotia, won in 2007 and 2008.

Like Salzman, Hudson had pretty good logrolling genes in his body. His uncle is Phil Scott, the dazzling roller who decades earlier had given Hayward's Fred Scheer fits on the log and had competed against Scheer in the epic matches that raised the profile of the event.

Logrolling began on a Friday, and JR Salzman had his ups and downs. At times he looked a little uncertain on the log, but with each match, when the results were tallied, you might say Salzman was the driest. He struggled, but he won. He was not as smooth as he used to be, but he won and advanced to the quarterfinals. There would not be much room for error in the final matches.

This is how it's done on the boom run. Mandy Erdman Sobiech makes a safe crossing at full speed. (photo by author)

Left: On the way up. Guy German of Columbus, Nebraska, a many-time champion, starts his journey upward in the 90-foot pole climb. (photo by author)

The Scheer Lumberjack Show is almost a spoof of the competition, a stage show making sure that fans leave with a smile. Master of ceremonies Will Hoeschler brings smiles to the faces of youngsters just learning what being a lumberjack is all about. (photo by author)

Dennis Daun holds the log steady as his daughter Lindsay readies for the start of single buck sawing. (photo by author)

Now white-haired, veteran Rick Halvorson still enters the occasional event such as the springboard chop. (photo by author)

Canadian J.P. Mercier makes the sawdust fly in the hot saw competition. (photo by author)

Jason Wynyard tries to pick a good spot to drive his ax in on the springboard chop. (photo by author)

Right: Jason Wynyard leans one arm on a log and holds his saw upright with the other hand. (photo by author)

Lindsay Daun with sawdust flying as she pulls. (photo by author)

Part of the typical crowd of four thousand fans at each session of the Lumberjack World Championships. (photo by author)

JR Salzman and wife Josie when the outlook was uncertain during the log rolling competition in 2009. (photo by author)

JR Salzman in log rolling match versus past champion Brian Bartow at the 2009 games as he makes his comeback. (photo by author)

Lumberjack in a Desert

When terrorists commandeered airplanes and crashed them into the Twin Towers of the World Trade Center in New York, the Pentagon in Washington, DC, and, after a struggle with passengers, an empty field in Pennsylvania on September 11, 2001, JR Salzman was a student at the University of Minnesota.

Inspired by patriotism and the call to arms, he joined the Minnesota National Guard in 2003, but mostly divided his time between study at the school, lumberjack sports, and the regularly scheduled guard meetings.

Following his Hayward upbringing, which resulted in his mimicking his older sister Tina's devotion to logrolling, Salzman developed into a world champion in 1998. From 1998 through 2002, Salzman won the title at the Lumberjack World Championships five straight years. Rival Jamie Fischer, the Joe Frazier to Salzman's Muhammad Ali, emerged in 2003 and won the first of his three crowns.

Back and forth they went from 2003 to 2006, with Fischer and Salzman meeting in epic logrolling showdowns reminiscent of the early days of competition when Fred Scheer came along to challenge Phil Scott. Fischer, from Stillwater, Minnesota, won the crown in 2003 and 2004, but in 2005 Salzman reclaimed the title for his sixth triumph.

Throughout the 2000s, Salzman was gaining a larger national following through televised exposure in ESPN's Great Outdoor Games. Over a six-year period, Salzman won fourteen medals in logrolling and the boom run, and in 2005 he won an ESPY, the Excellence in Sports Performance Yearly award chosen by the 24-hour sports network for being the best outdoor sportsman of the year.

By 2006, however, Salzman was living a different life. His National Guard unit was called up by Uncle Sam as part of the Thirty-fourth Infantry Division in 2005 and was sent to Iraq in the spring of the next year.

During his service in the Middle East, Salzman created a website to update his timber sports fans about his daily life and called it "Lumberjack in a Desert." It was a modern-day fish out of water tale. Salzman, whose success was based on keeping his balance on or running across logs floating in water, was surrounded by millions of acres of sand.

The website design was humorous. It pictured an exaggerated lumberjack with a thick beard, powerfully muscled shoulders, and a Cindy Crawford waistline holding an ax (reminiscent of some of the cartoonish Paul Bunyan pictures), with a bright, burning sun behind him and two cartoonlike camels trailing behind.

The entries were routine descriptions of a soldier's life, giving away no military secrets but commenting on a world far removed from most Americans' daily life experiences. Salzman's July 21, 2007, entry reads, "My unit, A Co-2-135 infantry, part of the Minnesota National Guard's 1-34 BCT is home from Iraq!" A simple entry.

War zones can be tense areas with long periods of quiet interrupted by short bursts of terror. The unanticipated can be the soldier's biggest enemy, the unseen encounter with the enemy a dreaded and hidden surprise. On December 19, 2006, which was marked by unusual fog for Iraq, Salzman was deployed on a night mission that placed him in the passenger seat of a Humvee. The vehicle led twenty empty fuel tankers through Baghdad to the Americans' Tallil Air Base.

In a place where the temperature regularly exceeds 100 degrees, American soldiers are weighted down with pounds and pounds of gear for their own protection. Besides his M4 rifle and to his knowledge more ammunition than anyone else carried in the field, Salzman toted two radios, a Global Positioning System (GPS) unit, and night vision goggles, and he wore body armor. Salzman is about six feet tall, and despite the muscles he developed through his athletic endeavors, he is slender. However, with all of the equipment on, he was as bulked up as a football player.

When they are deployed in foreign lands, enduring difficult conditions and adapting to the stresses of the moment, soldiers also look for minor ways to ease their discomfort. One of Salzman's trademarks was sitting on a cushy pillow in the Humvee, a bit of protection to soothe his butt as the vehicle bounced along. He had been running missions like this for a full year. He was hoping the December 19 ride would be more of the same—always on alert, but no damage done. Always the goal was to finish up fast and clean.

That's not how this trip ended.

"We were leading a convoy through Baghdad," Salzman said. "I was commander of a scout vehicle, and we were headed back."

The unexpected fog caused the Humvee to slow to 35 miles per hour, and as Salzman tried to scan the horizon with binoculars an enemy explosive device was hurled at him through an open window. There was a flash of light and the concussion of an explosion. Salzman took a direct hit, and his memories of the ensuing hours and days are sometimes very sharp and at other times blurry.

"All of a sudden, everything got really loud," Salzman said.

And then, as he lost consciousness, everything got really quiet. Whether it was seconds or minutes, Salzman awoke in the same position, pinned in his seat in a blown-up Humvee, blood splattered on the metal, windows shattered into small pieces. The point of impact from the explosive device was Salzman's door and window. The vehicle was stopped in its tracks, literally, with four flat tires. Among the things burning were his helmet and logbook, and his pistol had melted in its holster.

So much equipment was ruined, but Salzman tried to evaluate his bodily equipment. He was aware enough despite pain and a general feeling of dullness in his head to take an inventory of his limbs, innards, head, and face. He felt he should fight his way out of the vehicle, but when he reached for the door handle, he realized that his right hand and part of his arm had been blown off.

"I stayed calm," Salzman said.

As an athlete trained for years to size up situations and use all his physical strength and agility to succeed, Salzman compared this moment to his favorite lumberjack event. "In log rolling, you look around and evaluate the situation, and then you react," he later said. "The first thing I remember saying [to another soldier] is 'Give me a tourniquet.'"

Stop the bleeding. That was a simple, fundamental idea that made a lot of sense and was the first thing the first medic on the scene did. Salzman was in shock, with multiple pieces of shrapnel in his body—his left hand was also damaged—but at the moment the most urgent task was to cut off the flow of blood. The medic kept telling Salzman he was sorry that he had been wounded, and Salzman, partially in his delirium, possibly in denial, and perhaps just because it sounded good, uttered what seemed to be a flippant response. It was going to be alright, Salzman assured his distraught helper, because his legs were fine. That meant he could still logroll.

That optimism was helpful as he lay on a battlefield in Iraq, thousands of miles from Hayward, with his body oozing blood, but before he could logroll again, Salzman had to survive. In an earlier war, Vietnam even, it might not have been possible to treat Salzman at the scene of the injury or at an in-country hospital, and he might have died overseas.

As it was, Salzman could not be flown out of the country for a full day, so his initial treatment was in Iraq. He underwent two surgeries before being transported to an American hospital in Germany. Soon after, on Christmas Eve 2006, he was admitted to Walter Reed Hospital in Washington, DC. The ordeal to rebuild JR Salzman that had begun on a foggy street in Baghdad continued stateside for the next year.

After Salzman's National Guard unit was called up and he was sent to the Middle East, his wife Josie (whom he married in the spring of 2006 while on leave) moved back to Wisconsin. She was living in Menomonie when she was informed that Salzman had been wounded. Rather than pick up the phone and call Salzman's parents, and perhaps because she could use comfort herself, she drove to JR's family home.

As soon as Bonnie Salzman, JR's mother, saw Josie on the doorstep she was terrified. She feared that her son was dead. If JR was alive, she thought, everything would work out. As long as he was alive, the family could help nurse him back to health.

He was alive.

The explosive device had done considerable damage, and JR was at Walter Reed and the adjacent Fisher House for nine months of care. Most obvious was the loss of his right hand and arm below the elbow. He lost one finger on his left hand. The explosion resulted in a traumatic brain injury, and he has some short-term memory loss.

Salzman's rehab and recovery were long and painful and at times frustrating. Although his legs were not seriously damaged, it took some effort to maintain his balance and equilibrium at first, and the head injury was daunting at times. "It affects my concentration and memory," he said.

There was a lot to learn all over again without a right hand, especially as he was right-hand dominant. Salzman had to learn how to sign his name and tie his shoes one-handed, left-handed, with what had been his weaker hand. Because of nerve damage, however, the left hand can go cold and numb. "Without a ring finger, when it's cold I can't tie my shoes," he said.

Getting a good fit with a prosthetic arm, never mind learning how to use it properly, was an adventure in itself, and not a pleasant one. To Salzman's dismay, his first artificial arm did not work correctly and soon began to fall apart. When he approached the Veterans Administration for a replacement, to his shock there was at best a slow-motion response. In the end, the Internet played a role in drumming up support for Salzman's campaign. A Facebook group calling itself "Petition the VA to Give JR Salzman a New Prosthetic Arm" may have shamed the Veterans Administration sufficiently to replace the arm. Those "Lumberjack in a Desert" postings likely galvanized enough supporters nationally to ratchet up the pressure and help him when he needed it most. His congressman also got involved. In 2009, Salzman received a new arm.

By then Salzman was already back at logrolling. He began literally with baby steps when he got back to Wisconsin after his lengthy hospital stays. He pointed to the 2008 Lumberjack World Championships for a comeback. He didn't know what he could expect from his body, and he didn't know what he could expect mentally going head-to-head with the other top competitors. He just knew it was important to be out there at the Lumberjack Bowl, in his realm. He dreamed of winning again, of course, but he had to know how much of his skill had been lost and how much he retained. After all, very few people become a world champion at anything, and Salzman wanted to believe that the thing he was best at had not been taken from him by war.

Although he was a multiple champion with a glittering track record, Salzman had been out of logrolling for a couple of years. This meant he was not seeded in the top group when the brackets were prepared, and a tentative Salzman did not get the chance to ease his way back into competition. His first-round opponent, by happenstance of the draw, was Jamie Fischer, by then a three-time world champ and the number-one seed.

"It was a random seed," Fischer said. "I know he trained real hard. It was kind of bad luck."

Fischer won, and Salzman did not recover through the loser's bracket, so he was knocked out early. Was it too soon to come back? Was it so important mentally to try? A year later, in his analysis of that fledgling return, Salzman did not have much sympathy for himself.

"I did pretty terrible last year," he said. "I was a train wreck. I feel like I have a better handle on things this year. It's different. I know it's a young guys' event, but it's less about them than it is about me. I have to be calm, collected, and focused. You focus on one match at a time. I wasn't supposed to lose."

Salzman also featured some updated equipment that could be helpful in his pursuit of the crown. He waved his second artificial arm. It was made of stainless steel, and it wouldn't rust when he went into the water at the Lumberjack Bowl. More seriously, Salzman had experimented logrolling with the arm and without and found that he could better maintain his balance wearing the arm.

Salzman had a residue of confidence built up from years' worth of success, but that confidence had been shaken because of the damage done to his body. He was trying to recapture the swagger that had made him a multiple champion yet adapt to any new limitations imposed by his injuries. He was hoping there wouldn't be any but knew there might well be against the other top guys.

"It's all about strength and foot speed and tactics," Salzman said. "When I got splashed last year I wasn't sure enough about my balance. When I got mad I finally did splash him [his opponent] back."

Disappointed that he did not do as well as he hoped, in between his other activities—being a husband, returning to college at the University of Wisconsin–Stout with long-term plans to become a teacher, and fighting the battle to obtain a new artificial arm—Salzman rededicated himself to training for the 2009 championships.

This time, he believed, he could shine again.

The Idea Is Not to Go Boom

In a way, the boom run is tightrope running. Just as the circus performers do their stuff on the high-wire with the number-one objective being not to fall down and go boom, lumberjacks and lumber-jills in the boom run must maintain their balance at all times. The difference between the boom run and tightrope walking is that boom runners are running full out while leaping from log to log.

Competition in the boom run is head-to-head against another runner on a nearby length of logs. The entrant who stays upright and runs the fastest advances. The boom run requires balance and speed. It's an agility run on logs that are lashed together in the water, and slipping is discouraged, not only if you want to stay dry but if you want to win. Anyone who falls off the log and makes a splash can continue, but only by climbing back up on the log at the point where he or she fell.

The boom run looks like fun, but it is also a challenge. And it has its roots in real lumberjack work. During the winter logging season the cut trees were hauled to nearby rivers and stored until spring. The logs were penned up and circled by "booms," and then after the chopping season, when any ice on the water thawed, the corrals were removed and the logs began their journey downriver, herded by workers known as river pigs.

The sport is considerably safer than the work was, and no one has ever drowned competing in the boom run in Hayward.

Jenny Atkinson, who began competing in Hayward at age ten and was about to make her twenty-seventh consecutive championships appearance in the summer of 2010, discovered the boom run in 1990. She went to a log-rolling contest in La Crosse, Wisconsin, and at the end of that competition officials said, "Hey, we have this fun event." A boom run had been erected. None of the logrollers had seen it.

"For everyone, it was the first time we did the sport," Atkinson said. "It didn't hardly exist."

The race officials loaded everyone interested into a boat and transported them to the middle of a pond. Unlike the back-and-forth boom run between docks in Hayward, this one-time event called for an all-out, one-way sprint over the logs to shore with the reward being a medal and a hundred dollars. Atkinson won.

"I really loved it then," she said.

Starting the next year, in 1991, Hayward added the boom run to its program, and for four years, through 1994, the event was co-ed, men against women. Every year Atkinson made the finals, but she was the only woman. She earned the nickname "Boom Queen" for those performances because, as she said, it was "Jenny and all guys."

In 1995, the Lumberjack World Championships divided up the boom run competition into men and women, not men versus women.

Mandy Erdmann Sobiech saw her first timber sports event, logrolling, in her hometown of La Crosse when she was six, went home, and said, "Mom and Dad, I want to be a logroller." They rolled their eyes, but said OK. When she went to Hayward for the first time a year later she saw the boom run and discovered her true love.

"Logrolling is fun, but the boom run is my passion," she said.

She started winning the event in 1999 and has either been a champ or a contender ever since. "I've always been good at it," she said. "I love racing."

Nearing thirty and focusing on a career as a nurse in a cancer unit, Erdmann Sobiech is now living in a community without a boom run and has trouble squeezing in as much training on the logs as she would like. She runs sprints, practices logrolling, and lifts weights, but to actually get on a boom run involves driving two hours to Madison or two and a half hours to Minneapolis.

Although no one has ever seemed quite as passionate about the boom run as Jamie Fischer, Fred Scheer won the first men's title in 1995. JR Salzman, whose primary event is logrolling, won in 1996, 1997, and in 2000.

On the women's side, Atkinson, then known by her maiden name of Anderson, won in 1995 and 1996 and again in 2007 under her married name of Atkinson. Tina Salzman Bosworth, the log rolling savant, won in 1997. Erdman Sobiech owned the event in 1999, 2000, 2001, 2002, 2003, 2005, and 2010, and Abby Hoeschler, of the Judy Hoeschler clan, won in 2004 and 2006.

For the most part, it seems as if once you master the boom run you have a good shot at fending off all comers. The boom run, like logrolling, encourages lighter-weight athletes. If timber sports were comparable to football, the sawyers and choppers would be linemen and the boom runners and logrollers would be halfbacks or defensive backs. Body type is definitely a factor, Atkinson said.

"The less you weigh, the less you move the log," she said. "There have been some tremendously talented women in the past, but the smaller you are, it helps. Being light and agile . . . [is] important."

Unlike most other Lumberjack World Championships events, which are fairly self-evident just by their names, the boom run needs some explanation. The "boom" is actually a group of logs lashed together end-to-end stretching from dock to dock on the water inside the Lumberjack Bowl. When an official counts down to "go," the boom runners fly off the competition dock, land on a log and negotiate their way across as fast as they can. It is not an event where most spectators watch and think, "I can do that." More often they wonder just how many steps they would take before falling into the water.

It's important to be light on your feet and maintain balance, although anything can happen on the logs. At Hayward the two-person race begins at the logrolling dock. When the runners reach the other side of the pond, they leap up onto the chopping dock, turn around and run back on the logs. In a competition timed to the tenth of a second, taking a dip in the water can be costly. Anyone staying on the logs has the advantage, and once runners fall in the best they can hope for is that their competitor will, too. Typically, there is a lot of splashing going on, but the best boom runners stay dry.

Initially, in Hayward, not many women wanted to enter the boom run. Atkinson said they didn't want to get wet, didn't want to be embarrassed by falling off the log, and didn't like competing against men. But Atkinson worked as a cheerleader, exhorting the women to enter to show there was enough interest in the event to start a woman's division, and it paid off.

Fischer, who is from Stillwater, Minnesota, may be the best of the best among the men. He proudly proclaims that he "built the world's first personal boom run." Such a statement produces double takes. Fischer, who is now in his late twenties, discovered the boom run when he was seventeen. Already an accomplished logroller and the son and grandson of timber sports participants, Fischer fell in love with the boom run in 2000 when he first entered the competition in Hayward and placed second in the men's category.

"I found out I was pretty good at it," Fischer said. "I knew I wanted to get better at it."

When athletes discover a personal passion, fall hard for a sport, and sense that with some work they could improve, they typically throw themselves into repetition in the event, play the sport day and night to hone their skills, and devote themselves to long hours of training. Fischer, however, had a problem. The boom run was located in Hayward and he lived in the next state to the west. Unlike basketball, where there are hoops in backyards and gyms on every corner, boom runs are at a premium.

So in 2001 Fischer set out to build his own boom run. His parents' five-acre property featured a nice-sized pond, and there Fischer went to work. Applying his logging skills, Fischer employed a handmade lathe to shape timber into logrolling logs, then tied eight of them together so he could practice his boom running. This unique approach did not make national news, but in the small logrolling community athletes knew Fischer was up to something unusual.

Given that Fischer's family home was not on a main thoroughfare and the pond was well back from the road, few noticed what was going on.

"Not too many people stopped by to see it," Fischer said.

If they had, most of them probably would have asked, "What's that?" Those in the sport who learned Fischer was now a construction magnate reacted predictably: "He's building a boom run?" "They had to see it," Fischer said. And anyone who wanted to practice the boom run was welcome.

Fischer practiced and practiced in Minnesota, then showed up in Hayward and won the boom run seven years in a row, setting a world record time of 12.49 seconds for sprinting across the logs in 2005. "I won and set the world record, so it definitely helped," Fischer said.

Fischer is no longer the only possessor of a personal boom run, however. Atkinson, who is also from Stillwater but splits her time between there and Grand Marais, farther north, used to practice at Fischer's facility. She said she got excited when she heard he was building it and trained there many times. Then for her thirtieth birthday in 2003, Atkinson's husband, Neil, bought her the logs for her own boom run to use in a pond outside of

Grand Marais near the family cabin. That was a big-time gift from hubby. For one thing it probably kept Atkinson in the sport. It also presented new opportunities to make friends in the neighborhood.

It was either that or retire, Atkinson figured. She knew she had to keep up her training, and with the large amount of time the couple was spending in Grand Marais, the closest boom run was four hours away. Now Atkinson has about thirty logs arranged in different configurations. While the boom run in Hayward is composed of nine logs, Atkinson has one set up for fourteen logs and another for ten.

Atkinson spreads the gospel of the boom run everywhere she goes and to everyone who comes to her. In her mind, it's come one, come all to Jenny's boom run. The Boom Queen hosts a kid's competition each August but says young people, old people, passersby, and vacationing tourists are all welcome to try it.

"Even my sixty-four-year-old aunt has tried it," Atkinson said. "I bet there's been a thousand people who have tried it. Kids love it. The younger you learn, far and away the easier it will be."

Atkinson, a third-grade teacher, exudes about as much enthusiasm as one of the kids who give the boom run a shot. That attitude was a considerable help in December 2009 when she was diagnosed with breast cancer. Her treatment has progressed well, and she hasn't allowed illness or chemotherapy to interfere with the boom run.

"I'm doing great," Atkinson said about seven months after her diagnosis. "I'll live to be an old lady."

Fischer's success in boom run and the pleasure he has derived from timber sports made him rethink his original career goals. After earning a degree in elementary education at the University of Minnesota, he started a masters degree program. But he put finishing it on hold in 2005 when he incorporated to become Lumberjack Enterprises.

After Fred Scheer decided he wanted to downsize and stop traveling around the country with his long-running lumberjack show, Fischer stepped into the breach. Employing much of the same shtick as Scheer has, Fischer's All-American Lumberjack Show makes the rounds of fairgrounds and other palaces of entertainment throughout the land. Among the locations the show has played are Texas, California, and Michigan. The enthusiasm is out there. Just as Scheer suspected, Fischer continues to confirm that.

Families come out as groups to city festivals and fairs, places where they expect to have a good time with wholesome entertainment. Fischer supplies it. Some spectators are definitely first-timers who have watched timber sports on the tube but want to see it up close and personal.

"Their thinking might be, 'I've seen this on TV, but I've never seen it live,'" Fischer said.

And everyone who thinks about lumberjacks or participates in lumberjack sports is conscious of Paul Bunyan.

"Paul Bunyan was the lumberjack hero," Fischer said. "Everyone wanted to be his friend, according to folklore." Fischer does not overlook that part—Paul Bunyan as fiction.

Although his greatest triumphs have come in the boom run, Fischer is also a three-time Hayward logrolling champ.

"I'm a third-generation logroller," he said.

His grandfather, the late Harold Fischer, was a trick and fancy logroller. No longer contested, trick and fancy logrolling is as much about show business as competition. Two-man teams performed on logs for ten minutes while being graded for their ingenuity by a group of judges. Sometimes the on-log stunts involved jumping rope or juggling while balanced on the log. At times contestants even stood on their heads on chairs or roller-skated.

"He learned from the real lumberjacks," Fischer said of his granddad.

In 1972, Jamie's father Jim won the men's logrolling title at the Lumberjack World Championships. His career ended soon after, however, when he was hit by a car. Some thirty-one years later Jim's son Jamie came along and won the same crown.

"We're the first father and son to do it," Jamie said.

The younger Fischer was bred for logrolling. He was trying to balance on a log by the time he was three and says the earliest thing he remembers about his childhood is being on a log. If his first words were "log" and "rolling" instead of "mom" and "dad" it wouldn't surprise him.

Yet he does not for a moment claim that logrolling is easy.

"It is hard to pick up," Fischer said. "It is very popular in Hayward, and I think a lot of people there have tried it. They can appreciate the speed of it."

The good log rollers meet at the Lumberjack World Championships, ESPN's Great Outdoor Games, and other selected competition venues, and Fischer believes they have a bond; even if they are rivals and not all the best of friends, they are at the least friendly.

"It's such a small and tight group," Fischer said. "We're all on a first-name basis."

Fischer understands as well as anyone that logrolling is not a mainstream sport in the United States, but as a sidelight to his own competition and his traveling lumberjack show, he has produced a logrolling instructional video, complete with an instruction book. He will even make you a log and ship it. Figuring that kids love logrolling whenever they try it, Fischer is attempting to make the sport more accessible in places where logs are not handy. Following the general idea of building his own boom run, Fischer is trying to bring logrolling into communities where the only logs to be seen are in pictures.

"Our goal is to get as many kids as possible across the country wet," Fischer joked. "As long as it's nice out, they don't care if they get wet." He has been selling between fifteen and thirty instructional sets a year. And he says, "I'm backed up on log orders."

Yes, there is a wait for a log to be prepared for your pond or pool. Fischer is the middleman between trees in the forest and logs in your yard. He orders 60-foot-long western red cedars from a supplier in British Columbia, which are essentially the same size and wood as telephone poles. The wood shows up in Stillwater, Minnesota, at the workshop he maintains on his parents' land, and he goes to work.

"I put it on the ground and then it's mine," Fischer said.

It took a bit of vision to recognize that there might be a market for this sort of thing, but Fischer is working hard spreading the gospel of logrolling. He's been shaping competition logs for a few years now, and much of what he has done has been the result of trial and error. Originally, Fischer finished the sawing part of his work, then "slapped a postage stamp on it and mailed it." Naked. As is. Just a raw log. More recently he has shifted to using FedEx freight with the log traveling in a crate.

"Had to do it," he said. "Some of them got damaged."

Thus far Fischer has not volunteered to travel anywhere else in the country to build a backyard boom run. One log at a time, so to speak, and one Fischer logrolling at a time apparently. A recent father, Fischer said he took his newborn son Luke out on a log when he was seventeen days old. Luke was not such a prodigy that he stood up and attempted to balance on the log, and he did not try to splash water into Dad's face.

"I set him on the log," Fischer said, "and he fell asleep."

Does this mean Luke is naturally fearless? Fischer is not going to start the kid in logrolling just yet. "We're going to encourage it, though," he said.

Meanwhile, Fischer is still a student of the boom run. In fact, he is building Boom Run II at the same Minnesota pond because the first boom run is wearing out. "The logs just got worn out sitting in the water all of the time," Fischer said. The effort is also a signal that Fischer is not finished with top-level boom run competition either, despite being "more and more out of shape." He isn't building the Boom Run II for the heck of it. He plans to use it because he wants another crack at the title.

Trying to Carve Out a Living

Although he loved woodchopping from the time he first saw it as a kid at the Riverton Fair in Connecticut, Mike Sullivan had other athletic talents and he pursued another professional sports path.

There may have been sawdust in his bloodstream, but he didn't quite recognize that yet. His first dream was to become a Major League baseball player. Sullivan had the tools to become a very fine catcher and the top level of baseball is always trying to replenish its supply of catchers, the hardest position to play.

Hailing from Winstead, Connecticut, Sullivan was 6 feet, 1 inch and weighed 200 pounds, good dimensions for a ballplayer, and he was drafted by the Cincinnati Reds organization. He played for the Reds' minor-league affiliates but couldn't progress to the majors, and as happens to the majority of minor leaguers in their twenties, he was eventually let go.

It has been an intriguing journey for an athlete who began life with one set of goals, adapted, and is now one of probably only a handful of timber sports veterans who make the vast majority of their living wage from lumberjack activities.

Mike Sullivan's journey is in some ways symbolic of the lives of many top lumberjacks. He has excelled in Hayward, made a name for himself in the sport, and has scrapped and hustled to make a living through it.

Growing up to become president is supposed to be the American dream, but likely more kids picture themselves growing up to become baseball players and hitting a home run in the bottom of the ninth inning to win the World Series. It turned out that Sullivan was in the wrong sport. While he was rooting for Carl Yastrzemski to win the Triple Crown in 1967, he should have been rooting for Brian Herlihy to win his own Triple Crown of chopping in Hayward, Wisconsin.

More than thirty years ago, before he even started playing pro ball, Sullivan coincidentally did a chore for Connecticut sawyer Jim Colbert. Five years later both men, Sullivan then about twenty-two, were working for the state of Connecticut. Colbert was already a Hayward veteran, and they got to talking about timber sports.

By the time Sullivan watched the Lumberjack World Championships on *Wide World of Sports*, he had already seen some of the activities at his county fair and thought, "I know about woodchopping." When he started talking with Colbert his thoughts changed to "I always wanted to try that."

Sullivan made his first trip to Hayward in 1982 and was hooked. The Lumberjack Bowl was timber sports nirvana. For a baseball man like Sullivan, the comparison came easily. "For me it was like walking into Yankee Stadium. Now I was there. It was a good moment."

Sullivan was still raw at chopping and sawing, but he entered all of those related events. At the time the championships were less exclusive and allowed almost anyone to enter, even if they did not have a long track record. The top eighteen competitors in each event were seeded, and the battles went on and on until there were only six men left in each final. Sullivan did not take top honors, make money, or win major trophies, but he finished in the top six in everything he tried. That provided encouragement.

Energized by the experience of competing in Hayward, Sullivan determined to become a better lumberjack. He trained constantly, worked on technique, and improved his chopping and sawing. By 1984 he was competing down under, traveling to Australia and New Zealand not just for timber sports but to absorb the lifestyle and culture. He worked in a coal mine and on a deer farm.

"Going to Australia and New Zealand was all part of it," he said of his lumberjack self-improvement program. "I had some of the greatest highs being with the real people. It was not the touristy thing."

One year, chasing the hemispheric summer between North America and down under, Sullivan totaled the results on his record and realized that he had entered fifty-two competitions, averaging one a week for a year.

And Sullivan did improve. He saw the results of his devotion pretty quickly. From being just a new face on the block to becoming a world champion was not as great a leap for him as it is for many. More important, Sullivan kept building his résumé. In his forties, at a time when most athletes are retired, Sullivan was winning world titles. He gradually became one of the kings of the hot saw, buzzing wood so swiftly that he captured titles in Hayward in 2003, 2005, 2007, and 2008.

Sullivan teamed up with his old acquaintance Jim Colbert, and they won men's double buck titles together in 1988, 1989, and 1994. Sullivan and Nancy Zalewski won the Jack & Jill sawing in 2004 and 2008.

For Sullivan, weighing only 200 pounds is a competitive disadvantage. "We've talked about this a million times as a competitor," Sullivan said, "that the sport almost needs to have weight classes. A guy like Dave Bolstad who is 6 feet, 4 inches and 280 pounds, or Jason Wynyard, they're just too strong. The smaller guy who wins a chopping event is probably a better chopper because his technique has to be perfect. But you are what you are. I can get up to 280 pounds, but I'd be a fat blob."

Athletes of the twenty-first century are all bigger and faster than the athletes of decades ago. Basketball players are taller. Football players are wider. Baseball players field better with their bigger gloves. It is evolution, and Sullivan is not likely to see weight classes in timber sports. He should be celebrated as a top-level competitor who can hold his own and defeat the big guns.

Sullivan is also grateful that even though he is in his fifties he can still compete. That certainly would not have been true if he had made it in baseball. Yet, as the philosopher lumberjack he is, Sullivan also worries that there is not enough new blood breaking into the sport at the top level. He believes the college timber sports series sponsored by Stihl is terrific, but not even the best lumberjacks coming out of college seem willing to make the transition to pros.

"It's very, very hard," Sullivan said of the transition and the amount of time it takes to develop from good college lumberjack to prize-winning pro. "Not many people are willing to take a butt whipping for three or four years. It's a tough sport to get into and to stay in. You have to love it."

Sullivan loves everything about the Lumberjack World Championships and being part of them. He said he doesn't have a favorite event because it can change from minute to minute and day to day based on his performance: "Whichever one I'm doing the best [is my favorite] because I like them all."

Sullivan is one of a small number of lumberjack competitors who have taken a shot at making his living almost completely from the sport. Some competitors, like Dave Jewett, are chainsaw carvers. The Halvorsons run a sawmill. Many find ways to work with wood, but few take the professional aspect of being a lumberjack sports competitor as far as Sullivan has.

While Fred Scheer and Jamie Fischer have toured the nation with full-scale lumberjack shows, Sullivan has adapted and experimented to shape a show for audiences as well. He and Arden Cogar Jr. are partners, and they are as popular at state and county fairs as 4-H clubs, cow milking, and cotton candy. Some county fairs in Ohio and on Cape Cod have invited Sullivan and his friends to perform eight years in a row.

Generally, the game plan for the show that makes it different from the thoroughly scripted Scheer and Fischer shows is that real competition takes place. Sullivan and Cogar team up to face a couple of guys who challenge them in double buck sawing. And then Sullivan and Cogar go one-on-one. "It's head-to-head," Sullivan said. "It's real competition."

At one point, Sullivan employs a one-man crosscut saw against someone wielding a hot saw. "People who have never seen it think I'll be beaten easily." Sometimes Sullivan loses by a hair, and sometimes he wins. There is some banter in which a cast member says, "Do you have a hot saw, too, Mr. Crosscut?" Sullivan disappears backstage or behind a curtain and returns carrying a souped-up hot saw that makes his opponent's chainsaw look puny and ineffectual.

"It's a good show," Sullivan said. "We do fool around in some events, but we go head-to-head for real."

Until he was thirty-nine, Sullivan held a succession of jobs that paid the rent and helped him raise a family. Just about as passionate a bow hunter as he is a lumberjack, Sullivan obtained a job as a representative selling archery equipment and had his lumberjack travel sponsored. That has allowed him to concentrate on timber sports competition in Hayward and elsewhere, to train, to travel with the show, and to develop as a chainsaw carver, making appearances at Cabela's outdoors stores.

But Sullivan never makes enough money from lumberjack activities to break into the wealthiest tax brackets.

"My wife had a job," he said of getting his noncompetition lumberjack endeavors going. "If I didn't have the support of family, I couldn't do it. There's nobody in the sport who could support a family."

Getting paid fees for exhibitions helps pay the bills. So does chainsaw carving. But to obtain gigs a lumberjack must have a notable résumé. Just as it is in any other sport, corporations with products to sell want their front men to be accomplished. They want to be able to write a tagline on a commercial that reads "World Champion." They want to be able to create advertising copy that summarizes triumphs and lists titles.

"Being one of the upper-level guys in the United States is important," Sullivan said. "You've got to be a winner. You've got to be on TV and do a lot of exhibitions. The sponsorships are not going to keep coming just because you're a nice guy."

In many ways, what a competitor takes away from Hayward—if successful—can be more valuable than cash. Championships won are stamps of legitimacy. Reputations are enhanced. There is universal acknowledgment that if you have won a title at the Lumberjack World Championships you have done something special. That label sticks and is understood around the world. Organizers of an event in New Zealand might not know who you are, but if they see your name time and again on the results list, they might issue an invitation to compete down under or participate in a series of exhibitions.

The total purse paid out in Hayward in 2009 was fifty thousand dollars. It was divided equally between men and women in every event. The prize structure was separate but equal for men and women and was identical for each event whether it be chopping, sawing, or logrolling.

The cash prizes earned by the winners and top finishers were: first place, $825; second, $600; third, $375; fourth, $225; fifth, $200; sixth, $125; seventh, $110; and eighth, $100.

Given the cost of travel, either by plane or by car, the need to eat and the price of a hotel room, there is considerable pressure to perform. A lumberjack or lumberjill who does not place highly during three days of competition could end up losing money on the trip to Hayward.

"If you're doing it for the money, you're in the wrong sport," Sullivan said.

Sullivan is hoping to make enough money to be able to stay in the sport. Making money has never been the object, but the need to make money has been constant. Sullivan remembers sitting around with Mel Lentz, the former multiple all-around champion, telling stories and talking about how devoting years of their lives to doing what they love wasn't all that lucrative.

"We figured that if we put the same time and effort and work into it after saying 'I'm going to make money' as we did in timber sports, that we would have made a million dollars."

Instead, what Sullivan has is a million dollars' worth of memories.

"When I was twenty-three I decided I wanted to win a world championship," he said. "I didn't think about how much money I could make. Well, I won a world championship. I have stories to tell. I've been places around the world I never would have been. I actually had it pretty cool."

Powerful Women

 When sociologists discuss the evolution of American society since the 1950s one issue sure to be on the agenda is the empowerment of women. The typical married woman of the post–World War II period was a stay-at-home mom and homemaker whose job was to take care of the kids and make hubby happy.

Career options for women were limited, the most popular being secretary, nurse, or teacher. As Betty Friedan, Gloria Steinem, and other prominent women's rights activists led a revolution in the way women live their lives and participate in the job market, it's doubtful they spent much time dwelling on timber sports.

Still, much the same as opportunities mushroomed for girls and women in other sports following the congressional passage of Title IX, the act that required equal treatment by any organization that received federal funding, the Lumberjack World Championships expanded and offered more events for women.

It turned out women could yell "Yo-ho!" as loudly as a man.

Once given the chance to compete in more events, most previously restricted to men, women empowered themselves. While the men competing in the Lumberjack World Championships are the linear descendents of the men who worked in the forests cutting down trees in the nineteenth century, women had no direct link. The "fair" sex was not welcome in the woods. There were no women lumberjacks.

When Tony Wise founded the Lumberjack World Championships in 1960, he wasn't thinking of women's rights or women waving axes, either. Women were an afterthought. The only event for women in 1960 was logrolling. One of the oldest ways of measuring skill in the all-around lumberjack in the working camps was logrolling. Logging and timber sports were macho worlds. But unlike sawing and chopping, logrolling did not require the musculature of a professional wrestler. In fact, logrolling seemed a perfect fit for women from the start because generally the athletes who succeeded—male and female—were smaller boned, of slighter stature, and nimble on their feet.

It should be remembered that logrolling was the most established of the timber sports, with its own association and a hold on the community of athletes that predated Wise's program. Behavior on the log might not be ladylike or dainty, but nothing was going to take place to anger a chauvinistic world, either. The women could have their moment in the sun, be patted on the head, and sent to the sidelines. Wise did not have the foresight to realize that the lifting of the glass ceiling in the American corporate world, the creation of thousands of teams of high school and college women because of Title IX, and the entire attitudinal shift between what it was thought women couldn't do and what women could do was about to alter the landscape.

In 1960, Bette Ellis—who already owned a 1958 U.S. Log Rolling Association world title—became the first woman to win a Lumberjack World Championships trophy in Hayward. After getting married, she won again in 1963, 1964, and 1965 as Bette Ellis Toothaker. The fans seemed to enjoy the early women's logrolling, but no one considered it a monumental step forward for womankind. In fact, the Lumberjack World Championships was quite slow to expand its opportunities for women, and it only gradually added timber sports titles over the years. For quite some time, women's logrolling was a lonely event.

Penny Halvorson was no logroller. Her interests lay on the chopping dock and using her muscles to cut wood.

In 1984, as a way to ease women into a larger role in the championships, Jack & Jill double buck sawing was added to the program. Mel Lentz and Shirley Smith captured the inaugural title, and they won again the next year. The event proved to be a popular forum for husbands and wives working together, as well as the occasional father and daughter and brother and sister.

But that was the only event open to women who wanted to chop and saw. In fact, when Halvorson first accompanied husband Rick to Hayward in 1985, she was astonished to learn that women were not even allowed to set foot on the chopping dock. That rule was a red flag waved in the faces of women. Rick Halvorson was competing in the hot saw and realized that his chainsaw was running low on fuel. He asked his wife to go to his stash and bring him reinforcements. When Penny returned to the dock with Rick's supplies she was barred by officials from entering. That was like being invited out to a bar, then being stopped at the door and told it was a men's only club.

It was the last straw. Halvorson kicked down the gate blocking her way and gave Rick his fuel.

"It [the gate] hung there for three years," she said.

If ever there was a symbolic act of not being denied, that was it.

One dramatic gesture does not a revolution make, and Penny Halvorson said she lobbied long and loud for years to expand the women's program. She is not sure why it was so difficult to change minds but thinks the resistance was born of hidebound tradition, that the lumberjack world was always a man's domain.

It was not long before the debates over what events, how many, and opening closed doors to women were in full flower at the Lumberjack World Championships board of directors meetings. Some of the loudest voices in favor of expansion were those of Tina Scheer and Penny Halvorson.

"I fought very hard for many proposals for women on the chopping and sawing dock," Halvorson said. "I made it happen. It was a very big battle. The men had always dominated. I suppose that was it. I worked very hard for women, and it's so much better. It takes a lot of hard work for change to be made. Of course you have to have women who can compete. Whether it is men or women, it takes a lot of coaching and training and skill to get to where the women are today. There's a great sense of accomplishment for me."

An overdue evaluation of women's place in the lumberjack world was undertaken following the 1994 championships, and in 1995 the women's single buck sawing, underhand block chop, and boom run were added. The first all-around championship prize was awarded in 1997.

Peg Engasser had competed in timber sports in college and for one year, as she put it, as a "semipro." But when she learned that Hayward was expanding its opportunities for women she jumped in. Engasser won the women's underhand block chop in 2002, 2003, and 2004. "The women's events at the LWC really gave women choppers and single buck sawyers something to shoot for at a world championship level," Engasser said.

At long last, thanks to that hard-core lobbying by a handful of women, it was decided that if women were still expected to stand by their men, it just might as well be on the chopping dock.

The addition of women's chopping and sawing events was a milestone. Those were traditional preserves of men, and women had no historical link to that type of work in the forests. Just by adding the sawing and chopping events, the Lumberjack World Championships was providing an invitation to a different group of women. Prior to the addition of the Jack & Jill event, there really was no place for a heavyset woman in the proceedings except as a volunteer on the sidelines. No one told large women that they weren't welcome. No one held up discriminatory signs. But the practical matter was that if you had ever even looked at a glass of skim milk you probably would not score in logrolling or the boom run where one advantage of successful competitors was that their feet barely touched the ground.

The addition of the Jack & Jill, followed by the single buck and underhand chop, brought an entirely different class of women to Hayward. Logrolling and boom run body types conformed more with a man's view of what a female should be built like—if not quite frail, definitely slender. The women that handled axes and saws with ease were big women, with large muscles and broad shoulders, broad in the beam and sturdy in the thigh. They did not drive little foreign cars but flatbed trucks. Even if they had never shouted "Tim-ber" in the north woods, they looked as if they could handle the assignment of cutting down a 100-foot-tall pine without difficulty and with a few swipes of the ax or saw could reduce it to toothpicks.

Because the history of women in Hayward is limited, the legends of the women's events are mostly still active. Some are admittedly past their prime, but the late 1990s one day may be viewed as a golden era for the big woman in timber sports. Since that time some women have proved they can succeed against the best with wiry strength. Lindsay Daun of Illinois is built more like a rower than a weight lifter, and she might herald the wave of the future. But when discussing the first two decades of women recording their own feats of strength there are a handful of candidates deserving of special mention.

Sheree Taylor of New Zealand won Jack & Jill crowns with partners Dave Jewett and Dion Lane, two underhand block chop titles, and the coveted all-around trophy in 2001, 2005, and 2006. The 2001 competition marked Taylor's coming-out party because it was considered an upset that she bested Penny Halvorson for the all-around.

"That was a thrill," Taylor said.

At that point, Halvorson had won three straight all-around crowns, in 1998, 1999, and 2000, and while Halvorson let 2001 slip away to Taylor, she bounced back the next year, 2002, to win before age and other tough women began to catch up to her. Penny Halvorson and husband Rick won six Jack & Jill double buck sawing titles together, proving that the tension of being teammates need not affect a marriage.

Karmyn Wynyard did not so much burst on the scene as sneak up on the other top women. Wynyard, the wife of many-time men's all-around champ Jason Wynyard, has come to Hayward in the capacity of wife and mother. She has also come to Hayward determined to win gold. From a New Zealand family with considerable experience in forestry work, Karmyn did not pick up her skills just from her association with Jason. About the same time Jason and Karmyn teamed up for the Jack & Jill in the early 2000s, Karmyn emerged as a formidable opponent in other events.

Jason and Karmyn Wynyard won their first Jack & Jill championship in 2003, and then they pretty much took over the event, winning in 2005, 2006, and 2007, too. In 2009, competing against perhaps the best field ever assembled, Jason and Karmyn won a fifth title together, cutting through their piece of wood in 6.61 seconds, just shy of their 2006 world record of 6.17 seconds.

Remarkably, one of Karmyn Wynyard's finest all-around showings took place in 2009 when she came to Hayward six months pregnant. The couple knew they were expecting a daughter, and Karmyn jokingly noted, "She can say she did the world championships." That made Fischer's newborn seem like a veteran.

The runners-up were partners Mike Sullivan and Nancy Zalewski, with Dave Jewett and Lindsay Daun third and Rick and Penny Halvorson sixth.

As Penny Halvorson aged she mellowed, and after a bit of wifely resistance she admitted that Rick is a good coach.

"I didn't used to listen to him," she said.

Despite being a childhood lumberjill because of her family's ties to the lumber business, Penny wonders if she ever would have competed in timber sports if she hadn't married Rick.

"Once we got together, it was an instant agreement," she said, "that 'We're going to do that.'"

Halvorson knows there are other women on the rise who can beat her at her best events now, but through the 2009 event she still got a charge out of competing.

"You hear that whistle [to commence sawing] and your body takes over," she said.

In some ways that is making it hard for Halvorson to walk away after twenty-five years of competing, but she had a health scare at the fiftieth annual championships and chose to retire. Just fifty, she has diabetes, and after one chopping event in Hayward she started shaking. The effort was too much.

"The doctor said 'no more,'" Halvorson said. "What I used to chop in thirty seconds goes way too long. I'm retired, though maybe I'll do the Jack & Jill with Rick. I just wanted to go to the fiftieth championships. That was my goal."

Karmyn Wynyard's maiden name is Lane. She operated on the periphery of the logging world, but left New Zealand to play college basketball in Alaska. Again, as a large woman standing 6 feet tall and with appropriately proportioned big bones and muscle, Karmyn was no boom runner. She only spent two years in school, not because she didn't like the beautiful scenery but because of other considerations involving hemispheric differences.

"I was going from winter to winter," she said. "And I wanted to live in New Zealand."

When she got back to New Zealand after her second basketball season, Karmyn was in athletic shape but not lumberjacking shape. That's when she met Jason, and timber sports played a role in their courtship. They attended New Zealand championship events. Karmyn competed in the underhand block chop and single buck sawing. They soared when they linked up for Jack & Jill sawing, something Karmyn laughingly calls her favorite event now. "I like the Jack & Jill with Jason," she said. "He does all the work."

At thirty-six in 2010, Karmyn was a thirteen-year lumberjill, hardly retired, but also the mother of three children, which kept her busy.

As one anecdote that illustrates how high-level women in the sawing and chopping sports have added spice to the arena, Nancy Zalewski, probably the top all-around woman in the world now, offers her favorite story. In 2004, Zalewski, who grew up in Hayward and used to watch the championships as a little girl, and her timber sports mentor, Mike Sullivan, won the Jack & Jill sawing for the first time. The Wynyards were the defending champions but had not yet established their hegemony.

After three more titles in a row, the Wynyards were the boss couple of the event, but Sullivan and Zalewski kept after them. In 2008, Sullivan and Zalewski, the Wynyards, and Lindsay Daun and Dave Jewett were the three contending teams, and they all reached the finals.

"The team to beat each year is Jason and Karmyn Wynyard," Zalewski said. "It was a photo finish, so the judges had to go to the video to try to call the winner. The video showed it was a dead heat."

Close examination of the pictures eliminated the Wynyards, but the championships are not supposed to be declared a tie. So officials ruled that the other two teams would have a cutoff. They also shifted the teams' cutting locations to each other's previous station.

"The crowd thought this was fantastic because they're getting to watch the two best teams in the world battle it out in a second cut," Zalewski said. "Our two teams positioned themselves at the opposite block from where we initially cut and were poised for a second round, tensions high. When we finished, we all looked at each other, and still no one watching could call this race. Again the judges went to the video to make a decision, and this time we came out on top by 0.13 seconds."

The new champions of the world were Nancy Zalewski and Mike Sullivan, a few wood chips ahead of Jewett and Daun.

"That was pretty dramatic," Sullivan said. "That was unbelievable how close it was."

Zalewski, now of Manitowoc, Wisconsin, and a six-time all-around lumberjill champion after 2010, was always around the Lumberjack World Championships and the lumberjack show because her parents, Anita and the late Ed Zalewski, worked for it. Naturally, after years as a spectator, she became curious about her skills and potential. She also did not underestimate how much work it would take to do well, and part of her was intimidated. However, she was friendly with Sullivan, and in 1999 they were talking timber sports. That conversation changed her life.

"She used to hang out," Sullivan said of Zalewski. "She liked lumberjack stuff. One time I asked her, 'Did you ever think about doing it?' She said, 'Yeah, I'd like to try it.'"

Zalewski picked Sullivan to teach her how to saw properly because he didn't have a regular Jack & Jill partner, and she worked at it. A year later, in 2000, Zalewski competed in Hayward for the first time, something she truly enjoyed. Not only was she among friends, but it was a treat to compete against timber sports athletes she had seen on television.

"The rest is history," Zalewski said. "Mike and I have been sawing together for eleven years. Each year I tried to pick up a new discipline. I started with Jack & Jill and then learned how to single buck and eventually how to chop. The rest of the events just fit in along the way."

That casual mention of adding events along the way underplays the success Zalewski had when she threw herself into the new contests. She won the single buck title in 2002 and set a world record of 11.61 seconds in the 2006 prelims but lost the title in the finals to Sheree Taylor. In 2005, 2007, 2009, and 2010, Zalewski won the women's underhand chop and she set the the world records in 2007 and 2009. Her new record time was 28.19 in 2009.

"My favorite event is the single buck," Zalewski said. "It's a power event versus an accuracy event, which tends to favor me. There is technique involved, but if you've got the power you have an advantage. My most successful event is probably the underhand chop."

What might be miscalculated by some fans, Zalewski thinks, is how challenging it is to perfect the skills to win at the highest level of competition at the Lumberjack World Championships. Just because someone can swing an ax to chop wood for the fireplace does not mean she can chop wood with a clock ticking and other top-notch athletes standing a few feet away doing the same.

"It takes a lot of patience to learn the technique correctly," Zalewski said. "Each person saws a little bit differently, but as a female you need to use everything you have, arms, legs, core. Stance is a big part of being successful, and I just happened into it one day while practicing. It takes a lot of experimentation to get there. When you figure out the correct stance—how far away from the block to stand, how far apart your feet are—things start to fall into place. To understand the stroke, you need to be able to 'feel' your block as you cut it. I know it sounds odd, but when you can feel it, the stroke then just takes a bit of perfecting. Every stroke is the same, and you're maximizing the amount of wood you're cutting."

With only a handful of true contenders in Zalewski's class—Halvorson, Taylor, and Wynyard—there is little doubt in most events where the biggest challenges will emanate from. At each annual event that foursome is likely to be chasing the same gold medals, the same prize money, as small as it is, and bragging rights. Yet, unlike rivalries in some other sports, these women seem to have a bigger-picture image of the place of timber sports in their worlds.

Are they friends? Do they have solid camaraderie? Are they rivals? In Zalewski's mind, it is all of the above.

"When we're on the dock competing, there's definite rivalry," Zalewski said. "Once we step off the dock again, however, we're friends again. It's a sport to the women, so we're definitely competitive when we need to be."

Zalewski is blond and powerfully built, but she doesn't think that when the average person looks at her they see a lumberjill. She doesn't think they understand timber sports very well, even though television shows about Hayward and others featuring the events at the ESPN Outdoor Games have helped the comprehension level.

"Many people ask me why I would want to cut wood as a sport," Zalewski said. "Others, however, love to watch it and attend many of our competitions through the season. I don't think [fans recognize the level of skill required]. The elite performers make it look so easy because we're trained to improve and perfect our technique. There really is a lot of work that goes into being good at this sport."

Unlike Lindsay Daun, who said she encountered college guys who wanted to arm wrestle to test her toughness, Zalewski doesn't run into macho guys who want to show off in everyday life.

"The people I work with think it's pretty cool," Zalewski said. "So many ask me when my next competition is and where I'm going. When I return from a weekend of competing, they ask how I did. I think the TV end of it, and seeing someone you know, has definitely helped."

That awareness has come light-years since Peg Engasser was younger and competing on her collegiate woodsmen's team.

"When I first joined the collegiate team my friends didn't get it," she said. "They couldn't understand that it was the same as any other team sport, with the same motivations. They thought practicing on Saturday mornings in the middle of the winter was crazy. But I think they were a little jealous when the team traveled to other colleges to compete. My parents were worried that I would get hurt, but they traveled to many collegiate contests to support our team, standing out in the cold all day to cheer us on."

Engasser said she knew they understood her timber sports passion when they called her an athlete.

Familiarity has never done timber sports any harm. People who attend the competitions in Hayward are knowledgeable about the events and they know who the best athletes are. Almost any sports fan has seen timber sports on television, whether it was the old *Wide World of Sports* shows, ESPN broadcasts, or even other competitions in the Stihl series. It is easy to get hooked on timber sports. The games fascinate first-time viewers, draw them in because what they see is representative of fairly familiar activities and icons (chopping wood, Paul Bunyan), only placed in a new environment. Also, in no way, shape, or form should the overall impact of the popular state fair lumberjack show run by Fred or Rob Scheer or Jamie Fischer be overlooked.

At the very least the shows can serve as an introduction. Spectators see a performance similar to the real thing, and if they get curious they can up the ante and invest the time to see top-of-the-line competitors who are only secondarily putting on a show.

"I think the shows do give spectators the opportunity to see the events, but they are so different from the competitions I attend," Zalewski said. "The level of athletes in the competitions is quite a bit better than those that compete in the shows. I don't think the general public knows that there are many competitions that occur around the United States throughout the year."

Live and TV exposure do mean that some lumberjacks are recognized when they walk through airports, but it is not as if they experience top-tier celebrityhood where they can't step out the front door without paparazzi snapping pictures. But in Zalewski's experience there are definitely serious lumberjack fans.

"I do know that there are some really fanatic folks that will do anything to talk to you, to get a picture, to get your autograph," she said.

That's a kind of popularity for women on the chopping dock that Halvorson could envision but didn't know if she would ever see.

"I love to see the young women come," Halvorson said. "I started when there were no women competing, and now they are traveling all over the world." She also made close, enduring friendships with her keenest competitors, particularly Sheree Taylor. "Everyone wants to win, but we are all a big family. Sheree Taylor and I are archrivals. When the gun goes off, we're at war, but I'd do anything for her."

Engasser said when women's events were introduced in Hayward there was a special connection between the competitors, a sense that they were all in it together.

"The women had to prove that the new events wouldn't detract from the reputation of the LWC," Engasser said. "We had to support each other to be the best we all could be, to move the sport forward."

As Zalewski has experienced, the women have their own fans. Timber sports fame with the gallery is fine with Zalewski as long as the fanaticism is under control. Sign a hunk of wood here. Sign a hunk of wood there. That's OK. What Zalewski believes is that women have a more vibrant role to play in the Lumberjack World Championships in the future and in the expansion of the athlete base. She's not sure the universe will ever see a Paula standing next to Paul Bunyan perpetuating lumberjack legends, but she is certain that there is room for Paulas in general.

"The women's end of the sport is much younger than the men's," Zalewski said. "We're still breaking new ground in many of the events that they have been competing in for years. I think the men, for the most part, have accepted the women as competitors, particularly when they need a woman to cut in the Jack & Jill crosscut. If the sport is to grow, it's going to need both sexes involved. The men's end in the United States is younger than it is in Australia and New Zealand. Down under this is a sport that children pick up as young as five, so that by the time they're teenagers they've become pretty accomplished axmen. Here, in the United States, most kids don't try it until they're teenagers, so they're way behind the curve."

Maybe it's a case of mommas not letting their babies growing up to be lumberjacks or lumberjills because there are too many sharp objects lying around. But most likely in the case of girls, or young women, if they are going to jump into timber sports, it will be their own decision. Like Zalewski, they might attend lumberjack shows in Wisconsin or run across one at their county fair. They might see the best lumberjacks and lumberjills from Hayward on some cable network. They will stop what they're doing, stare at the TV screen or gaze raptly at the show in an arena, and think, "I can do that."

And they may be right. At least Penny Halvorson hopes so. As she retreats from the spotlight (except for those nostalgic trips to the chopping dock for the Jack & Jill competition), Halvorson plans to spend much of her free time with her nine grandchildren. She also has twenty-five years' worth of Lumberjack World Championships memories to reflect on for a perspective on just how far women have come.

"It was a pretty amazing adventure we were on," Halvorson said.

The Axman from Down Under

It is no surprise that someone named Scheer played a critical role in bringing perhaps the world's greatest timber sports champion to Hayward.

Jason Wynyard, born in a small town in New Zealand called TeAwamutu, grew up in a farming region, although his dad, Pae, was a logger, as was his father, Te Hurihanga, before him. Wynyard's grandfather was more commonly called Paddy.

Wynyard is descended from an English colonel who sailed across the ocean and ended up in New Zealand, and he has some native blood in him as well. In the United States the New Zealand natives are called Maori, but Wynyard's self-description is Maari.

Although he has never worked in the forest in the manner of an American lumberjack of the past, Wynyard has worked with wood. When Jason was younger, his father had a contract for log moving, and Jason drove some of the bulldozers. At the same time the family operated a deer farm. Wynyard was born in 1973 and watched his dad compete in timber sports events.

"He started out felling trees at a young age and eventually got into competition," Jason said. "He was very good. He won a few titles himself, and my grandfather was renowned in competition as well. So it's kind of in the family. I grew up watching Dad compete, and I took it up when I was about twelve years old, though I didn't really do serious competition until I was fourteen years old."

Pae Wynyard, Jason's father, worked in New Zealand forests, selectively cutting native trees called rimu and kauri, classified as softwoods. But in competition the wood was white pine, the same as the white pine used for sawing in the Hayward events. In Hayward, the chopping events use aspen.

Wynyard was well into his twenties when Tina Scheer, invited to compete at a major event in Australia, spotted him. She told him about Hayward and said she thought he had the talent to do very well at the Lumberjack World Championships. As it turned out, as far as sports scouting achievements go, this was like the New York Yankees spotting Mickey Mantle on an Oklahoma sandlot.

"Tina was doing a logrolling demonstration, and she saw the potential I had," Wynyard said. "She told me I had to get over to Hayward."

Wynyard stands 6 feet, 4 inches, and although he has trimmed down and muscled up, in 1996, during his first lumberjack stateside foray, he weighed 300 pounds.

"Thankfully for me, I'm big anyway," Wynyard said. "But it seems to be a sport that lends itself to bigger guys. You tend to have a little bit of an advantage over the smaller guys when you know how to use your weight."

Wynyard listened to Scheer's advice and planned an ambitious tour. Arriving in the late North American spring, Wynyard made his continental debut in British Columbia. He competed extensively throughout Canada and got into the Stihl series. By the time Hayward came around on the schedule in late July he was not quite the unknown he had been when he stepped off his flight on Air New Zealand.

It was a good thing that Wynyard was successful quickly because his plane ticket cost about two thousand dollars. When he mentions that figure, Wynyard hears gasps but then amends his expenditure to twelve hundred American dollars. It was not simply the outlay of cash that worried Wynyard. He had committed to a three-month trip, yet prize money was measured in the hundreds and he didn't know if he could even recoup his investment. Beyond that, Wynyard's job driving a concrete truck evaporated. He did not have enough vacation or leave time accrued to cover his planned absence, so he quit.

"I couldn't get much time off," Wynyard said. "It was a big gamble. There's no guarantee of making any money. There was pressure there. I'd already done reasonably well in New Zealand and Australia. I'd already won major titles. But I hadn't ventured off to the United States."

A professional athlete in another sport might be drafted by a team and given a contract that takes care of his needs. Timber sports resemble professional sports like golf and tennis where winnings are performance based. If a professional team sports athlete on a hockey or football team gets hurt, he goes on the team's injured list and continues to collect his salary. If an individual in golf, tennis, or timber sports gets hurt, he or she is out of luck. No play, no pay. And even if there is no injury to sideline the athlete an off day can be very costly. If a timber sports athlete places seventh in an event, he or she might not earn a nickel or perhaps a paltry fifty dollars.

While Tony Wise did his best to take care of his boys with room and board and the like, there are no major flat-fee appearance payments for timber sports athletes the way there are at some golf or tennis tournaments. And in 1996 Wynyard wasn't well enough known outside his own region to command such a fee anyway.

"It's not like someone is paying you to come over," Wynyard said. "It's not like you've got a job here and you're guaranteed X amount of dollars every week. It's kind of a leap of faith really. You've got to take your equipment over and rely on your own ability. It was pretty tough."

It was mentally tough, perhaps, but not physically. From his first appearance on the chopping dock in Hayward, Wynyard was the sensation from down under. He entered a lot of events and won a lot of events. He was an unknown at the Lumberjack World Championships no more, carting home as many trophies as could be handled in his luggage. As it turned out, Wynyard was better than he thought at timber sports. He made friends quickly in Hayward with his prowess and low-key, friendly manner highlighted by his appealing accent.

That year Wynyard won the standing and underhand block chops for the first time. His broad shoulders and muscular arms gave him the appearance of an NFL linebacker, and he quickly made it clear that he was pretty good at pulverizing wood.

"It was nice to know that I'd be able to survive for the time here and also be able to take a little bit of money home," Wynyard said. "It was really worthwhile."

Understatement is also part of Wynyard's repertoire. The culmination of his three-month sojourn to the United States in 1996 was the kickoff to one of the most decorated careers in Lumberjack World Championships history.

With his win in the 2010 championships in Hayward, Wynyard could claim twelve straight all-around titles. He was not the best in every event he tried, but he won most of his events and placed highly in the others. No one could touch him for high-level consistency.

At that point, Wynyard owned seven men's single buck sawing crowns. This is a one-man show event, man against a white pine log 20 inches in diameter to see how fast he can slice through to the other side and drop a round disk onto the ground. The world record is owned by Dion Lane, Wynyard's brother-in-law and toughest competitor. Lane has five single buck sawing titles, and his record of 10.78 seconds was set in 2006.

For the finals in 2009, Wynyard set himself in position, legs spread, eyes riveted on the log, and when the official yelled, "Go!" he was finished almost before the echo of the shout faded. Wynyard was the champ. His time was 11.01 seconds, a deep intake of breath shy of Lane's record and a whopping 2.35 seconds ahead of Brad Selosa.

When Wynyard and Lane, who did not compete in 2009, teamed up, they were nearly unbeatable in the men's double buck sawing event, winning in 2003, 2005, 2007, and 2008. When Wynyard linked up with his wife Karmyn they also scored big with five Jack & Jill wins.

For more than a decade, Wynyard and fellow New Zealander Dave Bolstad staged duels in the sun in the springboard chop. Between 1997 and 2009 Bolstad won eight times and Wynyard four. In the standing block chop between 1996 and 2010, Bolstad won two titles and Wynyard eleven. Between 1996 and 2010, Bolstad won the underhand block chop six times and Wynyard six times. The rivalry was intense.

More than fifteen years after his first visit to Hayward, Wynyard looked back at himself in 1996 as a different person. He has ultimate confidence. He has sponsors. He is married to Karmyn, who conveniently works for Air New Zealand so they can buy discount plane tickets to the United States each summer and afford to bring their children with them, too.

"The first three or four years I paid full price, and that was pretty tough," Wynyard said.

From his tentative beginnings, taking a risk on his future based on Tina Scheer's encouragement, Wynyard has become as much of an institution in Hayward as the boom run.

"I never thought it would end up like this," Wynyard said.

Teased that he probably took Karmyn woodchopping on their first date, Jason said that's almost how it happened. The two met at lumberjack championships in New Zealand soon after she returned from college in Alaska. They kept seeing one another and talking at the competitions. Next thing you knew they were sawyer and wife—or sawyer and sawyer, more accurately.

"She was a really good competitor as well," Wynyard said. "She started out sawing, and the Jack & Jill was her strongest event."

That may have planted the seed for a merger. While it seems sawing with your life partner can be fun, it's not always as easy as it seems from a distance.

"We've struggled with the training, and we kind of had these arguments," Wynyard said. "It's always difficult when you're sawing with your wife. It also makes it more rewarding when you do win together. It's a team effort. You can't say one person's doing all the work because they're not. You've got to work together with the saw, and it's really rewarding when you can break a world record or win a world championship together."

The Wynyards have three children age sixteen, six, and two. The kids have taken an interest in lumberjack sports already, especially Tai, the eldest. The middle boy, Tautoko, is years removed from competition, but he, like Tai, has shown that he is intrigued by lumberjack sports and the idea of following in his daddy's footsteps.

"Both of them are really interested in the sport," Wynyard said. "They want to have a chop every time I go out to train. So I let them have a little bit of a hack on a log. I've got a small ax for the six year old with a shorter handle. It's a regular ax, it's not plastic. And the older boy just uses a full-sized ax. But they're not really ready for competition.

"At first it was just, 'Go, Daddy!' I think my older boy understands how everything works with points and how you've got to do well in all the events to win the overall prize."

Wynyard is a true-blue New Zealander, but Hayward has become a second home. When in the area he stays with a longtime friend in Seely, about twenty miles away, and he even has American sponsorship now, something critical to being able to afford to bring his family with him for months at a time. Without the backup sponsorship and the prize money he wins, Wynyard might be forced to travel alone and be separated from his family.

The annual journey from New Zealand to Wisconsin, where he is based for much of the summer, is one long commute. Wynyard's trip begins in Auckland. He flies about twelve hours to Los Angeles, switches planes for

Minneapolis, another three-hour flight, and then drives the approximately 150 miles from Minnesota to Hayward in about three hours.

"I kind of play it by ear," Wynyard said. "I've been really lucky with the arrangements."

The recent recession has had an effect on timber sports, and some competitions have shut down. In the two months leading up to the Hayward championships in 2009, Wynyard entered only two events, in Columbus, Georgia, and Utah. In the years prior to that he was able to find competition almost every weekend.

It might be as he passes thirty-five that Wynyard can gain from a less hectic schedule since he competes year-round. The alternating summers in the northern and southern hemispheres mean that Wynyard does not have to choose between timber sports competitions at home and in the United States.

"I have about a month off from competition," Wynyard said. "Around November we start our [New Zealand] competition season."

Wynyard has become such a regular long-distance traveler that he has developed a plan to minimize hassles on airlines. Since the terrorist attacks of September 11, 2001, air carriers have become extremely sensitive about the transport of goods that might be construed as weapons, and certainly axes and saws, with their sharp blades, fit that description.

"I've seen so many big changes in the way you fly and carry equipment," Wynyard said. "It's really tightened security. It's a lot tougher."

Wynyard follows a meticulous routine in his travel planning. His first major change was to leave numerous axes, saws, and other implements of his trade behind in storage in Wisconsin. But he must always update the equipment and replace axes and saws that are wearing out.

The first thing Wynyard does when planning to leave New Zealand, besides pack everything up tight, is to inform his carrier that he is flying to the United States with saws and axes because he is a timber sports competitor. When he explains the situation in advance, Wynyard says, things go pretty smoothly.

"I still try to bring four to six axes every season and to circulate my equipment to make sure I've got the best stuff [in the United States]," he said. "Then there are chainsaws. I built a big, modified hot saw back in New Zealand and had to ship that over to the United States by FedEx. That kind of stuff it's normally better to ship over. You can only take so much weight on the planes anyway. That thing weighed like seventy pounds, so it had to be shipped. And then the crosscut saw's pretty difficult to carry. Sometimes I like to ship those over FedEx. FedEx is actually really good with equipment."

Of course, Wynyard can't afford to send too many hot saws because the shipping charges aren't cheap. It cost about five hundred dollars just to ship that one hot saw to himself.

"It's pretty expensive," Wynyard said. "Shipping's really gone through the roof. The thing is, even if you take your crosscut saws and axes on the plane sometimes they get damaged. So a lot of the time you are better off shipping them FedEx even though it costs a lot more money."

Even with all his efforts to foster understanding for timber sports, Wynyard has experienced some airline hassles. Once in a great while someone asks, "What's in the box?" And once, flying from New Zealand to the United States, Wynyard had a conversation with an airline official that was almost as heated as the hot saw.

"I had one guy try to say to me, 'Those are weapons.' I said, 'They're not weapons, they're sporting equipment.' I had a little bit of a heated discussion with him. This was about three years ago."

When it comes to transporting goods and equipment, Wynyard has a different list of items to declare on his way back to New Zealand—a lot of trophies and plaques. Sometimes they weigh more than the axes and saws.

"It does add up," Wynyard admitted. "It's really difficult. I have them put on a shipping container. It's cheaper. When I first came over to the U.S. all of the competitions had plaques for first place, but they also had them for second place. So I ended up with quite a lot of plaques. These days only the major competitions have them. I can usually get them in my luggage. That's not too bad, and they are nice things to have."

In order to compete, Wynyard has to invest thousands of dollars to buy the proper equipment and thousands more for travel. Yet he only competes for purses that pay in the range of eight hundred dollars for first place. The total purse for all events at Hayward in 2009 was fifty thousand dollars. Being a professional timber sports competitor is not an easy way to riches no matter how good you are.

Those who compete for the major sports franchises in the United States, playing basketball, basketball, football, and hockey, all make six-figure salaries at a minimum, and many of the top all-stars become multi-millionaires. Wynyard is to lumberjacking what Albert Pujols is to baseball, Peyton Manning is to football, Sidney Crosby is to hockey, and LeBron

James is to basketball. He is at the top of the heap. He is just not compensated in any manner, shape, or form that can compare to those sports stars. He reads newspapers when he is in the United States and knows how many millions those gentlemen sign contracts for each time they come up for renewal.

"It absolutely blows my mind," Wynyard said. "It really does. I think I've said a couple of times to some of the guys, if our sport just got half of what one person in Major League Baseball has made, we'd be really happy."

What would the timber sports worldwide prize money be? He doesn't know specifically, but he knows that it doesn't compare.

"It's pretty pathetic," Wynyard said. "The purses aren't very big, and they are spread out among all of the competitors. It's pretty low, but we're not in it for the money, you know. Even though I do it professionally."

Given that Wynyard can span the globe more readily than just about anyone else because of his access to discount airline tickets and being based in opposite hemispheres so he can compete in continuous summer, he can name no other full-time professional lumberjack competitor.

"I think I'm probably the only one, actually," he said. "None of the other guys in Hayward do. The other guys are holding down jobs. I feel really lucky. I really enjoy the sport and I feel fortunate to be able to come over to the U.S. and compete at what I love doing. We do it for pride. For pride and just to see who is the best man."

Wynyard recognizes that without Karmyn's job he would likely not be a full-time pro. "It's the only way I can travel and afford to do this. So we're really fortunate."

But as Wynyard was passing into his late thirties, an age when most athletes start to lose some of their youthful vigor, he was wondering how long he would be able to keep up his pace.

"I think age is starting to become a factor," he said. "I'm noticing it. I'm noticing it's a lot tougher to get ready and the body is a lot slower to recover after training. Training for me is just duplicating the events at home."

The home lumberjack kit includes having "a whole bunch of wood" handy for chopping or sawing. He knows he must practice to maintain proficiency, but the motions of the saw and ax threaten the muscles with repetitive strain injuries.

It was in 2008 that for the first time Wynyard felt his body start to rebel against the motions that had made his reputation. This was hard to acknowledge, as it would be for any successful athlete. He had to question and revamp his methods. There is reluctance to change what has worked all along, but there is a reality issue, too, facing the truth that the body might break down without change.

"There's a lot of jarring going on," Wynyard said. "There's a lot of impact, and I think after years of that it really takes a toll on your body. I feel it in my shoulders, arms, the tendons of the forearms. We use the forearms a lot when we're chopping. As I got older I tried to come up with new ideas for training. I'm not doing as much woodchopping in preparation. I've been mixing my training, doing a lot more cardio work, getting my weight down. I'm probably doing a quarter of the amount of woodchopping that I normally did."

It is not difficult for Wynyard to view his accommodation to age and his adaptation to circumstances in the same manner as a baseball pitcher. Pitchers might not be able to rely as much on the fastball, so they add a trickier off-speed pitch to their repertoire.

"I think change is really important in any sport," Wynyard said. "You've got to be in decent shape, and I think if you're doing the same thing repetitively, day after day for years, it takes a toll eventually. It's been a good discovery for me to find out that I can get by without doing as much woodchopping as I used to do."

Wynyard has been part of the scene and an overwhelming champion for more than a decade, so it is easy to forget he is only in his mid-thirties. But his résumé, his record, raises the issue of whether or not timber sports fans are watching the greatest all-around lumberjack competitor of all time.

"He would never say that," Karmyn Wynyard said. "He's very humble. He's very passionate about the sport, and he does everything he can do to make himself the best he can be."

Still, winning twelve straight all-around titles speaks very loudly. The time represented by those victories is more than a decade straight of excellence in a half-century-old event, so certainly if one could line up the greatest all-time timber sports stars in Hayward, Wynyard would be in the picture. There have been many great specialists who excel at one event or two. There have been only a handful of lumberjacks who have repeatedly won the coveted all-around award more than a few times. Ron Hartill, the muscular man who engendered excitement for competing without a shirt, won the all-around seven times in a row between 1974 and 1980. Mel Lentz won the all-around nine times between 1981 and 1994. His father Merv won it four times between 1967 and 1971, and venerable Dave Geer won it four times between 1964 and 1973. Matt Bush won three times in a row between 1996 and 1998.

But Wynyard has surpassed them all in all-around honors won. Maybe in cheers, too.

Dennis Daun, the now retired Illinois lumberjack who has followed developments in Hayward for years, acknowledges that there is a very solid case for Wynyard and that his accumulation of triumphs in Hayward seems untouchable.

"Eleven years in a row?" Daun said of Jason Wynyard's all-around championships in 2009. "You can't knock him. Dave Bolstad is probably the best chopper ever. In 2008, I think, he was straining so hard swinging the ax that he busted a tooth out. Jason, he's the best all-around. Jason's a very good competitor. It's a lifestyle for him in New Zealand. That gives him a real good advantage. He's the rare athlete where it's his life."

Daun also refuses to dismiss Australian Dave Foster. Foster came to Hayward just once and has built an impeccable record on the other side of the world, but while all of the other lumberjacks have gathered in one place, he has gone his own way.

Even Diane McNamer, executive director of the World Lumberjack Association, gives Foster his due. "Huge legend," she said. "Huge man. He could just chop forever."

Mike Sullivan, the Connecticut lumberjack, said it is very difficult to say who is the greatest all-around timber sports athlete of all because contenders competed in different eras.

"You really can't compare," Sullivan said, "but Melvin Lentz is really the best I've ever seen. David Bolstad and Jason Wynyard, they're pretty awesome. They're good, but Melvin in his day, versus David and Jason in their day, which is now, well, Melvin was very tough. He could do it all. Jason's close."

Wynyard, Daun predicted, could be the first "million-dollar lumberjack." If he does so it will be because he has built his fortune one log at a time in dozens upon dozens of competitions rather than with one major payoff.

Wynyard never expected to win the all-around trophy year after year. He reached twelve straight titles in 2010.

Still, Wynyard laughed at the idea that anyone would say he was the greatest lumberjack sports athlete of all time.

"I don't think so," Wynyard said. "I think there's been different guys throughout the years that have been the best in the era, and I don't think I'm the best that ever was. I'm just someone who does this for the love of it, and I get to make a bit of a living out of it. It's a pretty meager living, but we survive and I work together with my wife to make things happen."

That said, aches and pains and aging muscles notwithstanding, Wynyard doesn't see himself retiring soon. In 2009, Dave Geer competed in the masters underhand chop at eighty-four. Wynyard does not picture himself making such an encore appearance in fifty years, though.

"I don't know if I'll be going that long," Wynyard said. "He's a trouper. I'd like to think I can do it for another twenty years."

Another twenty years would be two lifetimes' worth of careers, too many axes and saws to count flying across the ocean, too many trophies and plaques to fit into luggage. Maybe by then the question of who is greatest will be settled. Or maybe there will be a new kid on the block from Wisconsin, New Zealand, or Australia whose finest efforts will be compared to Jason Wynyard's.

Tony Wise Lives On

If he were still alive, a smile would have crossed Tony Wise's face every time the words "Yo-ho!" were announced at the Lumberjack Bowl during the Lumberjack World Championships in 2009.

Each pronouncement of "Yo-ho!" would be a reminder that he got it right, that his idea to bring the championships to Hayward, Wisconsin, was a smart move, a bold move, and that fifty years later the premise and execution of the annual gathering of the best timber sports athletes in the world were still sound.

Just what overall attitude Wise would have brought to a fiftieth-anniversary celebration of his vision is unclear, however, because things did not end well for him from a business standpoint.

Wise was indeed a visionary, returning to Hayward after World War II with big ideas and big talk that he could back up. He gave the town Historyland, the Lumberjack World Championships, the Telemark Ski Lodge, and the American Birkebeiner and did his utmost to put Hayward on the tourist map as the focal point of the United States' most important distance ski race and a mecca for lumberjack competition. The shouts of "Yo-ho!" would always be sweet music to Wise.

In the same manner that Wise nearly burst with new ideas, once he got something new up and going he could not contain himself, could not hold back, and wanted to make it bigger and better. For that reason he became financially overextended and in a bitter denouement, after all of his hard work, he was forced into bankruptcy and lost his holdings and the projects dearest to him.

When he died on April 6, 1995, at the age of seventy-four, Wise was by most accounts soured by what had happened to him. Rather than being able to step back and admire all of the good he had done, and what he had accomplished to boost his home community, Wise was distraught at the end, angry about his losses, and unable to reconcile the balance between the financial bath he took with what should have been thriving enterprises.

One admirer is Fred Scheer, whose life has been linked to the Lumberjack World Championships in many ways, from youthful competitor to aging businessman. As the owner of the Lumberjack Bowl and the adjacent popular breakfast location, the Pancake House, Scheer even acquired some of Wise's holdings.

"Tony's got a legacy, for sure," Scheer said. "You certainly can't dispute his legacy. He put Hayward on the map."

That phrase, "put Hayward on the map," is used over and over again to describe Tony Wise. That was his goal, and he succeeded beyond most expectations.

Wise had an infectious way of selling his ideas. He had the grand vision and convinced others that what he was doing was going to work. He recruited volunteers and helpers and jump-started a Hayward can-do attitude.

"He had tremendous enthusiasm," Scheer said. "You don't get that kind of stuff done without getting other people onboard. He was the idea dude. He had a team behind him that got it done. Tony had a gigantic presence."

Scheer said some skeptics always thought Wise was making money hand over fist and squirreling away his profits—a belief proven incorrect. Scheer never viewed Wise in that manner. He did not believe that Wise worked so hard, dreamed so big, just to make money.

"He was certainly more motivated by ego than dollars and cents," Scheer said. "He was about the fame. He was a driven guy. I don't know if Tony had another big idea in his bag when he died, but he never slowed down, he never stopped thinking."

Wise was a promoter extraordinaire. He painted in bright colors on large canvases, and in many cases he left the details to be filled in by more technically oriented people. Wise was the kind of guy who would announce that he would "make it happen" and then call on others to take care of the nitty-gritty part of the planning. Whatever "it" was, however, it did happen.

Wise got the Lumberjack World Championships off the ground in 1960, and he was around to nurture it, observe its growth, and preside over its doings for most of the next thirty-five years until his death. Wise was the promoter type who worked the telephone to get what he needed, and his gift of gab persuaded more than one doubter that his plans were sound. They were sound. He had good ideas, great ideas, and he brought them to fruition. Wise delivered.

In the case of the Lumberjack World Championships, Wise knew his audience. Hayward was an epicenter of logging in the late nineteenth and early twentieth centuries, so what better place for lumberjacks to gather? The old-time links to the north woods were inescapable, and Hayward needed an infusion of something fresh to bring tourists to town. Let them catch muskies when they got there. Let them spend money in restaurants and on hotel rooms. All well and good. But let's give them something they've never seen before, too, and make sure they go home talking about the experience and wanting to come back.

The suggestion to bring the best lumberjacks to Hayward was inspired. There were regional and local lumberjack showdowns, but nothing was being held on such a grand scale in the United States. There was no timber sports union or clearinghouse to determine who was the best and convince them there was no finer place in the world to be than Hayward in late July.

Shyness would have been a handicap in Wise's business. In an era long before cell phones, he operated with a phone glued to his ear. If he didn't know someone, he found someone who did and could act as an intermediary. What Wise so shrewdly did in recruiting his initial group of lumberjacks was turn his first converts into salesmen for him. Soon enough, he had some of the most famous guys in the sport doing the work for him, telling other lumberjacks they just had to come to Hayward.

Dave Geer, one of the championships' early stars, played that role to the hilt, rounding up the usual suspects almost before they were the usual suspects. Axmen were recruited on the basis of their reputations, but the reputations proved to be solid.

There was always a buzz around Wise, almost as if he were followed by a swarm of bees. He exuded enthusiasm and energy, and it rubbed off on others.'

"He was a great man," Arden Cogar Sr. said of Wise. "He's the one who made the show."

Dave Geer put his faith in Wise. Geer was one of the first athletes telephoned, and he remembers Wise laying out the idea. "I'm interested in getting a lumberjack championship started," is the way Geer recalls Wise stating his case.

Geer flew to Minneapolis, about 150 miles from Hayward, wondering if he was really going to be picked up by this stranger he knew only over the telephone but sensed was on the up-and-up with a proposal that could be great for lumberjack athletes. "He was there to drive me to Hayward," Geer said.

Using Geer as a conduit to athletes he didn't know, Wise issued straightforward, optimistic marching orders as he turned over his telephone to the newcomer to the north woods. Geer has said it before, and he said it again fifty years into the lumberjack championships: "Tony Wise wanted to have the best."

It became clear to Geer immediately that Wise was sincere, and even after the first few lumberjack championships were held, word of mouth spread, and *Wide World of Sports* started televising the games, the bottom-line element that made Hayward such a popular place to visit was simple. "This is where the lumberjack was king," Geer said. "Tony was striving for perfection. He goddamn wanted to shock the world—which he did."

Wise did not operate on a shoestring. If he knew that a lumberjack star lived thousands of miles away and would enhance the lineup in Hayward, he went after him and paid his travel expenses.

"He wouldn't spare any expense to get the best in the world," Geer said. "He had some happy times after it was going. He knew it was the best. He was a great promoter."

In Ron Hartill's memory, Wise was a whirlwind promoter. The shirtless wonder called Wise "a great guy, a fun guy." That was whenever he sat still to talk.

Mel Lentz, the nine-time all-around lumberjack award winner, also got his time in the limelight through the Lumberjack World Championships, and said Wise treated him "first class all of the way," from transportation to taking care of his food and lodging in Hayward.

The crowds came and filled the Lumberjack Bowl, and the competition still plays to twelve thousand people during a weekend of events.

"Oh, he'd really be pleased," Lentz said. "He had a vision like that."

"Yo-ho!"

Judy Hoeschler said when she was a youngster she heard that Wise had set up a dry log spinning on an axle for kids to use.

"I was intrigued by that," she said. Her friendship with the Wise kids led her to play on the log before she got involved in logrolling in a more serious way. Wise, she said, seemed to innately recognize the appeal of logrolling because he always hired a talented female logroller to give exhibitions in the water.

"It was for the patrons of the Pancake House," Hoeschler said. "She was a dynamic, dynamic roller."

Hoeschler expressed admiration for Wise using a phrase commonly applied to him: "The man had such vision," she said. "What he had was a deep love of history. He loved the history of this area. He was a brilliant promoter. He wanted to create an event that would recall the history."

Dave Geer was probably the first lumberjack sports individual to suggest that Hayward erect a statue of Wise. But Hoeschler is out there making the case, too. "I'd really like to see a statue of Tony put up in downtown Hayward. He was an unselfish man. He didn't have a Swiss bank account. He put everything back into his projects. He was ahead of his time. He was bigger than life in a place that's hard to make a living."

Wise rolled with the ups and downs of entrepreneurship, but when deteriorating finances led him to court and the loss of Telemark and the Lumberjack World Championships, he did not bounce back.

"He was a very bitter man when he lost all this," Hoeschler said. "He had a huge ego, and it was very hard to lose this."

The same traits that enabled Wise to establish colorful, popular, enduring businesses that lured tourists and engendered pride in the Hayward area cost him in the end. He couldn't leave well enough alone and was determined to keep expanding. Wise's fatal mistake was investing in the construction of a coliseum in 1980. He had overextended his finances when a series of lean snow winters reduced traffic at Telemark. So at the same time Wise was struggling to stay afloat because of his expenditures, his steady income producer was faltering. He didn't have the cash to keep everything going and filed for bankruptcy in 1987. He could no longer spin the logs, and he took a dunking.

Liquidation of his prized properties wounded Wise. There was a sense that he had been wronged after all of the good things he had done for Hayward. After his death, one of his daughters, Fran, donated a large cache of Wise's papers to the Wisconsin Historical Society. These include personal papers and photographs and background materials on his pet projects, from Historyland and the Telemark Lodge to the American Birkebeiner and the Lumberjack World Championships.

Diane McNamer, who married a logroller, met Wise in the 1970s and admired his spirit. She is not sure why, but some people always doubted the long-term success of Wise's endeavors. "Maybe it's because you can't be a prophet in your own land," she said. "If you come from outside you appreciate it more."

Wise lived long enough that most of the early Lumberjack World Championships contestants would have had the opportunity to meet him. But he died long enough ago that most of the younger ones never did. Peg Engasser fits in that category. She never met Wise, but feels she owes him.

"I'm grateful to Tony for bringing his vision to reality," she said. "Although we never met, I think he must have been a big-picture thinker who didn't let the obstacles get in the way of his dream. In that way he is someone we can look to as a model—he did it, and we can, too, whatever 'it' is."

In 2009, to commemorate the fiftieth Lumberjack World Championships competition in Hayward, Wise got his statue. Sort of. It is not in the form of a life-sized bronze, but it is a tribute to the man who brought the ax-swinging, sawing world to Hayward.

The new addition, which stands outside the fencing at the Lumberjack Bowl, is less statue than sculpture. It is accompanied by a sign reading, "In 1960, the Lumberjack World Championships began here at the Lumberjack Bowl, the brainchild of Hayward businessman Tony Wise. A celebration of both our American heritage and the logging history of this area. This sculpture will serve as a visual legacy of our history for future generations to come."

Mounted on a three-legged wooden tripod is a steel globe with a man perched on top. It is Tony Wise on top of the world.

JR Salzman on a Roll

In 2008, JR Salzman wanted to have the feel of the logs under his feet as he fought through his recovery after being wounded in Iraq. He had been a six-time logrolling titleholder at the Lumberjack World Championships and the 2005 ESPN outdoor sportsman of the year.

But the Lumberjack in a Desert, as he dubbed himself after being sent to Iraq, fared poorly and he wondered if he would ever regain the innate sense of balance that had made him a standout in this popular event.

"He wasn't ready," said his mother, Bonnie Salzman. "His attitude was, 'If I do well, OK.'"

That's how Salzman talked, anyway. However, his riveting concentration, one of the attributes that made him a success, was out of kilter. In the past, when Salzman was on the log, spinning to dunk someone, he had been able to block out almost all sound. The one exception was his sister Tina's voice. His logrolling mentor could always cut through the white noise with her words.

"Last year," Bonnie said in 2009, "he heard everything."

Salzman had not regained the power to block out distractions. But after another year of rehabilitation and regaining strength, he returned to Hayward in 2009 with a little bit more ambition. He won his early matches, and on Saturday night, the second day of the competition, he dispatched Brian Bartow, the preeminent pole climber, in three straight falls. Was JR back?

While Salzman was at war and during the aftermath, coping with his wounds, Jamie Fischer won the logrolling title in 2006 and Darren Hudson won the title in 2007 and 2008. They were the guys to beat in 2009. It was a lineup of champions. There could be only one winner, and one wouldn't even make it to the finals. Nothing was guaranteed for Salzman.

If the logrolling competitors are so evenly matched that no one takes a tumble into the water, officials blow a whistle and halt the proceedings. They then substitute a smaller, 12-inch log to increase the challenge. Twice Salzman and Hudson climbed on their starting log and pulled out every trick they knew. Yet neither stumbled, and time elapsed. On a new log, Hudson made a move, and Salzman tumbled into the water.

They battled again, spinning the log, balancing with arms in the air, staring at one another's feet, trying to detect weakness or a hint of slippage. Hudson attacked, and Salzman fell into the pond again. It was 2-0 Hudson with Salzman looking doomed. His supporters had to be thinking, "Well, nice run" with a sense of resignation.

Even worse, Salzman's artificial arm was giving him trouble. It loosened and appeared poised to fall off. He worried it would fly off into the water or the crowd. Salzman adjusted the arm, an unusual injury time out, to be sure.

Back on the log they went, and this time Salzman made the critical move, dropping Hudson into the water. The suspense grew. It seemed unlikely that Salzman could rebound, but he did. Down went Hudson twice and the score was 2-2. Tina Salzman Bosworth could not contain her emotions. She yelled, "Put him down again!" In the next round, time elapsed for another draw. During a break, Tina came down to the dock and offered coaching advice.

"I told him to be steady," she said, "to keep his shoulders down and roll smart. I told him, 'It will be alright.'" In what felt like an eternity ago by then, when Salzman was bleeding in that Humvee, he had given himself the very same message.

She was right. It took eight rolls to decide the best three out of five, but Salzman prevailed. For him, it was a milestone victory in his newly revamped body.

"Tina told me what I needed to hear," Salzman said. "I was so hyped up. I was doing a lot of dances. She said to 'Go out there and play the game and calm down.'"

Given how close Salzman was to defeat, it was difficult to believe that he had advanced to the Sunday finale where he would face Fischer for the championship.

Salzman kept to himself getting ready for the title match, with headphones on listening to a punk rock band. His wife Josie was nearby. His mom and dad had staked out good seats near the logrolling start. Tina was in the grandstand.

In a pattern similar to the showdown with Hudson, Salzman fell behind 2-0 and seemed on the verge of settling for silver. Yet again, the man who had faced daunting odds rallied. Once again thousands watched a JR Salzman comeback. He took a roll and trailed 2-1. The suspense was intense. JR was a local boy, a homegrown Hayward guy who had been a crowd favorite before he went to war. He had given so much and now was trying to regain a part of his identity so important to him. Another roll. Salzman won again, and the score was 2-2. The circumstances were improbable—he was back in the game—but now it was anything goes.

One more roll and Salzman's comeback would be complete. Salzman and Fischer stood at opposite ends of the log, balancing on its curve as it floated in the water, four thousand pairs of eyes on them. Some fans yelled encouragement. Some fans were hushed. Two champion logrollers going head-to-head. And then it was over, one man down in the water and one man, the last man, still standing.

JR Salzman had captured his seventh lumberjack world championship crown in logrolling. Yo-ho!

Then, Salzman willingly plunged into the water. He shook hands—lefty—with Fischer, swam to the dock, leaned his head down on the boards, and let tears roll down his face. Tina burst from the crowd, knelt down next to Salzman, and patted him on the head. The fans erupted with cheers, clapping, screaming, and shouting his name.

He was back, back in so many ways.

"It was probably the most touching moment I'll ever have in logrolling, even though I lost," Fischer said. "It was emotionally pretty intense. It was back and forth. I know I did my best. I never trained harder in my life. It was so close."

Salzman joked later, "Why can't I win one three straight?" He also revealed how perilously close he had come to having his artificial arm disengage. He had taped it back in place. The victory was overwhelming for him.

"It's huge," Salzman said. "It's a culmination of everything that I've been through. Two and a half years ago I'm lying in a Humvee in Iraq bleeding out."

Only a short time passed before it was Salzman's turn to accept his championship trophy before the largest grandstand on the chopping dock. When his award was presented, Salzman held the trophy aloft, and the spectators rose and applauded, delivering a standing ovation that wouldn't quit.

When things finally quieted, Salzman started to cry as he began to talk. He couldn't get the words in his heart out at first. "Pardon me while I take a moment," he said. He said "Thank you" and choked up. He tried to tell a story and choked up. He said "Thank you" again and choked up. Salzman mentioned a friend in Iraq who didn't make it home and said the logrolling victory was for the sergeant.

As Salzman walked away, the fans rose again and gave him another standing ovation. Those annoying tears kept coming.

Men's logrolling is one of the final events of the Lumberjack World Championships, and an hour later the grounds had pretty much cleared except for officials compiling the results and competitors packing up their saws and axes.

JR and Josie strolled behind the grandstand. Salzman was carrying a plastic bag filled with popcorn. When asked if that was the trophy, he laughed. "It cost me five bucks," he said. "I hadn't eaten since breakfast."

Now he was smiling, his earlier tug-at-memory emotion replaced with the glow of victory.

Word of that victory spread swiftly and was highlighted in several media outlets. The comeback of the wounded Iraqi veteran was reported across America. Visitors to the JR Salzman website were happy for the Lumberjack in a Desert. Readers of the *New York Times* got to know him. Viewers of television programs learned his story. Congratulations poured in. Even he couldn't believe he had won.

A couple of months after his triumph, when things slowed down and he was back at college, Salzman described what he had heard and from whom. "I did hear from quite a few people," he said. "My winning is pretty inspirational to people. But that was not my goal. I just wanted to do what I love."

The logroller from Wisconsin who had been torn apart in Iraq was made whole in a way only he could understand. Despite all of the terrible things he had endured, JR Salzman was champion of the world in his favorite event once again.

And a year after this magnificent triumph, Salzman won again in the summer of 2010, claiming his eighth world title. He also learned anew about the sweetness of life as he and Josie had a baby. It was easy to envision Salzman, arm wrapped around the shoulder of his youngster maybe a few years down the road. Just maybe they'll be sitting in the grandstand at the Lumberjack Bowl when some hotshot teenager with great balance makes a show out of winning the logrolling.

And JR Salzman will say, "I used to do that. I used to do that better than anyone in the world."

Appendix: Lumberjack World Championships Winners

Men's Events

Tony Wise All-Around Champion

2010 Jason Wynyard
2009 Jason Wynyard
2008 Jason Wynyard
2007 Jason Wynyard
2006 Jason Wynyard
2005 Jason Wynyard
2004 Jason Wynyard
2003 Jason Wynyard
2002 Jason Wynyard
2001 Jason Wynyard
2000 Jason Wynyard
1999 Jason Wynyard
1998 Matt Bush
1997 Matt Bush
1996 Matt Bush
1995 Dave Jewett
1994 Mel Lentz
1993 Carson Bosworth

1992 Rick Halvorson
1991 Mel Lentz
1990 Mel Lentz
1989 Mel Lentz
1988 Mel Lentz
1987 Rolin Eslinger
1986 Mel Lentz
1985 David Foster
1984 Brian Trow
1983 Mel Lentz
1982 Mel Lentz
1981 Mel Lentz
1980 Ron Hartill
1979 Ron Hartill
1978 Ron Hartill
1977 Ron Hartill
1976 Ron Hartill
1975 Ron Hartill

All-Around Champion (*cont.*)

1974 Ron Hartill
1973 Dave Geer
1972 Sven Johnson
1971 Merv Lentz
1970 Clayton Stewart
1969 Merv Lentz

1968 Merv Lentz
1967 Merv Lentz
1966 Dave Geer
1965 Dave Geer
1964 Dave Geer
1963 Tom Kirk
1962 Arden Crogar Sr.

Hot Saw

World Record: David Bolstad, 5.55 seconds, 2007

2010 Jason Wynyard
2009 Jason Wynyard
2008 Mike Sullivan
2007 Mike Sullivan
2006 David Bolstad
2005 Mike Sullivan
2004 Dave Jewett
2003 Mike Sullivan
2002 Dennis Daun
2001 David Bolstad
2000 Mel Lentz
1999 Mel Lentz
1998 Matt Bush
1997 Gaston Duperre
1996 Gaston Duperre
1995 Gaston Duperre
1994 Rick Halvorson
1993 Rick Halvorson
1992 Rick Halvorson
1991 Chauncey Varney
1990 Ron Johnson
1989 Ron Johnson
1988 Mel Lentz
1987 Ron Johnson
1986 Sven Johnson

1985 Sven Johnson
1984 Sven Johnson
1983 Sven Johnson
1982 Sven Johnson
1981 Ron Johnson
1980 Ron Johnson
1979 Sven Johnson
1978 Ron Johnson
1977 Dave Geer
1976 Ron Johnson
1975 Ron Johnson
1974 Sven Johnson
1973 Dave Geer
1972 Alex Bildeaux
1971 Sven Johnson
1970 Sven Johnson
1969 Merv Lentz
1968 Bob Born
1967 Sven Johnson
1966 Gary Bradley
1965 Dave Geer
1964 Dave Geer
1963 M. Hendricks
1962 Ray Silvey
1961 Doc Parrett

Single Buck Sawing

World Record: Dion Lane, 10.78 seconds, 2006

2010 Jason Wynyard	1985 Rolin Eslinger
2009 Jason Wynyard	1984 Brian Trow
2008 Jason Wynyard	1983 Mel Lentz
2007 Dion Lane	1982 Merv Jensen
2006 Dion Lane	1981 Mel Lentz
2005 Dave Jewett	1980 Ron Hartill
2004 Dion Lane	1979 Ron Hartill
2003 Dion Lane	1978 Ron Hartill
2002 Jason Wynyard	1977 Ron Hartill
2001 Jason Wynyard	1976 Ron Hartill
2000 Dion Lane	1975 Ron Hartill
1999 Dave Jewett	1974 Ron Hartill
1998 Jason Wynyard	1973 Pete Holmquist
1997 Jason Wynyard	1972 Ede Rosemeyer
1996 Matt Bush	1971 Merv Lentz
1995 Matt Bush	1970 Dave Geer
1994 Mel Lentz	1969 Merv Lentz
1993 Carson Bosworth	1968 Merv Lentz
1992 Dave Hocquard	1967 John Miller
1991 Jack Patterson	1966 John Miller
1990 Rolin Eslinger	1965 Merv Lentz
1989 Mel Lentz	1964 Merv Lentz
1988 Bill Miller	1963 Merv Lentz
1987 Rolin Eslinger	1962 Paul Searles
1986 Rolin Eslinger	

Double Buck Sawing

World Record: Jason Wynyard and Dion Lane, 4.77 seconds, 2005

2010 Dave Jewett and J. P. Mercier	2007 Jason Wynyard and Dion Lane
2009 Dave Jewett and J. P. Mercier	2006 Dave Jewett and J. P. Mercier
2008 Jason Wynyard and Dion Lane	2005 Jason Wynyard and Dion Lane

Double Buck Sawing (*cont.*)
2004 Dave Jewett and J. P. Mercier
2003 Jason Wynyard and Dion Lane
2002 Dave Jewett and J. P. Mercier
2001 Dave Jewett and J. P. Mercier
2000 Dave Jewett and J. P. Mercier
1999 Matt Bush and Donald Lambert
1998 Rick Halvorson and Jeff Crago
1997 Dennis Daun and J. P. Mercier
1996 Matt Bush and Mike Slingerland
1995 Rick Halvorson and Jeff Crago,
    Dave Jewett and Carson Bosworth
    (tie)
1994 Mike Sullivan and Jim Colbert
1993 Giles Levesque and Gaston
    Duperre
1992 Giles Levesque and Gaston
    Duperre
1991 Matt Bush and Mike Slingerland
1990 Rolin Eslinger and Mel Lentz
1989 Mike Sullivan and Jim Colbert
1988 Mike Sullivan and Jim Colbert
1987 Jim Colbert and Jerry Scutt
1986 Jim Colbert and Jerry Scutt
1985 Rolin Eslinger and Rudy Dettmer
1984 Brian Trow and Cliff Hughes

1983 Alastair Taylor and Brian Herlihy
1982 Alastair Taylor and Eyler Adams
1981 Merv Jensen and Cliff Hughes
1980 Merv Jensen and Cliff Hughes
1979 Sven Johnson and Ron Johnson
1978 Ron Hartill and Merv Jensen
1977 Ron Hartill and Merv Jensen
1976 Dave Geer and Rudy Dettmer
1975 Dave Geer and Rudy Dettmer
1974 Sven Johnson and Ron Johnson
1973 Sven Johnson and Ron Johnson
1972 Sven Johnson and Ron Mahon
1971 Sven Johnson and Merv Jensen
1970 Sven Johnson and Clayton Street
1969 Dave Geer and Cliff Pitaim
1968 Sven Johnson and Gib Engel
1967 Merv Lentz and John Miller
1966 Dave Geer and Gib Engel
1965 John Miller and M. Hedrichs
1964 Arden Cogar Sr. and Vic Hewett
1963 Tom Kirk and Bill Johnson
1962 Paul Searles and Max Searles
1961 Arden Cogar Sr. and Benny
    Cogar
1960 Eli Miljevich and Vernon
    Miljevich

Springboard Chop

World Record: David Bolstad, 41.15 seconds, 2003

2010 Laurence O'Toole
2009 Jason Wynyard
2008 Jason Wynyard
2007 Jason Wynyard
2006 David Bolstad
2005 David Bolstad

2004 Jason Wynyard
2003 David Bolstad
2002 David Bolstad
2001 David Bolstad
2000 David Bolstad
1999 David Bolstad

1998 Matt Bush
1997 David Bolstad
1996 Carson Bosworth
1995 Mel Lentz
1994 Mel Lentz
1993 John Gossow
1992 Carson Bosworth
1991 Mark Etcheberry
1990 Mark Etcheberry
1989 Martin O'Toole
1988 Mark Etcheberry
1987 Martin O'Toole

1986 Martin O'Toole
1985 Bill Youd
1984 Mel Lentz
1983 George Quigg
1982 Brian Herlihy
1981 Rudy Dettmer
1980 Ron Hartill
1979 Ron Hartill
1978 Brian Herlihy
1977 Ron Hartill
1976 Owen Smith

Standing Block Chop

World Record: Jason Wynyard, 18.33 seconds, 1998

2010 Jason Wynyard
2009 Jason Wynyard
2008 Jason Wynyard
2007 David Bolstad
2006 Arden Cogar Jr.
2005 Dion Lane
2004 Jason Wynyard
2003 Jason Wynyard
2002 Jason Wynyard
2001 Jason Wynyard
2000 David Bolstad
1999 Jason Wynyard
1998 Jason Wynyard
1997 Jason Wynyard
1996 Jason Wynyard
1995 Mel Lentz
1994 Mel Lentz
1993 Mel Lentz
1992 Martin O'Toole
1991 Mel Lentz

1990 Mel Lentz
1989 Martin O'Toole
1988 Mel Lentz
1987 Laurence O'Toole
1986 Martin O'Toole
1987 Laurence O'Toole
1986 Martin O'Toole
1985 David Foster
1984 Brian Trow
1983 Jim Alexander
1982 Jim Alexander
1981 Jim Alexander
1980 Jack Bentley
1979 Jim Wass
1978 Brian Herlihy
1977 Mark Hughes
1976 Clayton Stewart
1975 Jim Alexander
1974 Arden Cogar Sr.
1973 Arden Cogar Sr.

Standing Block Chop (*cont.*)

1972 Arden Cogar Sr.

1971 Jim Alexander

1970 Arden Cogar Sr.

1969 Brian Herlihy

1968 Brian Herlihy

1967 Brian Herlihy

1966 Clayton Stewart

1965 Clayton Stewart

1964 Clayton Stewart

1963 Tom Kirk

1962 James Rope

Underhand Block Chop

World Record: Jason Wynyard, 15.94 seconds, 2006

2010 Jason Wynyard

2009 Laurence O'Toole

2008 Jason Wynyard

2007 David Bolstad

2006 David Bolstad

2005 Jason Wynyard

2004 Jason Wynyard

2003 Jason Wynyard

2002 Dion Lane

2001 David Bolstad

2000 David Bolstad

1999 David Bolstad

1998 Dale Ryan

1997 David Bolstad

1996 Jason Wynyard

1995 Mel Lentz

1994 Mel Lentz

1993 John Gassow

1992 Martin O'Toole

1991 Mel Lentz

1990 Mel Lentz

1989 Mel Lentz

1988 Mel Lentz

1987 Laurence O'Toole

1986 Mel Lentz

1985 Laurence O'Toole

1984 Mel Lentz

1983 Mel Lentz

1982 Mel Lentz

1981 Jim Alexander

1980 Jim Wass

1979 Jose Aria

1978 Jim Alexander

1977 Arden Cogar Sr.

1976 Clayton Stewart

1975 Jim Alexander

1974 Arden Cogar Sr.

1973 Jim Alexander

1972 Brian Herlihy

1971 Jim Alexander

1970 Arden Cogar Sr.

1969 Brian Herlihy

1968 Brian Herlihy

1967 Brian Herlihy

1966 Clayton Stewart

1965 Dave Geer

1964 Clayton Stewart

1963 Tom Kirk

1962 James Rope

1961 Bill Johnson

1960 Dave Geer

Masters Underhand Block Chop

2010 Warrick Halle
2009 Laurence O'Toole
2008 Jeff Schaut
2007 Alastair Taylor
2006 Alastair Taylor
2005 Cliff Hughes
2004 Cliff Hughes
2003 Gus Carlson
2002 Napoleon Mercier
2001 Dave Geer

2000 Napoleon Mercier
1999 Giles Levesque
1998 Dave Geer
1997 Jim Colbert
1996 John Postemski
1995 Jim Colbert
1994 Dave Geer
1993 Gus Carlson
1992 Dave Geer
1991 Arden Cogar Sr.

90-Foot Pole Speed Climb

World Record: Brian Bartow, 19.87 seconds, 2006

2010 Stirling Hart
2009 Brian Bartow
2008 Brian Bartow
2007 Brian Bartow
2006 Brian Bartow
2005 Brian Bartow
2004 Brian Bartow
2003 Brian Linville
2002 Guy German
2001 Dustin Beckwith
2000 Brian Bartow
1999 Brian Bartow
1998 Sean Duffy
1997 Wade Stewart
1996 Wade Stewart
1995 Dennis Butler
1994 Sean Duffy
1993 Wade Stewart
1992 Robert Scheer
1991 Robert Scheer

1990 Guy German
1989 Robert Scheer
1988 Guy German
1987 Dennis Butler
1986 Dennis Butler
1985 Glenn Erickson
1984 Dennis Butler
1983 Ed Johnson
1982 Ed Johnson
1981 Randy Campbell
1980 Clarence Bartow
1979 Clarence Bartow
1978 Clarence Bartow
1977 Marvin Trudeau
1976 Marvin Trudeau
1975 Marvin Trudeau
1974 Marvin Trudeau
1973 Larry Downing
1972 Armand Didier
1971 Armand Didier

90-Foot Pole Speed Climb (*cont.*)
1970 Dwight Carpenter
1969 Dwight Carpenter
1968 Dwight Carpenter
1967 Dwight Carpenter
1966 Dwight Carpenter

1965 Dwight Carpenter
1964 Dwight Carpenter
1963 Kelly Stanley
1962 Danny Sailor
1961 Danny Sailor

60-Foot Pole Speed Climb

World Record: Brian Bartow, 12.33 seconds, 2005

2010 Brian Bartow
2009 Brian Bartow
2008 Brian Bartow
2007 Cassidy Scheer
2006 Brian Bartow
2005 Brian Bartow
2004 Brian Bartow
2003 Brian Linville
2002 Tony Bush
2001 Sean Duffy
2000 Brian Linville

1999 Brian Linville
1998 Sean Duffy
1997 Wade Stewart
1996 Dustin Beckwith
1995 George Williams
1994 Roger Burger
1993 Dustin Beckwith
1992 George Williams
1991 Sean Duffy
1990 Randy Peters

Tree Topping

World Record: Wade Stewart, 36.50 seconds, 1999

2000 Guy German
1999 Wade Stewart
1998 Guy German
1997 Guy German
1975 Owen Carney
1974 Art Williams
1973 Art Williams
1972 Art Williams
1971 Leslie Stewart
1970 Ron Downing

1969 Ron Downing
1968 Ron Downing
1967 Ron Downing
1966 Hap Johnson
1965 Louis Kloewer
1964 Hap Johnson
1963 Mal Harper
1962 Hap Johnson
1961 Hap Johnson
1960 Hap Johnson

Logrolling

2010 JR Salzman	1984 Dan McDonough
2009 JR Salzman	1983 Fred Scheer
2008 Darren Hudson	1982 Fred Scheer
2007 Darren Hudson	1981 Fred Sayklly Jr.
2006 Jamie Fischer	1980 Phil Scott
2005 JR Salzman	1979 Fred Scheer
2004 Jamie Fischer	1978 Fred Scheer
2003 Jamie Fischer	1977 Phil Scott
2002 JR Salzman	1976 Phil Scott
2001 JR Salzman	1975 Phil Scott
2000 JR Salzman	1974 Phil Scott
1999 JR Salzman	1973 Phil Scott
1998 JR Salzman	1972 Jim Fischer
1997 Dan McDonough	1971 Phil Scott
1996 Brian Duffy	1970 Phil Scott
1995 Brian Duffy	1969 Jubiel Wickheim
1994 Brian Duffy	1968 Phil Scott
1993 Dan McDonough	1967 Ardiel Wickheim
1992 Brian Duffy	1966 Jubiel Wickheim
1991 Brian Duffy	1965 Jubiel Wickheim
1990 Dan McDonough	1964 Jubiel Wickheim
1989 Dan McDonough	1963 Jubiel Wickheim
1988 Dan McDonough	1962 Jubiel Wickheim
1987 Dan McDonough	1961 Ardiel Wickheim
1986 Dan McDonough	1960 Jubiel Wickheim
1985 Dan McDonough	

Boom Run

World Record: Jamie Fischer, 12.49 seconds, 2005

2010 Will Hoeschler	2006 Jamie Fischer
2009 Will Hoeschler	2005 Jamie Fischer
2008 Tyler Fischer	2004 Jamie Fischer
2007 Jamie Fischer	2003 Jamie Fischer

Boom Run (*cont.*)
2002 Jamie Fischer
2001 Jamie Fischer
2000 JR Salzman
1999 Cassidy Scheer

1998 Alex McLeod
1997 JR Salzman
1996 JR Salzman
1995 Fred Scheer

Women's Events

Tony Wise All-Around Lumberjill Champion

2010 Nancy Zalewski
2009 Nancy Zalewski
2008 Nancy Zalewski
2007 Nancy Zalewski
2006 Sheree Taylor
2005 Sheree Taylor
2004 Nancy Zalewski

2003 Nancy Zalewski
2002 Penny Halvorson
2001 Sheree Taylor
2000 Penny Halvorson
1999 Penny Halvorson
1998 Penny Halvorson
1997 Tina Salzman Bosworth

Single Buck Sawing

World Record: Nancy Zalewski, 11.61 seconds, 2006

2010 Denise Ott
2009 Karmyn Wynyard
2008 Karmyn Wynyard
2007 Sheree Taylor
2006 Sheree Taylor
2005 Sheree Taylor
2004 Lindsay Daun
2003 Lindsay Daun

2002 Nancy Zalewski
2001 Sheree Taylor
2000 Dany Boulanger
1999 Dany Boulanger
1998 Sheree Taylor
1997 Penny Halvorson
1996 Penny Halvorson
1995 Sheree Taylor

Underhand Block Chop

World Record: Nancy Zalewski, 28.19 seconds, 2009

2010 Nancy Zalewski
2009 Nancy Zalewski
2008 Sheree Taylor
2007 Nancy Zalewski

2006 Sheree Taylor
2005 Nancy Zalewski
2004 Peg Engasser
2003 Peg Engasser

2002 Peg Engasser
2001 Alyson Clarke
2000 Penny Halvorson
1999 Penny Halvorson

1998 Penny Halvorson
1997 Dory Kistner
1996 Christine Van Gee
1995 Dory Kistner-Morris

Logrolling

2010 Liz Hoeschler
2009 Katie Hoeschler
2008 Shana Martin
2007 Jenny Anderson Atkinson
2006 Jenny Anderson Atkinson
2005 Jenny Anderson Atkinson
2004 Liz Hoeschler
2003 Tina Salzman Bosworth
2002 Tina Salzman Bosworth
2001 Tina Salzman Bosworth
2000 Tina Salzman Bosworth
1999 Tina Salzman Bosworth
1998 Tina Salzman Bosworth
1997 Tina Salzman Bosworth
1996 Tina Salzman Bosworth
1995 Bonnie Pendleton
1994 Bonnie Pendleton
1993 Bonnie Pendleton
1992 Tina Salzman Bosworth
1991 Denise Marquardt
1990 Tina Salzman Bosworth
1989 Julie Janke-Hughes
1988 Bonnie Pendleton
1987 Bonnie Pendleton
1986 Bonnie Pendleton
1985 Julie Janke

1984 Bonnie Pendleton
1983 Jenny Janke
1982 Judy Scheer Hoeschler
1981 Judy Scheer Hoeschler
1980 Jenny Janke
1979 Jenny Janke
1978 Julie Janke
1977 Judy Scheer Hoeschler
1976 Judy Scheer Hoeschler
1975 Judy Scheer Hoeschler
1974 Judy Scheer Hoeschler
1973 Judy Scheer Hoeschler
1972 Penni McCall
1971 Phoebe Morgan
1970 Cindy Cook
1969 Cindy Cook
1968 Cindy Cook
1967 Cindy Cook
1966 Charlotte Hanson Janke
1965 Bette Ellis Toothaker
1964 Bette Ellis Toothaker
1963 Bette Ellis Toothaker
1962 Barbara Peterka
1961 Diane Ellison
1960 Bette Ellis Toothaker

Boom Run

World Record: Mandy Erdmann Sobiech, 14.42 seconds, 2005

2010 Mandy Erdmann Sobiech

2009 Shana Martin

Boom Run (*cont.*)
2008 Shana Martin
2007 Jenny Anderson Atkinson
2006 Abby Hoeschler
2005 Mandy Erdmann Sobiech
2004 Abby Hoeschler
2003 Mandy Erdmann Sobiech
2002 Mandy Erdmann Sobiech

2001 Mandy Erdmann Sobiech
2000 Mandy Erdmann Sobiech
1999 Mandy Erdmann Sobiech
1998 Taylor Duffy
1997 Tina Salzman Bosworth
1996 Jenny Anderson Atkinson
1995 Jenny Anderson Atkinson

Co-ed Event

Jack & Jill Double Buck Sawing

World Record: Dave Jewett and Lindsay Daun, 6.00 seconds, 2010

2010 Dave Jewett and Lindsay Daun
2009 Jason Wynyard and Karmyn
   Wynyard
2008 Mike Sullivan and Nancy
   Zalewski
2007 Jason Wynyard and Karmyn
   Wynyard
2006 Jason Wynyard and Karmyn
   Wynyard
2005 Jason Wynyard and Karmyn
   Wynyard
2004 Mike Sullivan and Nancy
   Zalewski
2003 Jason Wynyard and Karmyn
   Wynyard
2002 Rick Halvorson and Penny
   Halvorson
2001 Dave Jewett and Sheree Taylor
2000 Dion Lane and Sheree Taylor
1999 Rick Halvorson and Penny
   Halvorson

1998 Rick Halvorson and Penny
   Halvorson
1997 Carson Bosworth and Tina
   Salzman
1996 Rick Halvorson and Penny
   Halvorson
1995 Rick Halvorson and Penny
   Halvorson
1994 Matt Bush and Jill Bush
1993 Matt Bush and Jill Bush
1992 Gaston Duperre and Dany
   Duperre
1991 Matt Bush and Jill Bush
1990 Rick Halvorson and Penny
   Halvorson
1989 Jim Colbert and Marion Colbert
1988 D. Slingerland and Tina Scheer
1987 Jim Colbert and Marion Colbert
1986 Jim Colbert and Marion Colbert
1985 Mel Lentz and Shirley Smith
1984 Mel Lentz and Shirley Smith

Sources

Personal Interviews

Unless otherwise noted, interviews for this book were conducted between July 23 and July 25, 2009, in Hayward, Wisconsin, at the fiftieth anniversary celebration of the Lumberjack World Championships: Jenny Anderson Atkinson (telephone, June 2010), Brian Bartow, Dustin Beckwith, David Bolstad (July 2006), Tina Salzman Bosworth, Emmett Brown, Matt Bush, Arden Cogar Sr., Arden Cogar Jr., Dennis Daun, Lindsay Daun, John Dettloff, Peg Engasser (e-mail, June 2010), Mandy Erdmann Sobiech (telephone, June 2010), Charlie Fenton, Jamie Fischer (June 2010), Dave Geer, Guy German, Michael Glass, Max Goldstein, Penny Halvorson (also telephone, June 2010), Rick Halvorson, Ron Hartill, Judy Scheer Hoeschler, Katie Hoeschler, Will Hoeschler, John Hughes, Dave Jewett, Ron Lambert, Dion Lane (July 2006), Mel Lentz, Eric Mackey, J. P. Mercier, Maxime Mercier, Napoleon Mercier, Diane McNamer (June and August 2009), Laurence O'Toole, Bob Pendleton Sr., Shane Sabin, Bonnie Salzman, JR Salzman (December 2009, June 2010), Josie Salzman, Fred Scheer, Tina Scheer (July 2010), Dave Sievert, Mike Sullivan, Bill Swintkowski (July 2009), Sheree Taylor, John Wells, Jason Wynyard (July 2009), Karmyn Wynyard, Nancy Zalewski (e-mail, June 2010).

Books

Blanchard, Louie. *The Lumberjack Frontier: The Life of a Logger in the Early Days on the Chippeway.* Retold from the recollections of Louie Blanchard by Walker

D. Wyman, with the assistance of Lee Prentice. Lincoln: University of Nebraska Press, 1969.

Cowley, Mert. *Beyond the Shadows of the Pine*. Chetek, WI: Banksiana, 2003.

———. *There's Daylight in the Swamps*. Chetek, WI: Banksiana, 2002.

Dettloff, John. *Three Record Muskies in His Day*. Couderay, WI: Trail's End, 2002.

Edmonds, Michael. *Out of the Northwoods: The Many Lives of Paul Bunyan*. Madison: Wisconsin Historical Society Press, 2009.

Hoffman, Daniel. *Paul Bunyan: Last of the Frontier Demigods*. Philadelphia: Temple University Publications, 1952.

Kellogg, Steve. *Paul Bunyan: A Tall Tale*. Columbus, OH: Newfield Publications, 1984.

Lumberjack World Championships: A Pictorial History. Hayward, WI: Advance Printing, 2009.

McEnany, Jack. *Brush Cat: On Trees, the Wood Economy, and the Most Dangerous Job in America*. New York: St. Martin's Press, 2009.

McNamer, Diane, ed. and comp. *Lumberjack World Championships, 1960–2009: A Pictorial History*. Hayward, WI: Advance Printing.

Monte, Mike. *Cut and Run: Loggin' Off the Big Woods*. Atglen, PA: Schiffer Publishing, 2002.

Nelligan, John Emmett. *A White Pine Empire: The Life of a Lumberman*. Saint Cloud, MN: North Star Press, 1969.

Rosholt, Malcolm. *The Wisconsin Logging Book, 1839–1939*. Rosholt, WI: Rosholt House, 1980.

Singer, Eli. *Musky Chronicles II*. Park Falls, WI: Singer, 2002.

———. *Musky Chronicles III*. Park Falls, WI: Singer, 2004.

Wells, Robert W. *Daylight in the Swamp*. Minocqua, WI: NorthWord Press, 1978.

Articles

Boetcher, Terrell. "It's a Long Way from Papua . . ." *Sawyer County Record*, August 3, 1983.

Breining, Greg. "Lumberjacks Test Skills in Hayward." *Duluth News-Tribune*, n.d.

Daly, Matthew, and Shannon Dininny. "Timber Subsidies Grow Past $3 billion Sent to 41 States." Associated Press, December 6, 2009.

Dettloff, John. "Hayward's First Winter Sports Carnival." *Trail Blazer*, February 2, 1998.

Eifling, Sam. "The Recovery of J. R. Salzman." ESPNOutdoors.com, October 1, 2007.

Eldot, Walter. "Hayward Wows 'Em: It's a Year-Round Paradise." *Duluth Sunday News-Tribune*, January 22, 1967.

Freedman, Lew. "Great Muskie Feud Is Raging All Over Again." *Chicago Tribune*, March 18, 2004.

———. "Historian Reels in Truth about Record Muskies." *Chicago Tribune*, January 15, 2004.

———. "Logging in to Forest Games." *Chicago Tribune*, August 7, 2001.

———. "These Games All about Pulp Friction." *Chicago Tribune*, August 13, 2006.

Hamp, Leslie. "The American Birkebeiner Then and Now." www.birkie.com. [2009].

"Japanese Birlers Compete in 'World' Test at Hayward," July 25, 1965.

Kruckemeyer, Kate. "You Get Sawdust in Your Blood." *Journal of American Folklore* 115 (summer 2002): 301–31.

Leary, James P. "Birlers and Boosters." Unpublished paper, University of Wisconsin, Madison, 1998.

———. Wisconsin Sesquicentennial Celebration Folklife Survey. Interview research, 1996.

"Lumberjacks Chop for World Title." *Northline*, spring 1971.

"Merv Jensen, Master Sawyer, Dies." *Sawyer County Record*, April 6, 1983.

Morgan, Wallace W. "Japanese Trio to Enter Log Rolling." *New York Times*, July 26, 1965.

———. "Two Japanese Birlers Please Crowd at Hayward Events." *New York Times*, August 1, 1965.

"No Sissies." *Minneapolis Tribune*, July 29, 1956.

"Scheer Rolls Out of Retirement." *Sawyer County Record*, July 1981.

Stodghill, Mark. "Hayward Lumberjack May Soon Tell Tall Tales in Beer Commercial." *Sawyer County Record*, n.d.

———. "Lentz Wins All-Around Championship." *Sawyer County Record*, n.d.

Zgoda, Jerry. "Telemark Celebrates 55th Anniversary." *Minneapolis Star-Tribune*, November 29, 2002.

Programs and Brochures

Lumberjack World Championships, 2001 event program.

Lumberjack World Championships, 2006 event program.

Lumberjack World Championships, 2009 event program.

Lumberjack World Championships Rule Book, 1983.

National Fresh Water Fishing Hall of Fame and Museum brochure.
National Fresh Water Fishing Hall of Fame and Museum record book.
Paul Bunyan Logging Camp Museum brochure.
Pioneer Park, Rhinelander, Wisconsin.
The Rhinelander Logging Museum Story, 1940, 2004.